LENDING A HAND:

OR,

HELP FOR THE WORKING CLASSES.

CHAPTERS ON SOME VEXED QUESTIONS OF THE DAY.

BY THE AUTHOR OF

" DOING AND SUFFERING," " BROAD SHADOWS ON LIFE'S PATHWAY,"

ETC. ETC.

"If thou forbear to deliver them . . if thou sayest, Behold, we knew it not; doth not He that pondereth the heart consider it?"

Prov. xxiv. 11, 12.

SEELEY. JACKSON. AND HALLIDAY, 54 FLEET STREET
LONDON. MDCCCLXVI.

CONTENTS.

CHAPTER I.

CHAPTER II.

a

CHAPTER III.

THE WORKMAN'S HOME, AS IT IS.

CHAPTER IV.

THE WORKMAN'S HOME, AS IT SHOULD BE.

CHAPTER V.

THE WORKMAN'S HOME AT MULHOUSE.

CHAPTER VI.

THE WORKMAN'S SUNDAY—HOW SHALL HE SPEND IT?

CHAPTER VII.

DOMESTIC SERVANTS—WHAT WE MAY CLAIM FROM THEM, AND THEY FROM US.

CHAPTER VIII.

THE GENUS MENDICANT—WHAT TO DO WITH IT?

CHAPTER IX.

THE SICK POOR IN LONDON WORKHOUSES—WHAT IS AND WHAT OUGHT TO BE DONE FOR THEM.

Care of the Poor both a Duty and a Privilege—The *Sick* Pauper—
His Present and his Future—Gravity of the Subject as a Public
Question—Laying the Blame on the Wrong Shoulders—Ex-
travagant Hopes of the First Commissioners under the New
Poor-law—Aims to elevate the Pauper—Its Humanity—
Principles of Poor-law Relief—Necessity for Caution—Guar-
dianship of Rates reconciled with Guardianship of Poor—The
Lancet Commission of Inquiry—The Infirmaries of the London
Workhouses the real Hospitals of the Land—Character of the
Buildings—Of the Sick-Wards—Of the System of Nursing—Of
the Provisions and Cooking—Of the Dietaries—Of the Position

INTRODUCTION.

'F making many books there is no end.'
And in days like these, when the library
shelves are stored with modern books —
instructive, useful, interesting — of which, nevertheless, the leaves remain uncut; because the
leisure for reading which the owner of the library
can secure is small out of all proportion, compared with the books he wishes, hopes, and intends to read : in days, we say, like these, a separate
apology seems needed for every new book, which, if
purchased and read, consumes his time; if purchased
and unread, provokes his regret. There is, of course,
another alternative; but it is not one which authors
willingly contemplate.

We have, then, to apologise for turning our
thoughts loose upon the public. Our apology is,
that the public has itself forced the present subjects
upon our notice. The things written about have
been things talked about. They have engaged public
attention in Parliament and out of it; they have

taxed the powers of our Statesmen and the energies
of our Philanthropists. The necessities with which
they had to deal were urgent; imperatively demanding immediate attention.

But this being the case, are they subjects which
befit the pen of a lady writer ?   What has she to do
with Parliamentary measures and the perplexities of
Statesmen ?   Very little, if the subject is purely political; except to cultivate such a measure of acquaintance with it as shall enable her to share with
intelligent interest in the conversation of her father,
husband, or brother.

But if the subjects treated of in this book have
some of them a political bearing, because they treat
of evils and difficulties which have arisen out of
our national progress in commerce and arts, and
which cannot be remedied or met without recourse
to Government measures: yet this is not their
primary aspect, they are questions mainly philanthropic, which make appeal to the brotherly instincts of our common humanity.

It is not, we trust, out of a woman's province to
enter with keen appreciation into the danger which
threatens the domestic happiness of the workman,
if the house-mother is withdrawn from her family
and thrown alone and unprotected into the world
of labour.   The claims of a family, the demand it
makes on a woman's whole energies, the inestimable
value we set upon the shelter and privacy of domestic
life, are known to *us,* as they cannot be to those
whose calling lies in the outer world of action.

Again: a seemly and fitting dwelling for any
station of life in which God's wisdom may have
placed us, is a blessing which daily experience
prepares women to understand and appreciate.
Gladly and thankfully we recognise it as our office
and duty, to make a father's or a husband's home
happy and attractive. But, just because it is so,
we feel our hearts moved with tenderest sympathy,
when we think of the difficulties which beset our
working sisters in carrying out this legitimate object
of a woman's ambition.

A happy and attractive home!—the words sound
like a bitter mockery when we think of the foul
rooms, the crowded courts, where these working
women of England are herded with their husbands
and little children. We picture the war that such
a woman must wage with dirt and disorder—her
valiant endeavour to keep a bright hearth and a
tempting corner, where her husband may spend his
evenings at her side; and we note how pernicious
influences over which she has no control—bad air,
bad water, bad drainage—neutralise all her efforts;
her arm grows feebler every day; the sensitive frames
of her little children tell their unerring tale; and
her husband soon learns, after a hasty meal, to make
his escape from the nauseous atmosphere—probably
to a gin-palace.

We feel for her keenly; and we hear, with far
less blame than pity, that she has given up in despair
one of the dearest hopes of a woman's life.

Can we, then, do otherwise than watch with deep

interest any schemes which philanthropic men or a
philanthropic government are planning for mitigating
this crying social evil, and placing the workman in a
dwelling which has some prospect of being indeed a
home? Shall we not seek to diffuse among those
whose attention has not yet been drawn to it, any
information which, by a little painstaking, we may
have been able to collect on this subject, from various
sources, especially from the kindness of leaders in
the movement, who have answered our inquiries?
We acknowledge gratefully the kindness of Alderman
Waterlow, both in this respect and in the pains he
has taken to point out to us trustworthy sources of
information.

With regard to the efforts in the same direction,
which have been made with so much success now for
thirteen years by the Society of Mulhouse, near Bâle,
circumstances, which brought us into intimate acquaintance with Continental friends, had put it within
our power to obtain very full details as to the work
at Mulhouse. We did not find, judging by conversation with those whose attention was fully alive to
the importance of improving the workman's home in
England, that these details were generally known.

We have, therefore, given them as we received
them ; and must express our special thanks to Mons.
Bernard, père, Directeur-gérant de la Société de Mulhouse, for his kind and efficient help in answering
our inquiries, and bringing us within reach of sources
of direct information.

It was with some hesitation that we ventured to

touch on the subject of the Workman's Sunday,— a subject so widely discussed by those in a far better position to judge of its merits. But, in one view, it is within our province, for Sunday is the family-day in the workman's home; and the question, ' How he shall spend it ?' touches the happiness of his wife as nearly as his own. The labour of the week separates them — the rest of the Sabbath should bring them together; and any plans or efforts by which they may be helped to spend it profitably, rationally, and plea-santly, will have an important effect in cementing the bonds of family union. We are grateful to the Rev. H. Stevens for much valuable help afforded on this subject.

To the remaining subjects of the book we lay claim with some courage. The question of female domestic service is handed over to us with hearty consent by fathers, husbands, and brothers. It is our miniature government, and provided no family disturbance is created ·by our misrule or ineffi-ciency, they are willing enough to leave the reins in our hands.

We imagine, also, that they would look favourably on any attempt on our part to inquire or spread a knowledge of 'The Genus Mendicant,' as they have not the highest opinion of our discrimination when a plausible tale is told, or an appeal is made to our sympathy; they think we sometimes take too literally Milton's beautiful words :—

' Suspicion sleeps
At Wisdom's gate, and to Simplicity
Resigns her charge.'

The last subject in the book, the 'Treatment of
the Sick in Workhouse Infirmaries,' in so far as it
relates to the value and importance of engaging
efficient nurses to act under medical orders, certainly
lies within a woman's province; for every woman is
or ought to be, by instinct and practice, a nurse,
and should know how essential kind and skilled
attendance is, to the recovery of the sick. Such
knowledge, however, of the actual state of workhouse infirmaries, as could justify any attempt to
write upon it, must be gained in one of two ways—
either by reading all that has been written about it,
and keeping an open ear for what those who are
practically conversant with it have to say, or by
personal experience of the work itself.

We have no doubt as to which source of information will be most acceptable to the reader, or
which will place the subject before him in its truest
light. A medical brother-in-law, Dr. W. H. Cook,
has under his sole charge in a suburb of London,
a workhouse infirmary, to which he has devoted
very careful attention, not only because care for the
poor generally is to him one of the deepest interests
of his professional life, but because he has strongly
felt that the pauper, while under the chastening
hand of God in sickness, should be treated with all
the tenderness and consideration we accord to
the sick in our hospitals. To him, therefore, the
writer has deputed this subject, and is happy to be
able to secure for her readers the advantage of his
practical acquaintance with the question.

So far as to the subjects of which we have treated, we trust we have justified ourselves from the charge of presumption, and of stepping beyond our lawful province.

But we anticipate another objection. It may be said, 'There is much more philanthropy than religion in this book: does the writer imagine that working men and women are to be raised out of moral degradation, and made valuable members of society, by airy houses and pretty gardens? Why lay so much stress on these secondary means, and say so little of that radical change which must pass upon the heart, before any permanent and effectual change can be looked for in the life?'

In the first place we would say, that we trust no one who has the patience to read through our book, could rise from its perusal under any doubt as to our own solemn personal conviction, that godliness lies at the foundation of happiness and prosperity, whether individual or national; but the relative proportion which religious thoughts should bear to secular information in any book, must be determined by the subject in hand. For instance: we wish to study the physiology of plants, and purchase for that purpose a Guide to Botany; we are gratified to find, here and there, a trace that the author realizes that it is from God's open Book of Nature he is making his discoveries; we like, from time to time, to hear his tribute of admiration, as some marvellous adaptation of Divine wisdom has to be unfolded; but we do not wish our Guide to Botany to be encumbered with morals and lessons, we would rather have been left to draw for ourselves.

So with questions of social life, and the mutual relations of rich and poor, capital and labour, employer and employed. Every principle, really true, and trustworthy, and enduring, in social life, rests on a religious basis: but as in an edifice, having laid the foundation with care, we proceed to build upon it, and thereby cover it, and only if we doubt its security should we stay our work to examine it afresh; so in this attempt to suggest to the workman his true interests, and to remind the wealthy and the educated of their real responsibilities, we have stated that which we believe God claims from each; but our *selected* subject, that which we intended to enlarge and to dwell upon, was rather the mutual relations of these two classes as fellow-creatures, as brother-men, *one with another.* We have been engaged in the construction of a house for every-day uses, not of a temple.

It has been a question much debated whether attempts to civilise or to Christianise should lead the way in any social reform. Dr. Alison says, 'There is yet another class of reasoners on this subject, who distrust the efficacy of any measures for the benefit of the poor which go merely to the relief of physical suffering, and trust to religious and moral education as the only effectual remedy for this and all other evils of the social condition of our species. I should sincerely lament if anything that I have said should be construed into contempt or disregard of their opinions. But I beg to say that, in order that religious instruction may produce its due effect, the seed must fall on soil so far prepared for its reception. The philanthropist and the legislator can aspire to no higher object in the department of their duties, than to perform this preliminary duty. Occasional religious feelings exist in all ranks of society, and perhaps their most striking manifestations are in the lowest. It is easy to excite the sense of human dependence and of human unworthiness in the very outcasts of society; but all experience teaches us that we are not to expect them to regulate the character and permanently influence the conduct of those who are incessantly struggling for existence, and are unable to command any of the comforts, and enjoyments, and decencies of life. A certain degree of physical comfort is essential to the permanent development and habitual influence over human conduct, of any feelings higher than our sensual appetites.'*

So, then, the Christian philanthropist may rejoice, that in lending a hand to schemes for promoting the physical well-being of his fellow-men, he is preparing a soil in which the seeds of vital truth may germinate; he is showing brotherly sympathy in wants which are felt and recognized; he is establishing his claim to be regarded as a friend.

Convince a working man that you have his welfare at heart, that you are willing to put your

* Dr. Alison *On the Management of the Poor in Scotland*, p. 125.

shoulder under his burden, that you understand
how, and *where*, and *why* it presses on him, that you
will give time and thought and labour to set him
right with himself and with society; convince him
of these things, and you have gained your brother.
He will listen to your advice, he will try your
remedy. He will listen to you because you have
gone to work in the right way; you have recognized
that the mainspring of action lies in the heart and
the will; you have gained his heart, and thus you
have influenced his life.

It needs but to carry the same principle one
step higher—to remind him that there is an evil yet
more to be feared than social degradation, and that
a love higher and deeper than yours has measured
his danger and taken up his burden; that the
Highest has stooped down to him in his low estate,
to pity, to comfort, and to help. We do not say
that he will lend so ready an ear. *Your* help and
sympathy were tendered in troubles under which he
groaned in sensible discomfort; *this* succour is
offered for a need of which he is dimly conscious.
But by coming to his aid for the lesser want, you
have acquired a right to be heard when you speak
to him of the greater; he will listen to you with
attention—he will recognize the voice of a friend.

There is yet one other consideration which has
weighed with us in making our ground of appeal for
the workman, philanthropic and general. The evils
under which he suffers have grown out of the neglect,
the selfishness, the indifference to his wants, of

society generally: we mean, the classes of society above his own. It is not that we have intentionally wronged him, but that we have been criminally regardless of the fact, that in our keen pursuit of commerce and manufactures, the interests of the operative have been sacrificed, to the wealth he was the means of acquiring for us.

The evils have been of slow growth, they are now forcing themselves on public attention, and it is important that the sense of responsibility should be wide-spread; but that it may be so, we must make our appeal on grounds which will be generally understood, and the force of which will be generally admitted.

Happy, indeed, would the writer be, if the generous impulse to lend a helping hand should in any case result from this attempt to make known some of the difficult questions which perplex the workman's life.

LENDING A HAND.

CHAPTER I.

ESTORE! That is a serious word. Do we mean that family life has passed away from the workman's home, or that it is at least sorely endangered—ready to die? And why do we class it among the wrongs? Is Society chargeable with it? Is it because we have made haste to be rich? Is it because in this age of iron and steam, when workmen are called 'hands,' we have regarded him only as an intelligent machine, and have forgotten that he has a heart which must be satisfied with love? Is this the underlying cause which has sapped the foundation of domestic happiness in the workman's home? Let us inquire seriously; probably we shall find that the responsibility is neither exclu-

sively ours nor his, but is shared between us; and
that, as with the wrong so with the remedy, hearty
co-operation and a mutual understanding between
us, offer the best hope of cure.

Let us define what we mean by family life;—not,
certainly, the grouping together of individuals under
one roof in bodies corporate. This is true of a college,
a school, a workhouse; but these are not families.
By a family we mean those who, by ties of relationship and natural instinct, by mutual dependence and
bonds of affection, though *many*, are yet *one*—one
in interest, sharers in each other's sorrows and each
other's joys. A family is a corrective applied by
God himself to mitigate and soften human selfishness:
the husband loves the wife of his choice, the parents
love their children, the children love their parents
and each other.

Recent writers have spoken eloquently of the
power of the family as a moral regenerator. M. Jules
Simon regards it as the bow of promise, which spans
for the workman the dark clouds which have gathered
over his horizon. M. de Gasparin last year filled two
volumes with his own living, penetrating thoughts,
as to what the family is, and what it is intended
to accomplish. It is an agency for human happiness
which dates from Eden itself; when God found for
man his help-meet, He constituted the first human
family.

But family life has its laws, which cannot be
transgressed with impunity. The different lot assigned to the man and the woman, from the very

beginning, may be regarded as among the most essential of those laws. The man is to labour in his vocation as a bread-winner—the woman is to labour in her home; his life is to be outward and social—hers private and domestic. We cannot improve upon God's order; we may not violate it: in ordinary circumstances, *family life* flourishes only under these conditions.

It is not the daily toil in the sweat of his brow which threatens the workman's domestic peace; it is that we have taken the key-stone from his arch by tempting his wife away from her proper and natural sphere of domestic labour. Work! who would be without it?—it is the healthy exercise of our faculties, our courage, our perseverance, our enterprise! Let those answer who, having no fixed occupation, have tried to substitute for work a continued round of exciting pleasure. Are they happier than the honest working man, who comes back after his twelve or thirteen hours' labour with his basket of tools slung over his shoulder, and looks in at his own door to see the faces of wife and children brighten up at the sight of his smile and the sound of his voice? Every man, rich or poor, has, or ought to have, his work; the loving intercommunion of members of a family is far more likely to be endangered by idleness than by labour.

And assuredly, in pointing out that the house-mother's sphere of labour lies at home, we have not claimed for her a life of ease! If one woman, during the years in which a young family is increasing around

her, contrives, through all her days and hours of
weakness and incapacity, to nurse her children, bring
them up in good habits, cook, mend, and wash for her
husband and the whole family, and keep her house or
room in anything like neatness and order—whatever
else that woman is, she is not an *idle* woman.

Let the portrait of a Scottish mother, drawn by a
daughter's hand (the authoress of *The Pearl of Days*),
show what are the results when a woman, with honest
and loving labour, occupies her own place in the
workman's home;—she must have been a pattern to
women of her class:—'Her one aim,' says her daughter, 'seems to have been to make a happy and comfortable home for her family, and especially for her
husband. So careful was she in this respect, that
she would say, "It was disagreeable and improper to
be bustling about while father was within—the work
must be done up when he was gone out."' She was
too poor to send her children to school, but she carefully taught them herself. 'Four times a-day,' her
daughter says, 'we had usually each of us our short
lesson; and if it be considered that the whole of the
labour of the house devolved upon our mother, it will
be believed that this could be no light task. Nothing,
however, was allowed to interrupt our lessons; and it
was no uncommon thing to see her busy at the wash-
tub, while we, by turns, took our place beside her.
One child would be found attending to the baby;
another gathering sticks and keeping the fire alive;
a third engaged in reading; and a fourth bringing
water from a pure soft spring at some distance from

the house; while our eldest brother assisted father in the garden.'

We do not ask for a brighter picture than this of family life in the workman's home; but could it have been realized if God's order in the constitution of a family had not been observed? Is not the mother the central figure in this household group? If, instead of remaining at home to train and educate her children, and make a thrifty use of her husband's in-bringings, she had aimed at being herself a bread-winner, and had forsaken her own vocation to emulate his, would the few shillings added to the weekly income have compensated for the loss of family life, for the neglect of the children, for the discomfort of the home?

Compare with the honest content which reigned in the family of this Scotchman, where his chosen companion was truly his wife and the mother of his children, the domestic life in a workman's family where the woman, as well as her husband, goes forth with the dawn to non-domestic labour, and returns, like him, in the evening, wearied with a hireling's toil. 'In such a family,' says M. Jules Simon, 'the father and mother are absent, each in their respective work, for some fourteen hours of the day. A *family* under such circumstances is simply an impossibility. The mother must abandon her babe to some ill-paid substitute, and the sickly little life which results is often sacrificed; the children who survive, deprived of all maternal care and moral training, left for many hours in the day to wander at will in the streets

C

and the gutters, pinched with hunger and cold, grow
up puny, squalid, vicious,—to become, in their turn,
parents of an ever-degenerating race.'* When evening comes, and the family re-assembles, the father
and mother toil-worn, the children fretful and
wearied with neglect and wandering, what prospect
is there of comfort for them in the deserted room
which they call home? It has been empty all the
day; no one has been there to attend to the most
ordinary requirements of cleanliness; the hearth is
cold and desolate; no preparation for the evening
meal; the home-work is to begin; the mother, however weary, must address herself to the task; and if
after supper her weary eyes imperatively refuse to
keep open longer, and she takes to her bed with the
rest, it is with the uncomfortable conviction that the
clothes of her husband and children, to say nothing
of her own, are falling to pieces for want of a few
hours of thrifty mending. Is it very surprising if
the father turns from the comfortless home, the
hasty, ill-prepared supper, the half-wild children,
the wife who has become almost a stranger to them
and to him, and if, enjoying none of the sweets of
married life, he is tempted to shake himself free
from its claims, and to resume his bachelor evenings
among his mates in the public-house or gin-palace?
This, then, is the charge the workman has against us,—
that, while possessing ourselves superior education
and better opportunities of estimating consequences,
we have either overlooked or selfishly disregarded

* *L'Ouvrière*, Preface, v.

the disastrous results to his domestic happiness of
withdrawing his wife from her place in his household. *We* require women to serve our interests, either
private or commercial, and though employment for
single women is a crying want in England, we have
taken no precautions to secure the services of such,
rather than those of the house-mother.

We lay down our tempting wages before the
workman's wife (God knows, she can make plenty
of use of them, with the hungry mouths she has to·
feed, and the naked backs she has to cover!), and we
see her take them up,—we, whose range of vision is
so much longer than hers,—and yet offer her no
word of warning, no friendly hint that the shadowy
advantage she will reap if she leaves her husband
and children to do our work and receive our pay,
may cost her the best blessings of her life.

If one could be assured that the wife and mother
would only have recourse to non-domestic labour
under circumstances of extreme pressure; that her
heart would remain at home with her little ones;
that she would feel painfully the exposure of being
withdrawn from domestic privacy, and would fly
back to it as a bird to its nest when the pressing
emergency had passed by; then the danger would
be less: but we think those who are familiar with
the habits and life of the working classes will bear
us out in the assertion that this is not the case.   A
wife and mother who absents herself from the home
of her husband and children, and goes out to earn her
bread among strangers, does it at the imminent risk

of losing her domestic tastes, and finding the home-
life, when she returns to it, insipid.   We have an
instance in our mind at this moment—a remarkably
intelligent and respectable woman, who had been
cook in a gentleman's family.   Her husband, if we
remember right, was a bricklayer, and earned 18*s.*
or 20*s.* a-week.   She had two sweet little children,
the youngest a girl about three years old—just such
a rosy cherub as a mother might take pride in.
'*'* The woman *must* work now-a-days,' was her axiom,
' to make the weekly income sufficient.'   So she
went out to laundry-work, earning good wages, for
whatever she did, was sure to be done well.   The
children were carefully provided for, and a fair sum
for the charge of them was paid to a motherly body,
who, being an invalid, had no work of her own.
Some change in the circumstances of the laundress
who employed her, threw the woman for a time out
of work, and we found the door open, which was
usually locked.   Some such conversation as the following took place.   The pretty prattler was playing
about the room:

' Glad to find you at home, Mrs. ——; you
work so hard generally, you must be quite glad of a
little rest.'

' Well, no! you see it tires me more to be always
up and down after the child—that's what I ain't used
to; it tries me more than the work: and then, you
see, no work's no pay, and I can't afford the good
living I had at the laundry, and that tries me
again.'

'Yet surely, a time at home to look after your husband's things and the children's must be handy, and save in the end; you are such a good needle-woman.'

'Still, I miss the going, and feel dull like at home.'

'Well, there's one comfort: if you have smaller in-comings now, your cooking-knowledge helps you to make the most of them. I should think there's not a man in the place has nicer suppers than your husband, now you are at home to look after them.'

'Well, yes; he ain't a bad husband, and so long as he behaves hisself I don't mind doing for him. If he weren't a good 'un to me I should not be a good 'un to him; I can tell him that.'

Who does not see that the dry rot had begun in this family edifice, fair as it seemed with its industrious, sober husband, clever wife, and winsome little children? It had begun because the woman's heart was no longer centered in her home; because the excitement and gossip of the ironing-room had greater charms for her than the prattle of her child; because she liked harder work with more stimulating fare, better than the frugality of the meals her husband's earnings would supply : because, most of all, the wife-like feeling of dependence was giving place to the conviction that, being herself a bread-winner, she and her husband stood on equal terms.

It is true that the husband has often himself to

blame for the discomfort thus wrought in his home.
In the first months of his married life, when there is
less necessity for his wife's remaining at home, he
sometimes allows, nay, even urges her to add to
his earnings by her own. Mr. Weylland mentioned
to us the case of a man employed in an iron-foundry
at wages of 26s. a-week : he married the daughter
of a dustman; she could earn on the dust-heaps
12s. a-week. Tempted by the large addition to his
income he wished her to go. By-and-bye her work
was interrupted by the birth of her first child; now,
surely, the mother's duty was at home! but the father
persuaded her to pay 1s. 6d. a-week to have the
child taken care of, and when the family was increased by another, and yet another, till there were
five children, he still thought the mother might
continue her labour. 'Leave bread and dripping
for them,' he said, 'on the table: they won't starve
till you come home at supper-time.' The mother's
pitiful lament to Mr. Weylland was, 'It is killing
me, and it's the ruin of the children.'

Would that we could impress upon women, and,
for the matter of that, upon husbands too, how fallacious is the idea that they are really gainers in
a money point of view when the wife works away
from home! The appliances no doubt, are endless,
especially in the metropolis, for supplying to the
family her lack of service; but how costly! She can
buy ready-made clothes for the children, and does
so; but how do they wear? besides, her own busy
needle at home, mending and patching the old ones,

would have made the purchase unnecessary. So, again, with food: there is no chance of forethought or thrift, buying at advantage in the best market; the ready-cooked food is sent out for as it is wanted. 'I have been many a time,' said Mr. Weylland to the writer, 'on a Monday morning in a baker's shop, and have seen fifteen or sixteen women and children come in for their halfpenny hot rolls; this with a rasher, and a pennyworth of pickled cabbage, is their breakfast.' We know a lady who, during the Crimean war, when the price of wheat was enormous, had a tempting batch of bread baked by her own cook, in which barley-meal was mixed with the wheat; she wished to show her poorer neighbours how nice it really was, and that they might effect a considerable saving, at no sacrifice to their enjoyment. She sent round her loaves, and they were accepted; but not one housewife began the use of barley-meal. The woman whose work is away from home becomes almost hopelessly improvident, in spending her own and her husband's earnings.

In London, where non-domestic labour is not the rule for wives and mothers, it is difficult to make them realize that their wisdom is to be 'keepers at home;' but it becomes far more difficult in manufacturing districts, where other causes than those we have mentioned are in operation, to withdraw the house-mother from her family.

Labour now stands on a wholly different footing from that which it occupied in the days of our forefathers; as M. Jules Simon epigrammatically expresses it:—'Formerly the workman was an intelligent power, now he is only an intelligence directing a power.'* The department in labour where simple brute force was of avail, is now almost exclusively occupied by machinery: till lately this has been true only of manufactures, it is now rapidly extending to agriculture. Now, if the woman is found equally capable with the man, of directing and guiding the motive power of machinery, she will undoubtedly be preferred by the manufacturer: her labour can be had at a cheaper rate; she is less likely to stand on her rights, or strike for higher wages; and her manipulation being more delicate than his, she is, in many kinds of machine work, the better operative of the two.

Such being the case, it is not surprising that the demand for female labour is great: 'forty women,' we are told, 'can find employment where one man fails;' and the labour is by no means excessive which puts a comfortable income within the reach of the woman. The charge of one loom is paid by about 10s. weekly wage; but a quick, clever woman, can take charge, of two, three, or, at a stretch, even four looms. The evil is not in over-working the house-mother, but in withdrawing her from the family. Miss Barlee gives us some interesting details on this point, in a little book written by her during the cotton famine, for which she gathered material by a visit to the distressed districts:—

* *L'Ouvrière*, Preface, iv.

' From the demand for female labour, almost all the married women go, as they term it, " agate" (meaning to mill-work) ; and as their children must be looked after, they are committed to the care of a class of artificial mothers, who make child-nursing a trade. The poor little creatures are hastily taken from their cradles in the early dawn, in all weathers; and, enveloped in their mothers' large grey shawls, carried out with them, being left by them on their way to work, with their representatives. In the same way they are fetched again at night. If within easy access of her babe, the mother returns in the middle of the day to suckle it, though most of the infants are deprived of their natural aliment till night. The quantity of laudanum that is sold and administered to these children to stifle their cries, is said to be something appalling. I had some serious conversations with the men on the subject of their wives being called upon to work in the mills, to the neglect of their homes and their children. Many of them owned, that when they had first married they were very averse to the system, and that then their homes were far more comfortable, and they did not care to go to the beer-shop. It was when their families increased that they had been glad to supplement their own wages by their wives' earnings. One man said, most emphatically, " *His wife never had, and never should, work away from the house while he could help it.*" '*

This man had found the remedy—all honour to him for it ! We may spend a great deal of time and thought in striving to adjust the claims of political economy on the one hand, and the moral welfare of the operative on the other ; we may puzzle ourselves how it can be, that in God's world material perfec-

* *A Visit to Lancashire in December* 1862, pp. 28, 32.

tion and moral perfection can be at variance, so that
the one cannot be carried out to its natural limit
but at the sacrifice of the other: — the truth is, the
remedy lies in the hands of the operatives themselves,
— *husbands and wives;* let them present a united
front against the sacrifice of 'family life' for *any*
advantage, however specious; let them say — ' Trade
and manufactures may need women; they may have
daughters and single women, but *they shall not have
the house-mother.*'

M. de Gasparin thus encourages the workman's
family to assert itself, and believes that only in this
self-assertion will it be secure from the inroads of
trade and commerce. ' How beautiful,' he says, ' is
the real principle of family life in the workman's
home, and how mighty! — Commerce holds its head
high, but commerce must bow to it. When the
family — the true family — asserts its right to exist
as a united whole, to maintain the health and the
morality of its members, to guard the domestic hearth,
to harmonize the claims of daily labour with those of
family life — when it demands that the choice presented to it shall be no longer a choice between the
duties of the labourer and those of the father and
mother, — between physical starvation and moral ruin,
or, perhaps, rather the endurance of both—when the
family asserts itself thus, then it will be heard.
Public opinion, with an overwhelming force, will
take its side. Many will be found to plead its cause;
and among its advocates the manufacturers themselves
will be numbered. This 19th century of ours, be-

lieve me, will never consent to the annihilation of the *family*.'*

We recommend, then, most earnestly, to working men and their wives, an intelligent, thoughtful consideration of this subject. The remedy lies in their own hands; it must be applied by themselves; it is a matter in which, if they do not see their own interest, and do what is best for themselves, no one else can do it for them. We are not speaking of exceptional cases, as, for instance, the prolonged illness of the husband, where the necessity of paid labour is thrown upon the wife if she would not see him and her children starve. For such exceptional cases a most beneficent agency is now at work in London, which we are about to describe; but we are speaking of ordinary circumstances, in which we may suppose the husband to be in the receipt of regular wages. We say to him: 'If your wages are small for the needs of your family, increase them by any honest means in your power, *except* letting your wife work away from her home and her children, for that will work you woe which no money can compensate, and the apparent gain will be the greatest loss you ever sustained. Prize the dignity God has given you, and never let it be said that you, a brave-hearted English workman, use a woman's arm to under-prop your own.' To the wife we would say: 'You cannot *afford* to work away from home; in the long run your pocket will suffer, but in a much shorter time your husband, your children, will suffer: *no one else can take your place in*

* Gasparin's *La Famille*, p. 231.

the home—no one else can study as you can your
husband's comfort, and it is worth *everything* to you
to make and keep for him a happy fireside. Be content with his wages,—let it be your honest pride to
show how far you can make them go: we do not
deny that you will be sometimes pinched, but family
life and family love will amply repay the sacrifice.'

But if the working man's wife is pinched while
her husband enjoys good health and regular work—
if even then she is tempted to eke out his earnings by
being herself, to some extent, a bread-winner, how
will she fare in the dark days, which *will* come to
her as they come to all, when the husband is sick at
home, or in a hospital ward—when the incomings
are stopped, and the outgoings increased? Where
shall she turn when, to the dark days of sickness,
succeed the darker days of widowhood, and she looks
round upon the helpless children who will never more
eat the loaf earned for them by a father's honest
labour? Is there any agency at work which takes
account of her hour of need, and comes in with
friendly assistance, not offering her the pauperizing
and uncertain dole of charity, but putting within her
reach profitable labour, for those whom she loves?

A little inquiry will satisfy the reader that such
an agency *is* at work; till he can find, or will make,
the opportunity to witness its operations for himself,
we will ask him to trust our eyes, and to accompany
us to the Needlewomen's Institute, at 2 Hinde Street,
Manchester Square.

Our ring is answered by one of the very smallest

specimens of 'Buttons' we ever remember to have seen; active as a little sprite, however, and well up to the duties of his calling, which are, at the present moment, to usher us into the presence of Miss Ellen Barlee, whose interesting book, *Our Homeless Poor*, gave the first impulse to this scheme for the employment of women; and whose untiring exertions have maintained and fostered it, till it has reached its present proportions, and deals with an income of 10,000*l.* a-year.

From Miss Barlee we hear what classes the Institute is intended to benefit,—not married women whose husbands are in health and in work, but widows, or wives whose husbands are suffering lengthened illness, and single women. It is her plan to receive *respectable* persons only, and no woman can obtain work who cannot obtain a recommendation from her Clergyman or District Visitor, or the City Missionary of the district, or a Subscriber: by this care at the outset, such an honest class of workers has been secured, that out of some 390,000 shirts which have been made by the women, mostly at their own homes, not 40 cases of pawning or loss have occurred.

Miss Barlee's aim has been to secure for the worker the increased pay which ordinarily, in a large contract for work, goes to make the profit of the middleman. She is herself the middlewoman between her *employés* and Government, receiving and becoming responsible for the execution of extensive contract orders, while she pays to the workwoman

the highest price consistent with making this part
of the operations self-supporting. The advantage to
the workwoman will be apparent when we state that,
whereas formerly the price paid by contractors to
Government shirt-workers was from $3\frac{1}{2}d.$ to $4\frac{1}{2}d.$ per
shirt, Miss Barlee gives $7d.$ for each shirt, with the
additional help of the stitching being done by machinery, which is worth, in the worker's own estima-
tion of time, $2d.$ per shirt more. A quick worker
will make $2\frac{1}{2}$ or 3 of these shirts a-day.

Our kind conductor took us into her office, a
commodious room on the ground-floor, answering to
the dining-room of an ordinary house, where the
indefatigable Secretary, Miss St. John, receives
ladies who come with orders for work, gets through
her share of correspondence aided by a letter-copying
press, and presides over a large cupboard full of ac-
count-books relating to different departments of the
work, which might turn the brain of a less methodical accountant.

Into these books we were privileged to look — one
might be called 'a case-book,' and contained in a
fourfold column, the names of the women to whom
work had been supplied, the names of the parties
recommending, the circumstances of each case, and
the reason for help being discontinued. No eye
could glance down the column which told of the circumstances, without feeling the heart oppressed with
its brief record of misery and want, sickness, death,
misfortune, grinding poverty. A few words told the
tale, and a thick folio volume was rapidly filling

with such cases. Surely a blessing must rest on the
effort which has searched out this misery, and met it
with a fitting remedy! The column which recorded
cases of dismissal from employment was almost
empty, and for a most satisfactory reason.   'The
conduct of the women,' said Miss Barlee, 'is now so
uniformly good, that it is not once in the year I have
occasion to complain.'   Their sense of gratitude to
herself was marked by their subscribing together,
without her knowledge, to get for her a handsome
dressing-case.

Each woman is paid according to the quantity
of work she accomplishes. We opened the wages-
book, and taking a page quite at random, noted
down the figures it contained which represent the
weekly earnings; they are as under. Only in one case,
where the item is 1*l.* 1*s.* 3*d.*, was the sum earned by
mother and daughter; in all the rest they are single
earnings, and the earnings, in the case of in-door
workers, of five days in the week, nine hours per
day, for on Saturday the Institution is closed for
cleaning :—

s.	*d.*	*s.*	*d.*	*s.*	*d.*	*s.*	*d.*	*s.*	*d.*
7	2	6	11	6	5	7	6	12	6
5	11	4	7	21	3	4	8	10	3
4	11	4	11	6	5	6	10	5	1
4	7	7	8	5	2	9	10	7	10
8	10	6	2	7	1	7	2	6	8

This will give an idea of the substantial help rendered to these destitute women; about 100 work in

the house, the remainder take their work home; this, in the case of widows with little children, is an important advantage.

Rules both for the out- and in-workers are framed and hung in conspicuous places in the Institution; for the out-workers, they are as follows:—

'Out-door workers are to arrive at half-past nine A.M. on Tuesdays and on Fridays, keeping regularly to their own day, and are to bring in the full number of shirts they took away.

'No Tuesday-worker will be attended to on a Friday, and no Friday-worker will be attended to on a Tuesday.

'The gate will be locked at half-past two P.M., and no worker admitted after.

'Any worker going in or out of the front door will be fined 3d.

'Any worker detaining her work beyond a fortnight will be fined. In case of illness she is to write to the Secretary, and is to return the work, made or unmade.

'Any worker changing her residence is to inform the Secretary and the Inspectress.

'The work is required to be kept quite clean: any returned soiled, must be paid for by the worker.

'Cheerful obedience to the Inspectress's orders strictly enjoined.

'Any worker found guilty of pawning the work would be dismissed from the Society altogether.'

For the in-door worker they are as follows. (We have given these Rules in full, as we cannot but hope that this scheme for the employment of needlewomen will be transplanted to many provincial towns):—

'In-door workers are to arrive at five minutes to nine

A.M., and remain in the workroom until eight P.M., when a bell will be rung, and the workers are expected to leave quietly and orderly. One hour allowed for dinner, and half-an-hour for tea.

'At half-past nine the gate is locked, and no one admitted after.

'Any worker going in or out of the front door will be fined 3d.

'Cleanliness and punctual attendance required.

'Workers absenting themselves from the workroom without some valid reason will be fined.

'Every woman to do that portion of work given to her by the Matron.

'Industry and cheerful obedience to the Matron's orders strictly enjoined.

'Tea and milk will be provided from the Society's Funds. Workers must bring their own bread, butter, &c.

'One penny in the shilling will be deducted from the payment of in-door workers, towards the expenses of the Society.'

That is to say, for one penny in the shilling deducted from their earnings, Miss Barlee provides them with tea, milk, cotton for their sewing (which is an annual expense to her, of from 60l. to 70l.), gaslight, and fires both in the workrooms and kitchen, implying some ten or eleven fires burning all day, and a consumption of about a ton of coals in the week.

We paid a visit to the kitchen, where the in-workers take their dinner and tea, and thought it most inviting: a large airy room, with clean benches and wooden tables; a glowing fire on one side, where the rasher might be fried, an oven where a meat-

D

pasty might be warmed and made relishing, and the
tea-caldron ready for use.

A short prayer when they first arrive in the
morning, gives its tone to the day's industry.   On
Friday afternoon a short service, from half-an-hour
to an hour in length, is conducted in the large workrooms by a clergyman.   Miss Barlee is very glad
when London clergymen will volunteer assistance
for this little service.   It usually remains in the
same hands for a month : she can generally ensure to
her clerical friends a congregation of about 100
women.   She is also glad to provide for the instruction and amusement of the workers through
the kind assistance of lady-readers, who read aloud
in the workrooms.

The cutting-out department is a business in
itself; it is carried on in a separate room by two
men-cutters and one woman-sorter, whose proceedings we watched with no little interest.   On
cloth, folded so that 120 pieces can be cut at once,
an iron plate is laid of the shape and size of the
shirt-collar or wristband to be cut, and the sharp
blade of the cutter's knife is run five or six times
energetically round the edge of the plate, till it has
penetrated all the folds, and reached the wooden
board on which the cutting is done : it only remains
to separate the pieces which the knife has imperfectly reached with a pair of gigantic scissors.
Every Government shirt consists of 22 pieces, and
must go through the processes of cutting, sorting,
stitching by machine of collar and wristbands—

giving out the shirt to the worker, taking it in,
inspecting it (we saw some shirts in the Inspector's
room rejected and returned for alteration, because
one side of the collar was a quarter of an inch
higher than the other), folding it, tying the shirts
together in bundles of ten, and carting them away
to the Government depôts.   About 390,000 of these
Government shirts have been already executed by
the needlewomen of this Institution.

Our next visit was to the storeroom, a gloomy
place enough, but important for the wealth of goods
stored away there, waiting to be cut out and made
up: it frequently contains several thousand pounds
worth of material.   Our eye fell on masses of a
rough sort of rope in hanks.   'What is to be made
with this?' we asked.   'Oh, that is only string to
tie up the bundles of work.'   Two large worn-out
cutting-boards, hacked and hewed beyond all further
possibility of planing, won our respect in the storeroom: we thought how much hard, honest labour,
those roughened surfaces represented.

All that we had seen hitherto was on the basement and first-floor; now we proceeded up-stairs
to the workrooms.   The murmur of pleasure from
the women, as Miss Barlee entered the room,
showed how warmly her labour of love is appreciated.   In the first room, not Government shirts,
with the coarse strong work appropriate to them,
met our view, but delicate stitching and frilling,
which would bear comparison with the performances
of first-class sempstresses.   We were in the room

where orders for baby linen, ladies' under-garments, and *trousseaux* are executed. In a foot-note* we give the approximate prices for making such articles —we say *approximate*, because in all cases the

* LIST OF PRICES FOR PRIVATE FAMILIES.

				s.	*d.*		*s.*	*d.*
Making Gent's Shirts	..	..	.. from	2	6	to	3	6
„	„ Night Shirts	..	..	„	1	10	„	2	0
„	„ Collars	..	..	..	„	0	3	„	0	6
„	Boys' Shirts	..	..	..	„	1	6	„	2	6
„	„ Night Shirts ..	..	..	„	1	8	„	1	8
„	Ladies' Morning Gowns	..	..	„	6	0	„	10	6
„	„ Dressing „	..	..	„	4	6	„	6	6
„	„ Combing Jackets	..	..	„	2	0	„	4	6
„	„ Bodices	..	..	..	„	2	0	„	3	6
„	„ Night Gowns	..	..	„	2	0	„	5	0
„	„ Chemises	..	..	..	„	1	9	„	3	6
„	„ Petticoat Skirts	..	..	„	1	6	„	6	6
„	„ Drawers	..	..	..	„	1	6	„	2	6
„	„ Flannel Petticoats ..	..	..	„	1	6	„	2	0
„	„ Satchets	..	..	..	„	1	0	„	4	0
„	Children's Dresses	..	..	„	2	6	„	10	6
„	„ Petticoat Skirts	..	..	„	1	0	„	2	9
„	„ Pinafores	..	..	..	„	1	0	„	2	0
„	„ Night Gowns	..	..	„	1	3	„	2	0
„	„ Chemises ..	..	..	„	0	9	„	1	6
„	„ Drawers	..	..	..	„	0	9	„	1	6
„	Infants' Monthly Robes	..	..	„	8	0	„	15	0
„	„ Petticoats	..	..	..	„	1	9	„	3	6
„	„ Flannels	..	..	..	„	1	0	„	3	0
„	„ Shirts	..	..	..	„	1	3	„	2	6
„	„ Gowns	..	..	..	„	2	3	„	3	9
„	„ Night Gowns	..	..	„	2	0	„	3	0
„	„ Pelisses	..	..	„	4	6	„	7	6
Hemming Pocket-handkerchiefs	..	..	„	0	2	„	0	6
„	Hemstitched	..	..	..	„	1	3	„	2	6
Making Tablecloths	..	..	..	„	0	6	„	1	0
„	Sheets	..	..	..	„	0	6	„	1	0
„	Pillow-cases	..	..	„	0	4	„	0	9
„	„ frilled ..	..	..	„	2	0	„	4	0
„	Towels	..	..	..	„	0	1	„	0	2
„	Tray-cloths ..	..	..	„	0	3	„	0	6
„	Tea-cloths, Dusters, &c.	..	..	„	0	1	„	0	3
Marking, each letter or figure	..	..	„	0	0¼	„	0	0¼

woman is paid in this Institution *according to the actual amount of work done;* and it *is* possible to give orders for under-garments, implying an amount of work which will run them up to almost any price. We saw an enchanting baby-frock, which might have made any mother's mouth water —price, three guineas; but then, in addition to expensive embroidery, this little elegancy was decorated with a number of tucks we did not undertake to count, each about half-a-quarter of an inch in depth.

Our next visit was to the machine-room, where eight sewing-machines keep up a cheerful cackle, and eight young machinists (chiefly children or very young girls) turn off, with rapid movements of hand and foot, the collars and wristbands for the Government shirts, or any part of ladies' garments where machine work is preferred.

Upstairs again—on the next and highest floor occupied by the workwomen, was the Inspector's room, flanked on either side by ordinary workrooms. Every garment must be subjected to rigid measuring and overlooking from the inspectress, every button fitted to its respective button-hole, before the work can be passed and paid for. The Government work is inspected by women engaged expressly for that purpose. Indeed, few people would have an idea of the staff required to work the Institution effectively. The sum paid weekly in wages to the needlewomen themselves, sometimes amounts to 150*l.*

It is satisfactory to be able to state, that all the

operations of the Society we have hitherto described,
which may be called the *mercantile part, are now
self-supporting*, and the charitable aid afforded by
the public in the way of subscriptions and dona-
tions goes now entirely to the support of the Charity
Funds of the Institution.

The importance of having a Charity Fund at
command, can perhaps only be fully appreciated by
those who are daily brought into contact with grinding misery, by a work such as that to which Miss
Barlee has devoted herself. To use her own words,
she can tell ' of widows with young children struggling with gaunt famine, dividing a penny-roll
among four children for their entire day's food; of
emaciation and pain, unchecked, preparing their
victims for our hospitals; of women lying on bare
boards during frost and snow, without covering or
fire; of children born to deserted wives, without any
means to provide for them.'

For cases such as these, the Charity Fund committed to her for distribution, under the sanction of
a Committee, is invaluable. It is dealt out to the
very poor and the sick, by grants of coals, grocery
— chiefly tea — clothing, sending the sick into the
country for change of air, and the purchase of hospital tickets for those who cannot be nursed at home.
Grants out of the charity are also sent to all the local
clergy who manage branch institutions; as, for instance, at Chelsea, Whitechapel, Southwark, and
Camden Town.

It has been a great pleasure to Miss Barlee to

contrive some pleasures for her *employés*, as well as a bare supply of their necessities. At Christmas time all the workers share in a Christmas treat; and after a substantial meal, with tea, are entertained by musical performances or other delights, generally freely given by public singers, in connexion with amateur artistes.

Mrs. Gurney, of Carshalton, has also given, yearly, to 120 of them, a rural fête in her own grounds: the enjoyment of this to these worn-down, toiling women of London, has been something indescribable.

Thrifty habits are beginning to show themselves among these needlewomen: last year they paid no less a sum than 60*l.* into their clothing-club.

Miss Barlee is glad of any description of ladies' cast-off clothing: what is not suitable for giving away she sells, and with the proceeds purchases warm garments. A parcel of ball-dresses, lately, she sold for 4*l.*; and 4*l.*, with her judicious and wholesale mode of purchase, represents a great many comfortable shawls and water-tight boots.

She is also glad of any orders for fancy-work, for it would hardly be believed from what respectable classes of society many of her distressed applicants for work are drawn; this Institution provides an agency by which employment may be found for them, without dragging their calamities forward into public notice.

In conclusion, we have endeavoured to represent faithfully what we saw and heard; but we earnestly recommend our readers to verify our statements for themselves, and by all means in their power to befriend helpless women by such institutions as the one in Hinde Street, Manchester Square.

In endeavouring to do justice to this beneficent agency for the employment of women under circumstances of special want and pressure, we have somewhat wandered from the question with which we are at present occupied,—'How family life in the workman's home can be best restored and promoted?' yet it is a cognate subject, for the needlewomen employed by Miss Barlee are not withdrawn from their homes by the work with which she furnishes them; nay, on the contrary, many widows are enabled by it to keep their children about them, who must otherwise have gone with them to the Union, where 'home' is an unknown word.

But to return: the question, 'How family life is to be restored?' implies its present disorganization. In accounting for this disorganization we have spoken first of the withdrawal of the house-mother, because it seems to us a radical evil which carries many others along with it; but certainly, in the workman's family, *intemperance* takes only the second place in the destruction of domestic happiness. We have to show in a future chapter, in which we shall consider the over-crowded, unwholesome state of the working man's dwelling, that he has strong temptations to it. We have seen already how perilously the wife tempts him to it, if, by her own absence,

she leaves him without the home-comforts which
every hard-working man has a right to expect, when
the evening hour of relaxation succeeds to the day
of labour; there will be excuses for him if he yields,
but, unhappily, the excuses do not avert the disastrous
consequences: the drunkard demolishes, with rapid
strokes and a sure hand, all that was left to him of
a domestic sanctuary.   Do we want a picture from
real life? it is not far to seek: thank God that in
this case there is a reverse side to its melancholy
outline!

'I was asked,' said Mr. J., 'to visit a man whose
earnings as a workman ought to have placed him in a position almost of affluence.   He was by trade a glass-polisher;
and being very clever at his business, he could earn from
3*l.* to 5*l.* a-week.   I entered his room.   I found the man
seated on a rickety chair, suffering from *delirium tremens;*
and at the time of my visit, under the dregs of drink.
His wife had seated herself, as best she could, on a tin
kettle: it was the only other article of any kind in the
room.   He had no money, no food, no chance of work, for
he had pawned for drink the very materials for his glass-
polishing.   His wife and two children were sharing in his misery and starvation.   I knew that he had sunk down to the
very last resource of the drunkard, when he took out of his
pocket and showed to me, the pawn-ticket on his own body.'

It may be that the reader will share our bewildered astonishment when the narrative reached this
point; lest it should be so, we offer the explana-
tion we received ourselves.   It seems that the last
resource of the drunkard, when he has pawned goods
and clothes, and everything of marketable value on

which he can raise a penny, is to go to the pawn-
shop, throw himself across the counter, and offer
his own body in pawn! 'Five shillings, alive or dead,'
is his appeal; for the craving within him for drink
amounts to madness. It is a pledge which the pawnbroker accepts without hesitation: he produces the
five shillings, and pins a ticket on the man as a
proof of the transaction. *The pawnbroker never
loses a sixpence by a bargain of this kind;* it seems
to be a last relic of good feeling in the unhappy
drunkard, that he looks upon this as a debt of honour:
to redeem his body from pawn becomes his most
pressing care, and the first five shillings which come
to his hand is sure to be taken to the pawnbroker,
that his poor, much-injured body, may once more
become his own.

   ' Seeing that matters were come to this pass with him,'
said Mr. J., 'I took a little book out of my pocket, and
began to read to him. It set forth the advantages of
temperance. It was called *The Way to be Healthy and
Happy.* I took occasion, from his extreme misery, to urge
him to sign the temperance pledge, which he promised
to do.
   ' About a month after I was again in his neighbourhood, and called to see how matters stood with him. An
unwonted look of importance, as he came forward to receive me, was in itself a hopeful sign; but he had a tale
to tell, and his own way of telling it. " Come, old woman,"
said he, addressing himself to his wife, " bring out these
'ere clothes." The obedient " old woman" produced two
suits of clothes for himself, two for herself, two sets of things
for the baby-boy, and one complete set for the young

daughter. This was the first triumph. " Now, old woman,
the coppers." 16s. 6d. was counted out from a treasured
hoard. Triumph the second :—" That ain't all, master!"
A crowning look of exultation brightened his face when,
after a dive in his pocket, he produced two sovereigns. "Now,
master, take a pen and write." He dictated as follows :—
' " I, R. S., glass-polisher in —— Rosemary Lane, do
hereby declare the benefits I have derived from total absti-
nence. I have been twelve years a drunkard. I never
knew myself sober three weeks at a stretch but once, and
that was when I was in the London Hospital with a broken
leg. I have sold and pawned, many times over, everything
in my house. I have frequently pawned my own body;
and have gone about with a ticket on it,—' Dead or alive,
five shillings.' I return thanks to Almighty God for
sending Mr. J. to my house, and inducing me to sign the
pledge." '

Such was the man's brief history of a drunkard's
life; of domestic happiness marred; of the first
hopeful sign of its restoration. Happily, Mr. J.
can testify that his good resolution stood the test of
time. 'I saw him,' he says, 'fill that room with
furniture, take another room, and fill it too. The
next step in prosperity was to take a three-roomed
house for himself, and build another room on to it:
he always consulted me in his plans.' After a time
he was in a position to gratify his taste for music,
and he bought a piano, nothing daunted by the
consideration that no one in his house could play it;
that objection he hoped to obviate by paying a music-
master for three months, to give his daughter lessons.
However, the young lady's education was at a stage
when ' Reading made easy' was more appropriate

than music lessons; so the piano was rather a failure, and he exchanged it for a grinding organ which could boast a variety of fifty-six tunes, and on which his hopeful little son was delighted to perform. Mr. J. had the comfort of watching his steady improvement for several years, after which he went out to Australia with his family. Mr. J. had never reason to think that the change in the man went deeper than a courageous struggle with a ruinous habit, of which experience had taught him the bitter consequences, and with which he did battle bravely, as a reasonable man, a husband, and a father.

Nothing easier—alas, that we should have to say it!—than to multiply instances of the utter breakdown of family happiness from drinking habits in the husband, or wife, or both. Thus we hear of husband, wife, and ten children occupying one room. The man is a printer's press-maker; when he will work through the week he earns 2l.; his wife is a beautiful needlewoman, his boy works with him, and earns 8s. or 10s. a-week: but it is enough to say the father and mother both drink—we are prepared then to hear of abject poverty, and an utterly wretched home.

A compositor for the *Times* newspaper earns 2l. a-week—enough to secure plenty and comfort in a workman's home; but the household god is *Drink*, and his impoverished votaries, seated on the floor (for there is neither stool nor chair in the room), get their meals off an old box—their only substitute for table, drawers, and cupboard.

A man very successful as a commercial traveller, making his salary of 500*l.* a-year, driving his own trap, and looked up to as a thriving man, took to gambling and drink: the steps downward were rapid; family happiness was swept away; he was separated from his wife; and, when the writer last heard of him, he was to be found in a common lodging-house, earning a miserable pittance by picking up dog-dung, or going out early in the morning to gather together cast-off cigar-ends, which he sold, at a penny or halfpenny an ounce, to the people in the lodging-house.

But what need to say more? Every one must know of such cases, and must feel that a crusade against intemperance must form part of any scheme for restoring family life in the workman's home. There is this encouragement, that drunkards generally know they are their own enemies, and grasp at a friendly hand, firmly and kindly put out to save them: indeed, we recall an interesting conversation we once heard between two distinguished medical men, in which they stated, that when the habit of drunkenness has been of long standing a change is observable in one of the membranes covering the brain, which change is always found to consist in the drunkard, with the absolute loss of any power of volition in restraining his propensity. Such a man's friends must save him in spite of himself—he is helpless; they must keep rigidly out of his sight and reach, any possibility of indulging his vice. We remember an instance, in which Mrs. Bailey

thus exercised coercive guardianship over an unhappy woman, who came to her mothers' meeting,
and lingered to tell her miserable tale: Drink was
her master, and she was a helpless captive, irre-
sistibly drawn, in spite of her better wishes, towards
every public-house she passed on her way to the
meeting; so she must stay at home, for she dared
not come out. But Christian kindness and sympathy found a remedy, and the lady became the poor
woman's guardian on her way back to her home,
linking her arm in her own, and holding it firmly
when she felt the involuntary pull that told a public-
house was in sight.

One point we venture to urge, because practical
evils, where it has been neglected, have come under
our own observation,—' Never give spirits to working
men or women in return for services rendered;' for
anything you know to the contrary, that man or
that woman has made a brave effort to overcome
intemperate habits—has so far persevered that the
future is bright with hope, and your glass of brandy
or spirits may revive the pernicious taste, and plunge
them into a deeper ruin than before. It is told of
the Rev. Mr. Bardsley, who knows working men
well, and is much trusted and loved by them, that
he passed the door of a physician as a porter was
bringing up some load. The gentleman offered
him a glass of brandy. With all the possible consequences before his eyes Mr. Bardsley felt impelled
to step forward, and, apologising for the intrusion,
asked the gentleman if he could ' estimate the value

of the brandy?'—' Perhaps sixpence,' was the answer. —'Then, with your permission, I will put a question to the porter. My friend, this gentleman offers you a glass of brandy worth sixpence, would you like to receive the brandy or the sixpence?' Ready and unhesitating was the answer,—' Oh, the sixpence, of course!' It is quite true that money may and, in many cases, will be spent in drink; but, on the other hand, it *may* be kept to cheer an ailing wife or a sick child; and, at all events, your gratuity does not involve a possible injury, which you would shudder to contemplate.

The public-houses in London at the present time, as Mr. Weylland informs us, number 10,460: he feels how important any measure would be which would tend to limit the number of houses where working men may congregate to drink, and which would restrict the license to the *sale* of beer or spirits. Why should England be behind Russia in moral and sanitary laws? do we want to prove that an autocratic government would be better for us than English freedom? We give an extract, quoted by Mrs. Sewell, from the *Memoirs of Stephen Grelette*, who, being at St. Petersburg on one of his missionary tours through Europe, makes this record in his journal:—

' The Governor, Count Miloradowitch, has considerably reduced the number of places where strong drink is sold, *confining these, as formerly, to cellars, where no seats are allowed.*' [Contrast this with our brilliantly-lighted gin-palaces.] ' No kind of gaming is permitted, nor anything that can induce the poor objects resorting there to remain longer than to swallow the fiery water. During the absence of the Emperor (Alexander) the Minister of Finance, in order to increase the revenue arising from the consumption of strong drink, had allowed the sale of it in upper rooms, coffee-houses, &c., to the great demoralization of those people who would have been ashamed to go into the cellars. The very day of the Emperor's return to St. Petersburg the Governor said to him,—" Which do you prefer, the increase of your revenue at the expense of the morals of your subjects, or their well-being in not being enticed to evil?" The Emperor readily replied, " that the well-being of his people was far more dear to him than his revenues." On which the Governor said,—" In your absence they have considerably increased the consumption of ardent spirits, by allowing them to be sold out of the cellars, and thereby drunkenness and vice have proportionably increased; but, if it be agreeable to you, I will have those places shut up." " Do so," said the Emperor. That very evening the Governor had it done.'*

It may be altogether out of our province to let our thoughts run on such matters; yet perhaps wise men will tell us, why it is thought so much more impossible to restrain spirit-sellers by restrictive measures of the kind we have named, than to restrain graziers and farmers by restrictions—vexatious enough to them—which have arisen out of the cattle plague. They submit, though they live in a free country which trades on free principles, because they have the good sense to see that the interests of the class must yield to the welfare of the country. Yet, compare the evils, the known, recognised evils,

* *Thy Poor Brother*, p. 271.

which have arisen from drunkenness, with those we have already experienced, or even which our darkest forebodings anticipate from the cattle plague. In the one case men are the victims; in the other, beasts: in the one case, character, self-respect, wife, children, are sacrificed; in the other, property is at stake: in the one case, it is a question of moral and spiritual ruin; in the other, of a threatened scarcity of food. Which most imperatively demands the interference of authority? by which of the two evils are the best interests of England most seriously endangered?

God speed the day when we may see 'family life in the workman's home' spring up and flourish, because the helping hand has been found to roll off these encumbering weights—the withdrawal of the house-mother from her family, and habits of intemperance.

Next to these aggressive enemies, which make open war on his domestic happiness, we may place want of *education*, using the word less in the sense of acquirements than of mental training:—

' The father,' says M. Jules Simon, ' ought to be, in the midst of his family, a living, guiding *reason*. Every member of the family ought to feel itself enlightened, directed by him. He is responsible, not only for the bodily welfare of his children, but for their minds, their souls : up to the time when they become of age to judge and decide for themselves, he must think and decide for them. If, then, his own mind is undisciplined, unformed—if his own acts are the results of mere thoughtless impulse—if his own ignorance puts him in a position of perpetual childhood and minority, how can he fulfil his parental

E

duties? how can he inspire those around him with confidence and respect?'*

This was urged upon us the other day by one
very conversant with the habits of the working
classes, to whom we had communicated our eager
desire that their dwellings could be improved:—

'Bad dwellings,' he said, 'sometimes make bad people;
but bad people also make bad dwellings. It will be to
little purpose to improve their dwellings unless more effort
is put forth to improve their knowledge and habits. It is
astonishing how much gross ignorance yet lingers among
the masses; what large numbers of them cannot read; or
read so imperfectly, as to find neither pleasure nor profit
in it. Ignorance is the fruitful source of many of the evils
which peculiarly afflict the poor. Being themselves ignorant, they are indifferent to the education of their children.
The children of the weavers, for instance, choose their own
school, and go when they please. There is a very large
mass of our town population that education has scarcely
yet touched; and when human beings have no intellectual
pleasures, they are exceedingly apt to indulge in grossly
sensual ones.

'Coupled with ignorance I generally find improvidence
and extravagance—vices fatal to domestic comfort, even
if the working man had the best of dwellings. Generally,
he spends as much weekly in the public-house as would
provide him with an extra room and educate his children.
Many of the working men, who are not intemperate, yet
borrow loans at extravagant interest, send their wives
weekly to the pawn-shop; and I have even known them
to get goods from the tallyman, or travelling draper, at an
enormous price, and directly pawn them to raise a little
present money.

* *L'Ouvrière*, p. 384.

' They do require better dwellings, and they ought to have them; but it is, after all, mental and moral training which they peculiarly need: this will enable them, to a large extent, to do for themselves that which they now depend on others to do for them. I have seen the miserable room, inhabited by a whole family, converted by an intelligent Christian housewife into a really habitable dwelling, bright with an air of decency and comfort. She heroically wages continual warfare with dirt and disorder. It·is all around her; but it crosses not the threshold of her little room.'

We heard of a yet severer test to which an intelligent cleanly housewife was subjected, than the one just mentioned in our friend's letter. She lived in the extreme east of London, in a crowded district. The room, a good-sized one, was inhabited by another family as well as her own. Their habits were as dirty, as hers were clean. · Sights and smells *must* be shared, but she made a successful attempt at a division of territory. A chalk line drawn along the floor divided *meum* from *tuum;* dirt reigned on one side of the line, cleanliness on the other.

Yes, we agree with our friend; the workman must be trained to appreciate and desire for himself the higher moral and social standing to which we so earnestly wish to raise him: the *will* on his part wonderfully diminishes the difficulty of finding the *way* on ours. Not the most grinding poverty will keep back the man who has a steady purpose to raise and educate himself. Witness a poor weaver, who sat at his loom with a Hebrew grammar in the window — now

engaged with the intricacies of his pattern—now
mastering the perplexities of a point or the de-
viations of a rule. That man became afterwards a
colporteur.

Education for the workman is one of the subjects
of the day. Workmen's Reading Rooms, Workmen's
Institutes, Industrial Exhibitions, Educational Museums, a Workman's College, classes of various
kinds, books and periodicals written with special
adaptation to their tastes, wants, and circumstances,
with all these we are familiar. What we want is to
awaken rational and intellectual tastes in the lower
class of operatives, whose desires have been hitherto
bounded by physical comforts and indulgences.
We want to arouse in these men a sense of their
dignity and responsibility, as husbands, fathers, and
heads of families.

May we prescribe for the workman an old well-
tested remedy? There is an ancient, yet ever-new
book, which treats with him as a rational, nay, as an
immortal creature; which enters into his wants,
explains him to himself, sympathizes with his
anxieties, prescribes his duties, instructs him in
principles of the soundest wisdom, opens a door
of hope to him in the day of his calamity. We
have said, the workman's best education lies rather
in the training of his mind to think, and of his
heart to feel aright, than in the storing of his
memory with facts. If he will yield himself to the
teaching of this book; if he will make it his guide
and counsellor; if he will instil its principles into

his children, as he walks with them by the way or
sits with them in his house—then we may feel
a happy security that *family life* will flourish, and
bring forth fruits of domestic peace and joy, in that
workman's home.

CHAPTER II.

E can hardly avoid a feeling of shame as we place this second on the list of vexed questions. How came it to be so in England? the land of homes, the country which has ever been able to boast, as a counterbalancing advantage to her insular climate, with its changeful inclement weather, that *family life,* which, under more favoured skies, becomes almost merged in social life, is, in her own borders, concentrated and intensified within four walls and a sheltering roof, brightened into innocent gladness around the domestic hearth, so that to his latest years the strong man's heart melts into tenderness, as he remembers the home of his childhood.

Is there anything in the life of a working man which should shut him out from the joys of home? Will they make his arm less vigorous, relax his courage, weaken his powers of endurance? Why, then, has England been unable to secure them for her honest

sons of toil, on whom her greatness and prosperity
so largely depend? Why are we only now awaking
to a perception of the fact, that our working men
hitherto have been rather kennelled than housed?
We could wish it were possible to discuss a question like this with closed doors, and to hide from
our Continental neighbours,—who have begun to na-
turalize the sacred English word in their language,
because they are also beginning to appreciate that
of which it is a sign,—the humbling admission that
that portion of our population which needs it most,
and does not certainly deserve it least, finds its chance
ever lessening of obtaining any resting-place after a
day's toil which deserves the name of *home*.

We have given an early place to this subject,
because, as a recent writer has well said,—

' It is the home of the working man which, more than
any other single circumstance, affects his condition, his
health, his morals; and its goodness may almost be taken
as a measure of his civilisation. In a dark, dirty, crowded,
ill-ventilated court, or back street, common sense perceives
what is confirmed by the largest experience, that it is as
difficult for health or virtue to exist as for the vegetation of the tropics to thrive amid the snows of Iceland.
The improvement of the material circumstances of the
working classes is the condition precedent to all other
efforts for raising their moral character. In such places
the bodily system first becomes depressed, and then recourse
is the more readily had to alcoholic stimulants, which but
increase the evil. Not unfrequently the working man,
under the influence of these predisposing causes, falls a
victim to a cold, a fever, or some prevailing epidemic, and
then his wife and children are thrown on the world, to live

as best they can by the parish allowance, eked out by
mendicancy. Nor is the influence of such unfavourable
circumstances upon the moral health less disastrous. Under
emergencies men sometimes display a rare nobleness, but
the average mind is incapable of long resisting the daily
attrition of degrading associations. To see hardness of
heart, a selfishness of the lowest type, passing at slight
provocation into brutal violence—to see sensuality and intemperance in their worst forms, and men degraded to the
lowest level, we must visit the lowest class of dwellings,
hidden from public view in narrow courts and streets.' *

We are speaking, not of the agricultural population, but of those congregated in large towns, and
especially in London. The ploughman, who rents
his tenement under a parsimonious landlord, may
have his grievances, and heavy ones too, but they are
not of the kind which we have now under consideration. His home may be one of poverty, suffering,
and privation; but sunlight, pure air, and clean
water, are not to him scarce luxuries. The rain may
drip through the broken thatch, the wind may whistle
through many a crevice; he may feel an honest indignation when he counts out the hoardings for a
half-year's rent into his landlord's greedy palm, that
the small outlay is refused which would make his
habitation air-tight and water-tight: but still it is
home. To use his own expression, he can 'keep
himself to himself,' and the children thrive on a
crust and country air.

It is in London, where the honest artisan pre-

* Hole's *Homes of the Working Classes*, p. 2.

eminently needs a home; that difficulties have increased and thickened in the way of his finding it,
partly owing to the increase of population, and partly
to the wholesale clearance of houses inhabited by the
working classes for the erection of public buildings,
and the extension of railways into the heart of the
metropolis. Thank God, the very magnitude of the
evil is working its own cure! Parliamentary attention has been roused; private benevolence has
wrought out a problem, which proves that enterprise in this direction may rest on a commercial
basis; that the capitalist may do good to himself
while he does good to his neighbour. On all sides
there is light in the horizon, and we fervently hope
and believe that better days for the working man
are in store.

He has the greater claim to consideration, because classes, less deserving than his, have been,
to their own great advantage, taken up by the
State, and brought under careful protection and re-
gulation: we refer to the houseless poor, and to the
occupants of common lodging-houses. We shall
postpone for a little while the consideration of workmen's homes to show, first, what has already been
effected for this, the migratory portion of our London poor; the ebb and flow, who, for nights, or
weeks, or months, go to make up the aggregate of
the three-million peopled city, but who cannot rightly
be termed residents.

Among these, the lowest of all are those whom
the Houseless Poor Act is intended to benefit. Our

readers can hardly need to be reminded that this Act,
which has been in force somewhat more than two
years, provides that no houseless wanderer shall
henceforth be compelled to spend the hours of dark-
ness under a dry arch; that he may apply for a
night's shelter and a crust at the Workhouse or
Union nearest to him, without fear of being turned
back, cold and hungry, to hunt up an entry in his
parish register; that the burden upon rate-payers
shall be equalized by a Central Fund, levied upon
all equally, and chargeable with this nightly benevolence to the outcast.   There is something very
attractive about the general beneficence of such a
law.   We are ready to rejoice that one of those rare
occasions has been found in which human charity
is not bound to be discriminating, and the State may
in some measure shadow forth that Paternal Government which causes its 'sun to shine on the evil and
on the good, and sendeth rain on the just and on the
unjust.'

Recent disclosures have, however, somewhat
damped our confidence, and have made us realize
that the law of universal kindness, which acts safely
and beneficently in conjunction with absolute wisdom
and power, needs many a proviso and safeguard, if
we would act it out ourselves.   It is true that the
sight of misery silences for a time the question of
merit; but it is also true that, in extending a helping
hand to the misery entailed by vice, we must so regulate our charity as neither to foster the real cause of
the misery, nor to extend it by a moral contagion.

Let the sufferings even of the vicious be met by kindly commiseration, but, if — relieved from the pressure of immediate want, the vice begins to manifest itself and parade its deformity — stern repression becomes the duty of the ruler. For instance, last New-year's eve, when shutters were closed and curtains were drawn upon thousands of families gathered round the glowing hearth, each enriched with its holiday complement of sons and daughters, any one passing down Bow Street might have seen a sight to send him back saddened and thankful to his own fireside. A band of some forty men were gathered without the Police Station, waiting for the tickets which should admit them to casual wards for the night. Shoulder to shoulder, rank behind rank, huddled together like frightened sheep, these men stood, little trace of manhood in their countenances — it hardly needed the solitary policeman who paced the flags to keep them in order. Silently, each new comer took his stand in the rear, as they stood waiting for the pauper's humbling dole. Who could scan these faces, so visibly stamped with *misery*, for evidences of *crime?*—who could do otherwise than rejoice that the law gave them food and shelter?

But the feeling awakened in our minds is nearer akin to indignation than pity when we hear of professional idlers and thieves, who take their winter season in London as regularly as the titled resident in Grosvenor Square, begging or stealing during the day according to circumstances, and patronising at night all the casual wards of the metropolis in succession.

Public money, we feel, might be better applied than
in renewing the garments they wantonly tear up ; the
6 oz. of bread is superfluous for a young thief whose
'cap' is full of 'plum-pudding,' and his pocket of
'pence;' the need of a night's shelter is a delusion
for those who spend its hours in card-playing, riot,
and blasphemy, to the scandal and hopeless unrest of
the sprinkling of honest and decent men to be found
in the company. Humanity may, and does, forbid
that the vilest of our species should perish with cold
and hunger; but humanity has an eye to society as
well as to the individual, and will find means to
secure the one object without sacrificing the interests
of the other. The writer inquired of a friend residing in Utrecht how beggars were dealt with by the
government in Holland. The answer was as follows:
'Our police regulations on this subject have for the
last 10 or 12 years been well carried out. Any one
found begging is put into custody. Were it not that
funds are inadequate to meet the expense in every
case, all beggars would be transported to one of our
two colonies, or penitentiary establishments—Om-
merschans and Veenhuizen (in one of our northern
provinces)—where people are compelled to work.
To avoid this paupers contrive to get hawkers' li-
censes, and go about the streets with basketfuls of
matches, soap, thread, tape, &c., for sale.'

A glance at the different interests that have to be
adjusted, and the parties who must co-operate in carrying out the Houseless Poor Act so as to fulfil the
humane intention of its originators, will show us that

the subject is beset with difficulties, and that the
attempts of the last two years must be rather looked
upon as a series of experiments, by means of which
an enlightened government will be able to present us
with a measure as sound in its practical application,
as it is good in theory. That this is the intention of
the Government we learn from the answer of the
President of the Poor-law Board to Lord Cranborne,
who asked whether he meant to introduce any measure for more effectually securing the execution of the
laws relating to the poor in the metropolis? Mr.
Villiers replied that such was his intention, but that
during the last Parliament a committee had been
appointed to inquire into the subject, and any such
measure would be founded on resolutions in the Report it would make to the House. We see, therefore,
that the Houseless Poor Act must be regarded as at
present in a transition state.

That it may not break down in the working, very
varied, and in some cases rather antagonistic, interests have to be adjusted. Its well-working depends
on Boards of Guardians, Masters of Workhouses,
Poor-law Board Inspectors, Relieving Officers, aided,
according to a recent theory, by the co-operation of
the Metropolitan Police, and, not least, the paupers
themselves. Till very lately the dietary question was
left to the discretion of individual masters of workhouses, or of the Boards of Guardians, who respectively
regulate their actions. The result was a most unfair
distribution of the extra trouble entailed on workhouse masters by the Act. The casual, it will be

remembered, is allowed to choose where he will apply. What is likely to guide his choice? Nearness, for one thing—but many would walk an extra mile to get better treatment; and if one master were reported to have so much of the milk of human kindness that he allotted to wizen-faced babies in the arms of vagrant mothers half a pint of milk of another kind; or if he were known to argue that to a very cold and hungry man or woman the comfort of munching a dry crust would be more than doubled by the addition of a pint of hot gruel, why, inevitably there would be a run upon the casual wards where such a master was the presiding genius, and not only the sterner officials would enjoy an immunity from trouble at the expense of the kind ones, but the public must be taxed to find lodgings at 4*d.* per night per head, to relieve the overfull casual wards in one workhouse, while those of another were only half occupied.

To remove, as far as might be, this unequal pressure, a meeting, to which delegates from various unions and workhouses in the metropolis were summoned, was held on the 30th of last December, at St. Martin's Hall, to confer with Mr. Farnall, Poor-law Inspector, as to the adoption of a uniform system of dietary for the houseless poor of London. It was satisfactory, considering the weight which, in virtue of his official position, must attach to any opinion of Mr. Farnall's, to hear that he considered that the Houseless Poor Act had been, on the whole, a success. ' He could safely say that there were now nothing like the number of vagrants that had formerly been seen

in the streets at night; and whereas complaints had
been at one time frequent of the denial of admission
to applicants, he had only received one letter on the
subject in the last nine months.'

Fortified with assurances of the good already
accomplished, the delegates proceeded to their task.
The discussion was not meant to be facetious. The
dole which is to keep an outcast from starvation is
not a natural subject for merriment; yet a smile
must have had an irresistible tendency to play round
the lips of some who were present, as the debate waxed
warm. The guardian of the poor is also the guardian
of the rates, and which interest lies nearest to his
heart and uppermost in his thoughts, depends on individual character. There are guardians in whose
minds pauperism is hopelessly confounded with crime,
and to add a relish to the casual's fare would be, in
their view, a premium upon vice. ' Bread! yes,
let him have it, and welcome: but don't talk to us
of buttering it, adding cheese to it, soaking it in hot
gruel: we are business men, who can calculate to a
nicety, wholesale and retail profit and loss. The public purse is taxed heavily enough, without ordering
in stores of cheese and oatmeal.' Some one hinted
at tea. It was an adventurous thing to do. Did he
not know the pretty little story about 'guardians
and tea,' which had found its way into public journals—how a devoted Board of Guardians had been
made the victims of a parsimonious curtailment of
expense on this very head? How, having talked
themselves hoarse for the public benefit, they were

wont to take a friendly cup together before they
parted? But the government auditor would not see
it in the right light, and actually disallowed the
item for its payment; and then the guardians felt
bound to give strong expression to their disapproba-
tion at such an attempt on their liberties and luxuries, and consequently withdrew, to a man, from the
board-room, leaving the affairs of the poor at the
next meeting to settle themselves. He was a bold
man who hinted at tea, if he knew all this. Was
tea, which had been denied to the guardians, likely
to find its place on their dietary table for the
casuals?

The conclusions actually arrived at were as follows:—'That the supper served out to adults shall
be six ounces of bread and a pint of gruel; and to
children, four ounces of bread and half a pint of gruel.
The same allowance is made for breakfast; but during the summer months, from Lady-day to Michaelmas, bread only, without the addition of gruel, is
allowed for the evening meal.'

The labour test has proved to be a more difficult
question than the diet table. When the Act first
came into operation it was proposed that all able-
bodied casuals, who were fed and housed over-night,
should earn the next morning's breakfast by doing
an allotted portion of task-work. The proposal
seemed reasonable enough, and valuable as a deter-
rent to the idle and vicious. In one case, that of
the Camberwell Workhouse, where about fifty-five
casuals weekly claimed the benefit of the Act, the

work done by them about repaid the cost of their
food : but some important objections had not been
taken into account. The hour to which casuals were
detained in the workhouse by their morning task,
prevented them from obtaining work the next day,
and so obliged them to be casuals the next night.
One of the more intelligent of them said, with much
force, 'When I am kept in till twelve o'clock I must
be a pauper and a vagrant for the rest of the day, and
I shall get into the habit of it.'

Besides, the task-work cannot be enforced in all
cases. When casual wards are full, and vagrants are
sent out to sleep in certified lodging-houses, the
guardians have no lawful means of compelling them
to return and do their task-work in the morning.
Out of 500, Dr. Brewer tells us, provided with
lodging certificates from St. George's, only forty-five
had returned, and even that proportion was steadily
diminishing.   Dr. Brewer further stated (at a meeting of the guardians of metropolitan unions, held
at his own house, Feb. 3 of this year), that he had
conversed with some of the more respectable among
the vagrants, and the suggestion made by one of
themselves was, that all applicants should be made
to come into the wards at five o'clock, and be made
to work till nine o'clock ; that those who had worked
well should have tickets for supper, bed, and breakfast, and be allowed to go out at seven o'clock in the
morning, to see if they could not obtain work in the
day.   This seems very sensible, because the idle and
unemployed can as well come in early as late, and

F

men who are at work ought to have earned what will
pay their night's lodging.

Difficulties about task-work are not the only ones
which beset this vexed question. The professed thieves
who frequent casual wards know how to turn a penny
out of their lodging-ticket: many of the vagrants obtain tickets, sell them, and then turn to other institutions for relief. No way has been found as yet
which can prevent their doing so. Another variety
of vagrant misconduct was more frequent two or three
months ago than at present—we mean, the mania for
tearing up clothes; but as cases of this kind still appear in the police reports, it may be worth while to
give the experience of the Chairman of a Union, as
communicated to the *Times*:—

'Sir,—Many years ago I was Chairman of a Union
much infested with tramps.

'One morning the master of the workhouse begged I
would come up, for several able-bodied tramps—about a
dozen, I think—were very riotous, had torn their clothing
to atoms, were in bed, and refused to get up unless new·
clothing was provided.

'On arrival I found matters as reported. The tramps
were somewhat insolent; but, taking no notice of that, I
told them we were bound to supply the destitute with food
and shelter, but nothing was said about clothing; that if
they preferred nakedness, it was the same thing to us; that
they could stay in bed as long as they liked, and should
be provided with food, but not with new clothing.

'Shortly afterwards they began making holes in the
roof, but a shower of rain fortunately coming on they
desisted from that amusement, and stopped up the holes
again as well as they could.

' They told me on my visiting the ward next day, that
unless they had clothes they would set the place on fire.
" All right," I said: " do as you like, we shall not in-
terfere : if you set the place on fire you can stay in the
flames, or adjourn to the yard, as you like." Still, food
was regularly provided. About the third day, I think,
two or three disappeared in the night, carrying off rugs or
blankets. No notice was taken, no inquiries made, but
food served as usual to the remainder. At the end of
about a week, as well as I can recollect, every one had
vanished.

' Now, whether this system was legal or no I cannot
say, but it certainly was effective ; for, though we lost a
few rugs, not a tramp came near us for months — I may
almost say, for years : so I recommend the plan to the notice
of the Guardians of the East London Union.'

Worse, however, than even the wanton and un-
grateful waste of the public funds which succour and
feed them, is the unbridled license which vicious and
depraved vagrants give themselves in the casual wards,
making them a very hell upon earth to the decent
and honest wayfarer. No wonder that at a meeting
lately held in the rooms of the Reformatory and Refuge Union, under presidency of the Earl of Harrowby,
the following resolution was recorded : —

' The managers of the night refuges are of opinion that
the Houseless Poor Act, while effectually providing, if
properly carried out, for the class of regular vagrants and
tramps, cannot meet the case of the honest and deserving
destitute poor, who, from various causes, are for the time
houseless, and who need such aid as can alone be afforded
in voluntary refuges.'

All honour to the Refuges for stepping in to do that which the Act has hitherto failed to do! but the framers of the Act will not let it rest here—they will not sit down under a sense of defeat. It was, undoubtedly, intended to meet the emergencies of the really houseless poor, who migrate from place to place, seeking for work, and become temporarily destitute; not to maintain in idleness audacious vagabonds, who alternate between workhouses and prisons. It can never be too strongly impressed on our minds that poverty in itself is no crime, homelessness is no crime; we are disciples of One who 'had not where to lay His head.' To take it for granted that because a man is poor he is also criminal, and to put him in consequence under penal regulations, is unjust; but so soon as a man adds to his pauperism daring exhibitions of criminality, our duty towards him is altered—not that we should abandon him, cast him off, leave him to starve; on the contrary, we must the more rigidly take him in hand; but in a way suited to his moral condition.

Classification, separation of the well-conducted from the vicious, seems to be an important object to keep in view. At the meeting at Dr. Brewer's house, to which we have already referred, he says that, from his investigations he is satisfied that if two wards were established, one for early and one for late applicants, all the deserving poor would be found in the early ward, and the worthless, law-breaking vagrants in the late ward.' That of itself would be the commencement of a discrimination between the worthless and the deserving classes of vagrants.

The Poplar Union has adopted another method of discrimination,—it has placed its casual wards under the supervision of the police, and with very striking results. The *Times* says of this measure:—

'Its great object is to divert public charity from unworthy to deserving recipients, and to provide especially that the relief designed for the houseless poor, should not be monopolised or intercepted by notorious thieves. The dangerous classes in the metropolis are pretty well known to the police, and the police are well known to them. A thief has a natural antipathy to a constable, and to all places under a constable's supervision. Such characters, it may be safely assumed, will not present themselves where the police may be expected to receive them. In the workhouse of the Poplar Union provision is made, as' elsewhere, for the admission of houseless poor to shelter and relief. During the month of November last, when the place was under the old system of management, the admissions under this head were 1821 in number. In the following month the casual wards appropriated to these applicants were placed under the supervision of the police, and the consequence was that the number of admissions dropped to 580. It appears, therefore, that of the whole number of people receiving assistance in the character of casual poor, two-thirds at least have reason to avoid the observation of the police.'

Of the 1821 admitted in November, 1251 were men, and 1180 of these men called themselves labourers. In December, when the police were employed, only 476 men were admitted, of whom 440 called themselves labourers.

The remarkable results obtained from the Poplar experiment have led to a serious agitation of the question, whether the plan shall not be adopted and acted upon, throughout the unions and workhouses of the metropolis. Sir Richard Mayne has signified his readiness to the President of the Poor-law Board, that the duty shall be undertaken by the police. It must, however, be remembered, that should the measure be adopted, and should all casual wards be placed under the supervision of the police, with the same results as at Poplar, we should have succeeded in scaring the vicious from the workhouses, but we should have left them altogether outside the benefit of the Act. We should have purged the casual ward, and left it fit for the reception of the decent wayfarer, but those who cannot show their faces as honest men would have to perish from starvation in the holes and corners to which their iniquities have driven them.[*]

It has been suggested that there should be special houses of detention for vagrants, where men who can give no account of themselves, nor show that they are following any lawful calling, shall be sent, and maintained under a proper state of discipline, being kept closely to work until suitable employment can be provided for them. This corresponds with the system pursued in Holland, to which allusion has already been made.

Meanwhile, until the inquiries and investigations

[*] Inquiries made in the present spring (March, 1866) from an Inspector of Police, elicit the fact that the police are now engaged in many parishes, by the request of the guardians, in the application of the Houseless Poor Act, and the Inspector gave it as his opinion that the carrying out of the Act would be in their hands before long, through all the metropolis.

which have been or are being made by those in authority shall result in the establishment of the Houseless Poor Act on a practical and efficient basis, every board of guardians and workhouse master must surely see it to be their duty to enforce such discipline and restrictions in the casual wards as shall protect honest and decent men from riotous outbreaks, and silence the revolting blasphemies of which they have been unwilling auditors. The rest of a labouring man should be sweet and refreshing—better to secure it under a dry arch, than have it broken and dispersed by the uproarious mirth of daring thieves and profligates.

Five suggestions were sent to the *Times* on this subject, as to regulations to be adopted in casual wards, which appear worthy of attention. They are as follows:—

'1. All cards and gambling implements to be taken from any person admitted, at the time of admittance, and not to be restored until the period of departure.

'2. No persons to be admitted after (say) half-past nine o'clock, unless when it shall appear that they could not apply earlier for admittance.

'3. At (say) half-past ten o'clock a gong to be struck, and after that time silence to prevail throughout the building, and to be maintained till the hour of rising, except in necessary communication with the porter or police, or any officer of the workhouse.

'4. Before silence is proclaimed no person to use any bad language or sing any song.

'5. Any person infringing the rules may be turned out of the shed, first having his clothes handed to him or her;

and if refractory, may be taken before a magistrate in the morning.'

The writer continues : —

' I do not offer these suggestions as either new or as the best that can be adopted, but. in the hope that they may lead to further discussion of the important question how we can prevent our night homes of charity, from continuing to be schools of vice.'

Before leaving the question of the houseless poor we must say a few words on efforts of private benevolence which have been directed to the same end as the Houseless Poor Act itself. It must not be supposed, that until the passing of the Act the outcast and the vagrant were generally left to perish unheeded. The action of a representative government on such a matter as the one we have under review, implies that a social evil has attained proportions which arouse general attention ; but the eye of philanthropy detects it in an earlier stage, and takes the initiative in supplying a remedy. Twenty years ago the Field Lane Refuge had commenced the work which is now so widespread and beneficent; for sixteen years the Leicester Square Soup Kitchen, founded by Mr. Cochrane, has attracted the hungry and the weary, by its savoury messes and night accommodation. Playhouse Yard, Whitecross Street, has housed its 700 nightly, good and bad, young and old, English and foreign, on the sole plea of want and misery. The managers of the Dudley Stuart Night Refuge, in addition to immediate unquestioning relief, have sought to trace

the history of applicants, and to stretch out a helping
hand to raise them from the moral and social slough
into which they have fallen.   But it is needless to
enter into any details on the subject of these Refuges,
as they are fully described in Mr. Blanchard Jerrold's
very interesting book, *Signals of Distress*, which,
up to the date of its publication in 1863, gives information and statistics on these and other kindred
operations of benevolence, more or less public, carried on in the metropolis.   One only of his suggestions we would venture to reproduce.   At the Field
Lane Refuge, while bread and coffee are distributed
in the morning to those who have been housed through
the night, the master reads from the advertisement
columns of the newspapers all the advertisements
which apply for *labour*, by which most sagacious
proceeding hundreds of men find employment.   Mr.
Jerrold advises that this Field Lane plan should be
copied in other Refuges; and may we not add a hope
that each workhouse master will adopt it in the casual ward ?   The blessing of the honest man who
longs to trade with his sole capital, the power to
labour, but who finds it locked up for want of information as to where it can be invested, will be sure to
be upon him; though he may gain small thanks from
the idle vagrant or the professional beggar.

Thus far we have had to do with gratuitous
lodging, provided either by law or by love for the
houseless; now we advance a step, to consider what
accommodation he may hope for, if the close of the

day should find him with a few pence in his pocket. He will inquire in such a case for a common lodging-house, the poor man's hotel.

Fifteen years ago, what would he have found? He would have paid three pence for the privilege of lying down, under circumstances compared with which the wild beast in his lair is surrounded with comfort,—floors encrusted with filth and swarming with vermin, on which, without bed or bedding, the healthy, the fever-stricken, the decrepit, lay promiscuously side by side, sleeping, or gaming, or drinking, with now and then the ghastly variety of a corpse waiting to be carted away.

What would he find now?* Clean and well-ventilated houses, drainage, and the necessary accommodation connected with it; good water, amply supplied. Each sleeping-room furnished with clean and separate beds, and a sufficient supply of bedding. The number allowed in each room apportioned according to space. The houses have each a kitchen, with fire and other accommodation for cooking, for the use of the lodgers, and some houses are provided in addition with a library or reading room.

What has wrought so beneficial a change? A system of Government Inspection. The former state of the common lodging-houses was brought before public notice by the representations of the General

* The writer is indebted to the courtesy of Sir Richard Mayne, in replying to questions sent to him at the close of last year, for information and statistics as to common lodging-houses up to that time.

Board of Health, and the Report of the Constabulary Commissioners, as constituting a great source of contagious and loathsome diseases on the one hand, and as a hotbed of crime and moral depravity on the other.

We have already hinted that overcrowding in its most repulsive form was the rule in common lodging-houses, arising from a rapacious desire on the part of those who owned or rented the house, in whole or in part, to squeeze as much profit as possible out of their interest in it. Captain Hay, one of the Commissioners of Metropolitan Police, states in a Report made to the Secretary of State, — "It is difficult to ascertain who is the really responsible keeper of the house : there is, first, the owner; secondly, his tenant for the whole house; thirdly, the sub-tenant for a room ; and fourthly, five or six persons occupying one room as lodgers. Each grade of tenants endeavours to obtain as large a profit as possible for the wretched accommodation afforded." As a specimen of the money wrung out of a house of a small yearly rental, he mentions one in Church Lane, St. Giles's, which was rented of the owner for 25*l*. per annum ; the rents received from the sub-tenants occupying rooms in the house amounted to 58*l*. 10*s*. The sum received by these sub-tenants from lodgers would, as nearly as can be calculated, be more than 120*l*. per annum. Thus, a house worth only 25*l*. a-year was increased to a value of nearly five times that sum by charges to the poorest classes.

To meet evils such as these the Common Lodging-

house Act of 1851 was passed, by which all keepers
of common lodging-houses were compelled to register
their houses; and all registered houses were put
under a code of regulations, and subjected to visits
of inspection from officers, who were empowered to
enforce the carrying into effect of these regulations.

They include such points as these,—The windows
in every room must be capable of opening—Floors
and stairs must be clean—Walls and ceilings lime-
whited—Bedding clean—Holes for ventilation
opened, where there is no open fire-place—Persons
of different sexes not to occupy the same sleeping-
room, except married couples, or parents with their
children under ten years of age—Restriction of the
number of the lodgers in proportion to the number
of cubic feet of air contained in the apartment—
Removal at once of any cases of infectious disease.
We have given, however, in an Appendix, the regulations in full contained in the Act, that visitors
of the poor may be acquainted with its terms, and
may thus be prepared to deal with cases in which
they suspect the law is evaded. Within the metropolitan police district the Commissioners of
Police of the Metropolis are the local authority to
carry the Act into execution.

After five years of diligent reform from the time
of the passing of the Act a very different tale could
be told of the state of common lodging-houses.
With scarcely a dissentient voice, the different
Medical Officers of Health of the metropolitan
districts report to the General Board of Health a

complete radical change for the better. To give two or three instances among many.

The Medical Officer for St. George's, Southwark, reports:—

'The present state of lodging-houses, with few exceptions, is very satisfactory. There is now, and for some time has been, but little sickness in these houses. I was parish surgeon for seventeen years before my appointment to my present office, and I can therefore speak personally to this fact. Then the worst cases of fever occurred in the common lodging-houses ; and a very large proportion, and by far the worst part of the duty of the parish surgeon, was the visiting of the sick in these houses. Now, very few cases of fever or any other disease occur, and by cleanliness and prompt removal in case of attack, the spread of · disease amongst a class so likely to take it, is prevented. I think it is almost impossible to overrate the good that has resulted from the operation of the Act. *It would be most desirable if the same benefits, such as limitation of the number of inmates, compulsory cleaning, &c., could be extended to a class of houses very numerous in St. George's, Southwark, which are underlet to families not coming under the operation of the Lodging-house Act. Such houses are, at present, greatly over-crowded, filthy, abounding in bad arrangements, and the haunts of the worst and most infectious diseases.*'

The Medical Officer of St. Olave's, Southwark, reports:—

' I find the regulations under which lodging-houses are placed in this parish strictly carried out. *The cleanliness, ventilation, and comfort of the licensed rooms, offer a very marked contrast to those occupied by the families of the poorer classes, residing even in the same houses.* No

disease has occurred in the lodging-houses of the district
for nearly twelve months, though previously disease was of
common occurrence.'

The Medical Officer of St. Margaret's and
St. John's, Westminster, reports:—

'In these parishes the common lodging-houses are
generally well-conducted, cleanly, and wholesome; *and if
these advantages could be afforded for families, I am
quite sure the death-rate would be materially diminished.
Under the existing law, a family, however large, may
occupy a room, however small and unfit it may be, not
only for convenience, but for health. I would wish the
Legislature to adopt such measures as may appear desirable to secure to the poor, not living in common lodging-
houses, more efficient ventilation.* For lodging-houses
themselves, I can state that their condition, under the
present system, is a very vast improvement upon the
former state of things.'

We would draw the reader's attention to the
passages we have put into italics. These letters are
selected from many others contained in the Report,
and in almost all of them concurrent testimony is
borne to the existence of a great evil lying side by
side with the one which has been remedied, which is
rapidly forcing itself into notice, though as yet
scarcely touched by legislation—we mean, the condition of what may be called Family Lodging-houses.
The overcrowded condition of the *families* of London labourers and workmen, and the unsuitable and
debasing character of the only accommodation accessible to them, is the subject we have still to con-

sider. We will close our present chapter with a few of the details kindly furnished by Sir Richard Mayne:—

'The number of houses surveyed as common lodging-houses up to October, 1865, amounts to 8110, of which 3400 have been registered under the regulations of the Act.

'The price for a night's lodging is on an average 3*d.*, though it ranges from 6*d.* as the highest, to 2½*d.* as the lowest.

'The lodgers still consist principally of the vagrant class, who follow no legitimate occupation, such as thieves, tramps, and beggars. Many exceptions, however, exist; licensed hawkers, and other members of the industrious classes, such as sailors, shoemakers, tailors, market, dock, and other labourers, cabmen, &c., lodge in the best houses.

'Many gentlemen interested in the measure have personally inspected the registered houses, and borne testimony to the satisfactory working of the Act.

'Much of the success of the Common Lodging-house Act is due to the assistance rendered by the police magistrates, on cases brought before them by the police.'

CHAPTER III.

HOMES FOR ENGLISH WORKMEN, AS THEY ARE.

WE approach now a subject of graver import. We are no longer considering the temporary succour to be accorded to the vagrant, or arrangements for the well-being of the passing lodger; but the *home* of an English workman, as it is to be found in our large cities, and especially in the metropolis.

Home? Of all countries in the world we ought to know best in England what it means, what it implies. It has passed into a proverb, that 'an Englishman's house is his castle.'

Family life is one of God's most effective instruments for preserving and renovating the moral health of a nation. It is a germ in which lie folded domestic happiness, education in its truest and highest sense, social purity, loyalty, and order; the germ is encased in a protecting sheath, and that sheath is *home*. When God created the first parents of our human family, He placed them in a *home* which

His own hands had not disdained to prepare and decorate.

The intimate connexion between the healthy unfolding of family life, and the home in which it is developed, must be evident to all. What should a workman's home be? What is the ideal called up to our imagination when we speak of it? It should be the place to which his heart has turned during the day, while his head or his hands have toiled faithfully to promote the interests of his employer; the place to which he returns at night, laying aside his calling as a servant, to resume the simple and natural dignity with which God has invested him, as head of his family.

It is his place of repose, of refreshment, of endearment. In the factory or workshop he is a 'hand,' esteemed or despised in proportion as he is efficient or inexpert; at home he is the husband, the father, the centre round whom all revolves, the prop of his wife, the example and instructor of his children.

With an honest pride he cuts up and distributes the loaf earned by the willing labour of his own right hand; and as the helpless little ones cluster round his knees, his heart grows big with protecting love, and he calls himself a *rich* man, measuring wealth by God's estimate, and not by the standard of the capitalist.

An hour or two later in the evening these thoughtless youngsters will be in dreamland; and then home is the place where the workman and his wife take counsel together as long-tried friends over family

G

plans and possibilities—'another half-year's schooling for the eldest,' or 'a place for our little maid,
where folks are kind and careful, and won't let her
come to harm.'

The talk, it may be, is prolonged, and goes back
to old days; and as the wife looks with full, trusting
eyes into his face, and her tongue utters fondly the
old familiar name, he smiles to remember how shyly
it passed her lips for the first time, on the day from
which he dates his happiness.

Life may not have been all smooth to these two;
some of the children's places may be empty: there
have been times, perhaps, when work was scarce and
health failed, and debts were unwillingly contracted:
nay, troubles and rough places may be in the road
before them now, but they have not given in hitherto,
and they will not now—partly because they meet
troubles together, and the strongest carries the heavy
end of the log; chiefly because they believe there is
a God above them who is the poor man's friend, and
they nourish their faith out of an old book which
never grows dusty on their shelf, where they read
that 'He giveth food to the ravens,' and that He hath
'chosen the poor of this world rich in faith, and heirs
of the kingdom.'

Will any one say this is a highly-coloured ideal
of a workman's home? We ask, why? Have we
introduced one element of happiness beyond domestic
affection in the life present, and hope for the life to
come? We have confidence enough in our industrial
classes to believe that this is often realized, and would

be realized to a far greater extent if the physical, moral, and spiritual welfare of the working classes in our large towns were not exposed to deteriorating influences, *over which they have no control.*

How, we ask, is the sanctity of the family home to be preserved?—how are children to be nurtured in self-respect, and kept free from moral pollution?— how is the father, the bread-winner (whose failing power to work reduces the whole family to pauperism), to be kept in health under such circumstances as are daily brought to light by our public journals?

Mr. Weylland, for several years employed as City Missionary to the public-houses in Marylebone, whose talents and untiring zeal have won for him a position of influence with some of our ablest statesmen, gave to the writer some curious facts which bear on this subject. His work in public-houses was night duty: about five in the morning he was accustomed to see gangs of workmen, fifteen or twenty in number, crowding to public-houses for what they called ' a freshener,' consisting of gin and milk.

' Why do you take this? it is a bad breakfast.'

' Oh, it isn't breakfast: but we must have it the first thing—we feel so queer and tired when we wake up in the morning.'

' Why, where do you live?'

The answer explained the need for ' a freshener;' they lived in a place which, by a bitter mockery, bore the name of *Paradise* Street, Conway Court. The missionary knew it well, with its overcrowded rooms and stifling atmosphere; under depressing influences like these vital powers flag, and nature craves a stimulant.

Again: he was speaking of Sabbath traffic, and the impossibility of purchasing the Sunday dinner overnight, because, in the *close foul air in which these human beings sleep, neither meat nor vegetables will keep.*

'It is often a very small room,' he said. 'At night the Punch-and-Judy bedstead, which stands against the wall, is let down for the father and mother, and the room seems almost filled with it: for such of the children as cannot be crowded into the bed, a bundle of rags is thrown down by the door after it has been closed for the night; and what the air soon becomes you may judge by the fact, that meat and vegetables become putrid in a few hours: yet if they were left outside, or in the yard, of course they would be stolen.'

Speaking of the state of Devonshire Court, (his acquaintance with it dates nine years back), he says, 'there were 122 rooms in it, and they accommodated 129 families—nearly 700 souls.' Just recently he has met with a room where, in consequence of the scarcity of accommodation from pulling down for railways, the rent has run up to 6s. 4d. for a week's lodging. This is paid by two families, who share the room between them; the women go to bed and hide themselves up, after which the men come in to undress and follow their example. Washing, of course, is not thought of; even if it were not rendered more difficult by the scarce supply of water, and its foul quality.

This missionary spoke earnestly of the importance of getting penny baths for the working classes; he spoke of twopence as a prohibitory price, and, even though space is so valuable in London that we hear its value is now estimated at so much the square *inch*, he expressed his belief that a penny bath might be made a paying concern.

The absolute neglect of any personal washing, beyond that of the hands and face, was curiously brought out in a circumstance which befel a Lancashire labourer, a particularly decent-looking fellow, whose white shirt and well-brushed coat on Sunday attracted attention by their respectable appearance. He had been engaged to clear out a pond, and consequently stood for several hours in water with bare feet and legs. When work was done, and he was about to put on stockings and boots to walk home, he was struck with dismay at the unusual appearance of his legs,—they were *white,* and he thought the skin had come off!

But to return to the houses. What is the condition of the rooms themselves? Dr. Druitt* says of them : —

'It appears absolutely necessary to utterly remove the old, dilapidated, dark, squalid, damp tenements, which cover a large area of this metropolis. Practically speaking, they are perfectly incurable; and they serve only as a

* In a paper read Feb. 20, 1860, at the General Meeting of the Royal Institute of British Architects.

nursery of an enfeebled and sensual population. There are houses from which disease is never absent; the soil is sodden with damp and riddled with drains; the walls damp, and saturated with the exhalations of years; the wood, decayed and spongy, full of vermin, never looking clean, and from its porosity refusing to dry if washed. Such houses are utterly hopeless, and it is evident that it would be a boon to humanity if the districts where they prevail could be razed to the ground, the surface excavated, and then covered with dwellings which would admit the light and air, and encourage cleanliness.'

Dr. Jeaffreson gives an account which is yet more detailed, and in this respect more valuable, that he brings information down to the present date. We invite the reader's attention to extracts from a letter he addressed to the Editor of the *Times* on the 1st of January of the present year, containing the results of a house-to-house inspection he had lately made, as closely as one person could, of the worst quarters of Lambeth; St. George's, Southwark; Bermondsey; Rotherhithe; Bethnal Green; St. Luke's, Middlesex; St. Pancras; and St. Giles's. Dr. Jeaffreson was late Medical Officer to the London Fever Hospital, and therefore speaks with authority as to insalubrious influences.

But, while inviting the reader's attention, we warn him that he will be pained, perhaps disgusted. We are sorry to have to drag him with us through such scenes. Yet if he cannot bear to hear of them from a distance, how have the pioneers, as we trust, of extensive reformation, borne to investigate them? and how—far more appalling question!—have men,

women, and children, less delicately nurtured indeed
than ourselves, but with human nerves, and frames,
and feelings like our own, how have they borne to
live in them during the weeks, months, and years of
their miserable existence? There is a significant
proverb which rebukes an over-sensitive shrinking
from hearing of human misery and degradation—
' If thou forbear to deliver them that are drawn unto
death, and those that are ready to be slain ; if thou
sayest, *Behold, we knew it not,* doth not He that
pondereth the heart consider it, and He that keepeth
thy soul doth He not know it? and shall He not
render to every man according to his works ? '

Dr. Jeaffreson thus states his object :—

' It has been to acquire a correct idea of the real state
of such localities. *The more the very intricate question of
the sanitary condition of various parts of the metropolis
is inquired into, and the subject of reform considered, the
more supreme do the difficulties appear ; but at the same
time the importance of energetic action assumes imperious
proportion, and calls for the earnest consideration of all
classes of the community.*

' Although varying somewhat in particular localities,
the general characteristics of low house property, and its
surroundings, where fever is continually rife, are of such
painful and offensive monotony, that the matters mentioned in my communication are more or less applicable to
all; and each person, familiar with but one district, will
believe the sketch taken solely from it.'

He enters first into details as to the water supply
of these fever-nests as follows :—

'This is extremely deficient. Those houses the best supplied have each a butt holding about 80 gallons, into which water flows from a stand-pipe for from ten minutes to half an hour each day.'

This is supposed to supply the wants of 20 persons, for cooking, washing their persons, house, and linen, and every variety of domestic use.

'At other places a larger butt, but in relation to the number of persons proportionally smaller, supplies a whole court of ten or more three-roomed houses, which have no back-yard, and a population of 150 people, members of 30 different families. On Sundays even this supply is absent; the water of the day before is gone, and in many houses that for the Sunday cooking has to be begged from neighbours who may have provided themselves with a larger butt, who are more provident or more dirty. Sometimes, for part of Sunday and Monday a whole court has to borrow for their scant necessities from a " public" at the corner. Thus the day of all others when the houses of the poor are crowded, the means of cleanliness and comfort are even less than on the working days, while in those instances where continuous week-day toil precludes the housewife from cleaning on any day but Sunday, she then finds it impossible to make up the compulsory neglect of the week.'

Dr. Jeaffreson next remarks on the state of the water-butts themselves:—

' More than nine-tenths of these water-butts have no cover, and fully half are so placed as to catch the drippings from the foul eaves of the houses, and are lined internally with scum and slimy vegetation. More than a few are so rotten that one's finger can be pushed through

them, and they allow the water to run rapidly off—an
evil for which there is some consolation, as it is better than
that the water should be swallowed, after it has imbibed
the soppy sewage, sometimes of the foulest description, in
which the water-butts not unfrequently stand.'

Even this is not the lowest degree of misery in the
matter of water-supply.   Dr. Jeaffreson further tells
us :—

' In some courts and alleys not even such appliances
are to be found.   Several such, containing say eight two-
roomed houses and sixty-four inhabitants, are thus supplied.
A half-inch pipe projects a few inches through the wall of
the court, so that any small can or tub may be placed
under it, on the soppy ground, by such of the inhabitants
as possess them, for the purpose of catching the water,
which flows for twenty minutes only, in the course of the
day.   Those who have no vessels, or are out, or not up as
early as the water flows, must go entirely without.'

Want of water means dirt—dirt on the person,
dirt in the cooking, dirty clothes, a dirty house.
A very little reflection will show that a family compelled to live in dirt will soon lose self-respect and
become brutalized and degraded.   There *are* instances which now and then refresh the eyes of City
Missionaries in the worst localities, where poor struggling women *will* be clean, where the visitor turns
in from the filthy common stair, to a room whose
bright window-panes, well-rubbed furniture, and
general neatness and order, bespeak the character of
the inmates; but the instances are as rare as the
circumstances are difficult, and many who have come

up from the country with ideas and habits of cleanliness, and have striven hard—and perhaps for months
successfully—to maintain them, at last succumb, and
come to acquiesce in that for which they see no hope
of remedy.

Dr. Jeaffreson divides the houses themselves into
three classes :—

' First, such as cover acres of the ground of London—
small four-roomed tenements, with wet walls, sodden floors,
and loose ceilings, and roofs permitting the rain to come
through. Two of the rooms are upon the ground-floor,
and two above; and, with few exceptions, they give covering to four families, and to from twelve to twenty persons, rarely more. The rent of each room is from 2s. to
4s. a-week. The largest room of the house will barely
give 250 cubic feet to each of five inmates; while sometimes ten persons crowd into the same space, which is often
used as workshop as well as dwelling-room. In many such,
where typhus had been, or was raging, I saw smart, warm
children's clothing, and good cloth garments, being made
for children and men.'

The second class of houses is still worse; he
describes them as follows:—

' Miserable two or three-roomed buildings, which are
placed back to back, without any back-yards, any staircase window, or any means of through ventilation ; so
that the upper one or two rooms are the receptacle of part
of the air from the lower. The inhabitants of those upper
rooms often imbibe typhus from atmosphere which was a
little too pure to give disease to those on the ground-floor
room. In such cases it was generally the " party up-stairs"
who first had the fever, and from whom the poison spread
over the house.'

The third and last class includes old rambling houses, which were originally built for those in better circumstances, and were formerly occupied by single families. They are now let to as many families as there are rooms in the house; ordinarily eight or ten. Till within the last few years the cellars were inhabited. Each family is composed of from ten to two persons, and lodgers are not unfrequently taken in under the rose. This kind of house is open to two or three special objections. Family privacy is still more impossible than in the three or four-roomed house, because, as it was originally built for the use of one family only, offices and conveniencies, which must be used in common, imply still greater discomfort and heterogeneous mixture of families. Commonly, also, in such houses, water is only conveyed to the ground floor, and the women inhabiting the upper rooms have to drag up several flights of stairs all the water required for cleaning and cooking.

Dr. Jeaffreson's letter next treats of the invariable connexion between filthy over-crowded dwellings and the outbreak of typhus. Speaking of the last-named class of houses, he says:—

' In some houses of this kind, known to me from the prevalence of typhus in them, I found the cellars communicating with the main living-rooms on the ground-floor by an open staircase, through which and the cellars there used to be traffic to a small yard behind; but which are now impassable, because of the cellar and stairs being filled up level with the floor of the room and the yard by the dust,

garbage, and sweepings of the house, which have literally
not been removed for years, and which, if disturbed, are
found alive with maggots, and those other forms of animal
life which swarm in decaying matters.'

But it will be said—'The tenants, and not the
houses or the landlords, are accountable for abominations like these; and it is true that in too. many instances dirt and disorder are the *preference* of the
families who inhabit these houses. They would not
thank you to whitewash their walls; it would make
them feel uncomfortable to see anything so clean
around them. Many of their windows do not open
from the top, but where they do, the inmates will not
be persuaded, however many may have to crowd into
one sleeping-room, to open the veriest crack for the
admission of fresh air: they prefer the warmth of
the stifling fœtid atmosphere, many times breathed,
though they feel and complain of its depressing consequences. Could the horror of the workhouse, so
universal in our poorest classes, be analysed, one
element would be found to be, dislike of the cleanliness, the order, the regularity which reign there.
The Marylebone Association for Improving the Dwellings of the Poor, at a heavy cost, fitted their apartments with plate-rack, shelves, cupboards, and other
appliances for comfort and cleanliness; very shortly
all was broken up and burnt for fire-wood. Some
contrive to evade rent altogether by constant migra-
tion, and of course have no interest whatever in the
dwellings where their abiding is so short; they are
not troubled by dirt, nor would they be at any pains

to be cleán in houses, however decent and well-appointed. Taking, however, all this into consideration, and allowing that the character makes the home, and not the home the character, the question still remains—How did they sink so low? We believe the answer is chiefly contained in one word—*Over-crowding*. Give them *space*—they cannot abuse that—and we shall begin to see improvement.

Meanwhile, whatever may be the cause which lies most at the root of all this squalor, whether bad houses or bad habits, and whatever may be the proportion in which these causes act and re-act on each other, there can be no doubt as to the effect. Dr. Jeaffreson says:—

'In one such room that I more particularly examined the whole of a large family had had typhus. Numerous instances came to my knowledge of family succeeding family in typhus-infected houses, each succumbing in succession, till at last the house was for a time shut up and lime-whited. Then fever ceased, and has not returned, though the house has since been inhabited by the same class of poor. In one street there were, within a short time, more than one hundred cases of typhus. Three fathers of families lay dead at the same time, leaving orphans to raise the rates and swell the ranks of pauperism. After a time fever died out; but nothing effective has been done to yards or houses which belong to a landlord who, in other parts of London, owns nearly similar typhus-nests. It is hard to say to what extent the now too prevalent typhus may not extend.'

On selfish grounds only no time is to be lost, but we can hardly believe that a generous English public will need that so much stress should be laid on the personal risk the wealthy and educated would incur if these 'nests of typhus' remain undisturbed. One-eighth, they are told, of the 2000 cut off annually from typhus fever in London would be drawn from their own ranks. The disease generated in the slum might be propagated to the adjacent square. The gentleman's dress-coat, stitched in the upper room Dr. Jeaffreson has described, has perhaps very lately been heaped, with other infected garments, on the shivering patient in the first stage of his complaint. 'The smart, warm children's clothing,' made up in rooms where fever is or has been raging, may strike a death-chill to the heir of a noble house.

All this is said and reiterated, and it is very important as an additional reason why no time must be lost in applying a remedy to an evil of long standing; but we should not like to think that the wealthy and educated are open to conviction on no higher ground. We should be reminded of a captain who was called out with his men to quell a town riot; he restrained them with admirable coolness from avenging the insults of the mob, till a missile caught him in the face, then the affair became personal. 'Up lads, and have at them!' said he; the signal for action had come at last.

It was not thus that the royal penitent of Israel argued, when having a terrible selection to make between war, famine, and pestilence: his choice fell upon the ill to which the prince was exposed equally

with the peasant. Death is a great leveller; and
viewing the poor man's home in the metropolis in
its sanitary aspect only as a ' fever-nest,' we think
the sevenfold proportion of poor, who die year by
year, cut off by remediable causes which their wealthy
neighbours might have prevented, is a still more
serious consideration than the small remainder of
victims from other classes of society.

Fever is not the worst evil bred in such homes
as Dr. Jeaffreson has described; the higher the
organization, the more sensitive is it to surrounding
influences; over-crowded, filthy dwellings, mean
something more than bad air, which enervates the
frame and undermines the constitution: they mean
moral deterioration, the loss of self-respect and
decency—a degrading process, by which men become
drunkards and women slatterns, and young maiden-
hood loses the power to blush.   How is a man to
bring up his young family decently who, at a ruinous
rent, can command nothing better for himself, his
wife, his boys and girls of all ages, than one room in
a crowded court?   The next room to his, perhaps, is
occupied by a nest of thieves; above or below him,
with such ruinous floors and ceilings that sound is
scarcely deadened, a drunken virago is filling the
air with foul language; in the opposite room, but a
step across a narrow passage from his own door,
lodgers are smuggled in without a license; the
appointments of the house are such that cleanliness
and decency are next to impossible, and the landlord will not remedy them.   For a time self-respect

may hold out; for a time he may keep his head above the infecting stream of moral pollution; but unless he is partaker of a hidden life, which draws its sustenance from a higher source than his own good resolutions, the chances are serious that, sooner or later, he will give in: he will choose the bright, cheery gin-palace, with its pleasant cup of forgetfulness, for his evening resort; domestic affections will become deadened, and at last extinct; brutalized by drunkenness, he will be ripe for crime, and his former place in society as the honest, industrious workman, will know him no more.

It is an affecting proof of the stupefying effect which over-crowding and its attendant evils exercise upon the workman, that he has so little heart or courage to use even the remedies which the law has put within his reach; probably many are never even at the pains to inquire with whom complaints may be lodged. In conversation with one who had had twenty-six years' experience of going in and out constantly among the lowest classes, the writer learned that *fear of their neighbours* generally deters a poor man from making any complaint of those living in the same house with himself: for instance, in the matter of taking in lodgers without a license, the law offers a remedy; a man who knows that his neighbour is thus over-crowding his room, and rendering its atmosphere pestilential to all inhabiting the same house, has only to go the clerk of the vestry and state his complaint, giving the name of the street and the number of the house; the

clerk will send an inspector, who will at once redress
the grievance, or, in case of opposition, report to
the vestry; the vestry will then empower the inspector to summon the offending party before a
magistrate: but this remedial power is little used
in the lowest neighbourhoods, because a man feels
neither his person nor his goods would be safe, if he
made enemies of his neighbours.

It may be well to mention here, for the benefit
of the working classes themselves, and of philanthropic persons who visit and advise them, the steps
which should be taken where the grievance lies
against the landlord who will not incur the expense
of remedying or removing a nuisance. The sufferer
from the landlord's remissness or indifference must
apply to the local board of health at the vestry;
the board will send an inspector, who, after verifying
the complaint, will serve a notice upon the landlord
for the removal of the nuisance: should he prove
refractory, the board can send workmen in to remedy
the evil at the landlord's expense. It is a pity that
information is not more generally disseminated as
to the proper parties with whom complaints should
be lodged, and to whom application may be made.
Why should not every holder of a tenement or head
of a family be furnished with a list, telling him
where to find the vestry-room, the fire-engine room,
and the relieving officer of the district? Every facility
should be put in a poor man's way for obtaining the
protection allowed to him by the law.

It is a disgrace to human nature that dens of

H

filth like those visited by Dr. Jeaffreson, where no prudent man would kennel his dogs or stable his horses, are yet *valuable property* to the landlord. Dr. Whitmore, Medical Officer of Health in Maryle-bone, after describing to the representative council a narrow court running from tenements 'which,' he says, 'it is almost a fiction to say give *shelter* to between sixty and seventy human beings,' makes a general statement that property of this description, let out in separate rooms to weekly tenants, con- stitutes *a most profitable investment;* the amount of profit varying, of course, with the degree of firm-ness and flinty determination in collecting the rents. There are various ways known to second-class agents of 'putting on the screw,' but one adopted in this court strikes us as rather a novel expedient for ejecting an unprofitable tenant, who would *stay,* and would or could not *pay.* Not a stick of furniture remained to seize for rent, and, except the bundle of dirty rags on which she slept, and which (as not likely to command any market value) had been left, the room was bare; but a strong hint to 'move on' had been given *by taking the grate out of her fire-place,* that she might be starved out by cold and hunger. Her wits befriended her in this case, and she contrived a fire without the grate.

Of another poor emaciated woman in the same court Dr. Whitmore says:—'I found her engaged in slop-work; her sad tale, not obtrusively, but hesi-tatingly told, was this: Her husband, by trade a plasterer, was sick in the hospital. She had four

young children to maintain, and by sitting up four
nights out of seven she could earn about seven
shillings; of these, *three* went to her landlord for
rent!'

There are causes always in operation for the
congregating of masses of the labouring classes in
our great industrial centres. They are attracted
there not only by the demand for labour to which
commerce and manufactures give rise, but also as
purveyors to the numerous conventional wants and
luxuries of the wealthy inhabitants of a great city:
over-crowding is not an evil of yesterday. But
there are circumstances at the present time which
have exaggerated the evil, and caused it to assume
proportions which can no longer be overlooked. The
march of improvement in London, in the erection
of public buildings and the advance of great railway
lines towards the heart of the metropolis, has compelled extensive clearances, and the pulling down
of streets, and even districts, inhabited by the
labouring classes. Dr. Jabez Burns says, in a letter
dated December 2, 1865:—

'In London, unless steps are taken, the poor bid fair
to be thrust out of house and home, and to have no place
left to dwell in. Our Street-improvement Acts and our
Railway demolitions are turning out the poor by thousands.
Even in our crowded and deplorable districts, such as the
streets and alleys running out of Drury Lane and to the
region of the Seven Dials, apartments are not to be had,
and the rents in some neighbourhoods have been raised 50
per cent.'

For the erection of the New Law Courts the
eviction of some 5000 persons, principally labourers
and artisans, has been necessary. Mr. Wilkinson,
Diocesan Home Missionary, thus writes of them,
October 25, 1865:—

'The notices to quit to the poor of the district to
which I am appointed by the Bishop of London are being
served, and in many cases immediate expulsion is involved.
The present misery is, therefore, grievous to witness; but
it will be infinitely greater when, probably in mid-winter,
the majority of the 5000 will have to seek a not less
miserable shelter at enhanced rentals, away from those who
have long known, cared for, or employed them.'

The Railway Bills actually before Parliament
contemplate the demolition of 8000 tenements of
the lower kind.   If, indeed, previous provision had
been made for the accommodation of the evicted
poor, the wholesale demolition of their present
habitations would have left nothing to regret; but
as the case stands, the period of transition is one of
unmitigated suffering.   The inhabitants of the back
slum, crowded enough before, have squeezed yet
closer to the wall, to take in, *sub rosâ*, fresh tenants:
the labourer, the mendicant, and the rogue, are
huddled together in polluting proximity, to the
physical injury of all, and the demoralisation of the
labourer.

Truly the time is come to act; 'the wonder is,'
as the editor of the *Telegraph* well observes, 'that
we have still time to sweep away the national disgrace, without being terrified into the performance

of the duty by pestilence, or coerced into it by revolt.'

We hope, in the next chapter, to speak of what has already been done, or what it is now in contemplation to do, to meet this urgent want, to provide town-labourers with suitable homes, and to enable, as we trust, Englishmen of the next generation to look upon this eminently vexed question as a question satisfactorily solved.

CHAPTER IV.

HE task is great. London has 648,000 of labouring inhabitants, and out of these more than 600,000 are vilely lodged: the problem is to house them well; will philanthropic effort solve it? will wisely-directed commercial enterprise? will co-operation among the labouring classes themselves? or, finally, must the State come forward with Government assistance? We will endeavour to show what has been or is being attempted under each head.

Philanthropy, as usual, held the honourable office of pioneer in the way of improvement; benevolent individuals formed themselves into associations for improving and re-constructing the dwellings of the labouring classes; the health and comfort of the poor man and his family was with them the primary object, the realisation of a dividend secondary, though not ignored, as it was their purpose to render their scheme in the end self-supporting. Among such associations we may name 'The Metropolitan

Association for Improving the Dwellings of the Industrious Classes,' formed in 1842; 'The Society for Improving the Condition of the Labouring Classes,' formed in 1844; 'The Marylebone Association,' formed in 1854.

We will take the Metropolitan Association as typical of the class, and state its objects in its own words, as contained in the first Report of the Directors to the Shareholders, in March 1846:—

'The founders of this Association, impressed by the evidence adduced of the deplorable physical and moral evils directly traceable to these wretched dwellings, conceived the plan of attempting some improvement in the general construction of the poor man's house, and some addition to its convenience and comfort. They did not, indeed, imagine that it would be possible for any private body of men to provide suitable habitations for all the poor, even of the metropolis; but they thought that it might be practicable, by the combination of capital, science, and skill, to erect more healthy and more convenient houses for the labourer and artisan, and to offer such improved dwellings to these and similar classes at no higher rent than they pay for the inferior and unhealthy houses which they at present occupy.

'It appeared further to the Association, that if it were practicable to present some examples of houses well built, well drained, and well supplied with air, water, and light, and to offer these dwellings at no greater charge than is at present demanded and obtained for houses in which no provision whatever is made, or even attempted, for the supply of any one of these essential requisites of health, cleanliness, and comfort, a public service would be rendered beyond the mere erection of so many better con-

structed houses; that the influence of this example could
scarcely fail to be beneficial; that, especially, it might help
to make it no longer easy for the landlord to obtain an
amount of rent for houses of the latter description which
ought to suffice for those of the former; and that it might
thus indirectly tend to raise the general standard of accommodation and comfort required in all houses of this
class.'

The Association distinctly repudiated any attempt to pauperise the labourer, by offering him a
better house as a dole of charity.   The Report from
which we have quoted goes on to say:—

'It was no part of the plan of the Association to attempt to assist the poor by offering them any gift, or doing
anything for them in the shape of charity; experience
having shown, that while the means afforded by charity for
the removal of extensive and permanent evils are always
inadequate, because always too limited and too transient,
her gifts, in such cases, do not really benefit the recipients,
but, on the contrary, have a tendency to injure and corrupt
them, by lessening their self-reliance and destroying their
self-respect. The proposal of the Association was, therefore, that the industrious man should pay the full value for
his house, but that for the sum he pays he should possess a
salubrious and commodious dwelling, instead of one in
which cleanliness and comfort can find no place, in which
he can neither maintain his own strength nor bring up his
family in health, but must constantly spend a large portion
of his hard-earned wages in the relief of sickness.'

It was stated to the Government that while, on
the one hand, the essential principle of the Association was self-support, so that. its founders

would regard their scheme as a failure if it did not
return a fair profit on the capital employed, yet that,
on the other hand, it was not their design to set on
foot a money-getting speculation. The dividend
was limited to five per cent, it being determined to
devote any profits which might accrue beyond this
to the extension of the plan.   The Government approved, and a charter was granted in October, 1845.

The enterprise was then primarily philanthropic,
though intended to be self-supporting.   The same
was true of the other Associations we have classed
with the Metropolitan.   In the Marylebone Association especially, the amount of return for capital
invested was more entirely subordinated to the
primary object, and a considerable sum in money
and shares was given to the Directors solely for the
object of improving the condition of the dwellings of
the poor, the donors not wishing to receive *any*
profit.

Now let us glance at results. In the last-named
Association, 300 families are comfortably domiciled
through its operations—about 50 families of artisans,
and the remainder the poorest classes of Irish
labourers and costermongers. Among such it is
up-hill work to enforce any rules for the maintenance
of order and cleanliness, owing to the inveterate
personal habits of the tenants; yet the Medical
Officer of Health of the parish reports, in May 1865,
concerning Gray's Buildings : —

' These buildings furnish a satisfactory illustration of
the advantages which result from efficient drainage and

ample water supply. These buildings consist of 21 houses,
inhabited by about 500 men, women, and children, principally Irish of the lowest class. The habits of these poor
people are dirty in the extreme, and all the care and
pains bestowed upon them by the excellent Association
to whom the property belongs cannot prevent, in the
dwellings, yards, &c., constant accumulations of filth and
other abominations. Yet, with all their noxious surroundings, owing to excellent drainage and water supply,
the sanitary condition of these people is by no means unfavourable. Cases of fever rarely occur, and when they
do they are isolated; whilst deaths among the children from
contagious epidemic diseases are very infrequent.'

The Metropolitan Association provides in ten
establishments for 420 families and 362 single men.
The Labourer's Friend Society has lodgings for
64 single women and 280 single men, single-room
accommodation for 275 familes, and household
accommodation for 74 families: the sanitary principles maintained are,—

1. The thorough drainage of the subsoil of the
site.

2. The free admission of air and light to every
inhabited room.

3. Complete house-drainage.

4. An abundant supply of water.

5. Provision for the immediate removal of all
solid house refuse by means of dust-shafts.

The result has been a perfect success, as to the
improved sanitary condition, and the decrease of the
death-rate in these localities. Dr. Southwood Smith,
the father of sanitary reform in this country, closes

a Report, in which he has carefully analysed the
death rate in various parts of the metropolis, in the
following remarkable words (he is speaking of the
years 1851 to 1853):—' If the whole of the metropolis
had been as healthy as the Metropolitan Buildings,
Old Pancras Road, on an average of the three years,
there would have been an annual saving of about
23,000 lives.'

The primary or philanthropic object has been
obtained, and that among the lowest classes, where
the experiment is of course put to the severest test.
The monetary aspect of the undertaking is less
encouraging. The Marylebone Association Report
for 1865 declares a dividend of 2 per cent for the
shareholders. In the Metropolitan, the dividend
for the year 1864–5, was at the rate of 3½ per cent
upon the whole of the capital. The twentieth Report
of the Labourer's Friend Society shows a dividend
of about 4¾ per cent, from which, however, the
working expenses of the Society must be deducted.
Renovated dwellings are better, as a commercial
speculation, than *new buildings;* some which
were bought by the Marylebone Association, under
specially favourable circumstances, are now producing
8 per cent: but taken as a whole, the philanthropic
pioneers cannot be said to have presented an investment which will tempt the capitalist. The man of
wealth, who is also benevolent and public-spirited,
may let a few hundreds lie at low interest in these
associations, but they will not command the support
needed to meet the present emergency.

We have next to consider as a remedy, *wisely-directed commercial enterprise.* It is peculiarly gratifying to Englishmen, to whom the memory of their late lamented Prince is so justly dear, that among the many enlightened schemes which he originated or promoted, the improvement of the dwellings of the labouring classes was one which lay near to his philanthropic heart, and in which he took the initiative, by causing to be constructed on his own account, in the Cavalry Barrack yard, opposite to the Great Exhibition of 1851, model buildings for the occupation of four families of the class of manufacturing and mechanical operatives. Each tenement consists of three bed-rooms, living room, lobby, scullery, sink, closet, dust-bin, &c.

The intention of the Prince Consort was to initiate an enterprise which could be proposed and maintained, purely on commercial grounds. To use his own words,—'Unless we can get 7 or 8 per cent we shall not succeed in inducing builders to invest their capital in such houses.' He estimated that the ordinary cost of a tenement of this character would be from 110*l.* to 120*l.*, and if let for 4*s.* a-week, after deducting ground-rent and taxes, a return of 7 per cent on the outlay would be realized. This estimate, however, did not include architect's fees, working expenses, or wear and tear—expenses which cannot be avoided, and necessarily reduce the percentage of profit.

The idea thrown out by the Prince germinated in the minds of men who, being at once capitalists

and men of enlightened philanthropic views, were
determined to try his experiment on a large scale,
and to prove that a priceless benefit might be conferred on the working man without taxing the benevolence of the rich. No one has, perhaps, more
thoroughly vindicated the success of this leading
principle than Alderman Waterlow. Taking as his
model the tenements built under the direction of the
Prince Consort, he determined to mass together in
one block forty of such tenements, keeping the main
features of the Albert Cottages—such as a central,
open, fire-proof staircase, communicating with the
external gallery, and a flat roof which may be used as
a drying and recreation ground ; features which command advantages of the utmost importance—security
in cases of fire, the perfect independence of each
family, without even the comparative publicity of the
common corridor, and, not least, the exemption from
house duty, which results from rendering each
dwelling independent.

Mr. Waterlow secured a lease for 99 years of a
plot of ground situated in the most populous part of
Finsbury. To make way for the Langbourn Buildings, the noble structure he has erected on this
ground, he had to clear away a number of the most
wretched habitations imaginable. He was thus for-
tunate in his selection of a site, for he not only
substituted healthy and decent dwellings for hovels
which were scarcely fit for the accommodation of
pigs, but he did this in a crowded neighbourhood,
and in close proximity to the scenes of labour of

... might be expected to become his tenants.
... within a quarter of an hour's walk of
... England. Every tenement which Mr.
... has built is complete in itself. Nothing
... common use of the inhabitants but stair-
... way, and roof. Every domestic office and
... is provided for each household separately.
... degree of thoughtful consideration which has
... expended in securing to the working man and
... family domestic privacy in the buildings of
... Waterlow, will be shown in an extract
... a pamphlet on Overcrowding, which he kindly
... to the writer. The question was that of a
... common laundry, which was decided against on the
following grounds : —

' In the first place, the arrangement necessarily brings a
great number of women together from time to time, and in
the enforced familiarity thus created a good deal of gossip, and
' chaff," and irregular conversation, is likely to be indulged,
which tends banefully to the breaking down of that reserve
and seclusiveness of family life which is one of the strongest
safeguards of its peace and purity. Then, contentions for
place and precedence are almost sure to arise; and these
go far to disturb that feeling of good-neighbourship which
it is so desirable to maintain where numbers of families are
living in such immediate proximity to one another. Thirdly,
the finest delicacies of a woman's nature are necessarily
taxed by such an arrangement. The woman whose linen
is not quite so ample or so good as another's, even should
she not be wounded by unpleasant observations, will find
her instinct of self-respect painfully touched ; will feel that
her inferiority of circumstances involves a social penalty
... it is hard to bear. These may be esteemed trivial

disadvantages, but those who know most of human nature know that the mightiest spring-force of its noblest progress is always to be found in its very finest sensibilities, and that in all successful efforts for its moral improvement and elevation, those sensibilities must be taken tenderly and faithfully into account.' *

The sound commercial views of Alderman Water-low and his associates may inspire the capitalist with confidence; but we think words like these have a higher mission — they tell the working man that his interests have been taken up by those who recognise that his social *status* as an operative, comes into no necessary collision with the existence and exercise of all the more refined instincts of our common humanity. Such words will make him feel that he is respected, and will thus nurture in him self-respect, and the manly, social virtues of which it is the parent.

Mr. Waterlow endeavoured to render the appearance of his building as attractive internally as it is externally. In order to reduce the cost of construction, the joinery is made to a uniform size and pattern, so that the use of machinery may economise the cost of its manufacture. The principal saving, however, is in the use of an extremely hard, durable, and light artificial stone, composed of clinkers, culm, hard broken coke, and similar rough, porous, calcined substances, in the proportion of four parts to one of Portland cement. The floors, lintels, arches, chimney-pieces, stairs, window-sills, &c., are composed of

* *Overcrowding : The Evil and its Remedy,* p. 43.

this material, which, readily moulded into any form, speedily becomes harder than stone.

We have had occasion to notice, in speaking of the 'fever dens,' the soppy back-yard, with its dilapidated brick walls and open water-butts; in place of these, at the back of Mr. Waterlow's buildings, the eye rests on a space enclosed from the street by neat iron rails, and laid out in flower-beds and gravel-paths. This is true knowledge of a workman's nature and tastes. Mons. Jules Simon thus speaks of the delight taken by French operatives in the smallest approach to a bit of garden-ground; and we believe the Englishman in this respect is not behind his continental neighbour. He is speaking of the workmen of Sedan, to whom the public-house and 'St. Monday' are scarcely known, and who have gained well-earned credit by their orderly and respectable habits. This he attributes in part to their passion for gardening:—

'The poorest will have his garden, though it be but a hand's breadth. Lovingly he tends it on the Sunday,* and dreams of it in the week. Many among them have purchased their gardens, others are simple tenants. Several of the manufacturers have allowed their workmen to contrive a little garden-space out of the ground allotted for hanging out the cloth in the fabrication of which they are employed—mere little plots, which may be stepped round in a few paces, but objects of most eager desire, and considered to belong of right to the oldest workmen. Mr. Charles - Cunin Gridaine offered a retiring pension to an aged workman. " Impossible, sir !" was the answer : " I

* The Sunday of the Roman Catholic peasant in France is, as our readers are probably aware, simply regarded as a holiday.

should lose my garden." These gardens have been a
death-blow to the public-houses, and have fostered into
vigorous life the family and domestic spirit of the operatives. They have done more than any exhortations or
good advice could do, to train them in habits of thrift and
economy.'*

One little touch more we must indulge in to show
the animus which directed the construction of Langbourn Buildings. The windows are constructed on
a somewhat novel principle, being made to open out-
wards like ordinary French casements; but the two
lower panes are *not made to open,* that little eager
heads may crowd round and enjoy their favourite
point of observation, *without the danger of falling
out.*

The larger lettings consist of three rooms and a
wash-house; the smaller, of two rooms and a wash-
house. At a rent of 5s. or 6s. 6d. a-week, a comfortable and thoroughly healthy home may here be
obtained.

The conditions of occupation are six in number,
and we think it will be allowed that there is nothing
in them to which any exception may be taken in
respect of stringency. They are as follows:—

' 1. Rents are to be paid in advance; no arrears will be
allowed. Each tenant must also deposit the sum of five
shillings, which will be held as security for the proper use
of the fixtures, and returned at the expiration of the tenancy,
subject to any deduction for breakage or loss of keys, &c.

* *L'Ouvrière,* p. 364.

I

' 2. The collector will call for the rents every Monday, between the hours of eight and ten o'clock.

' 3. Broken windows must be repaired by the tenants, and the chimneys must also be kept properly swept. In case of neglect the collector may cause this to be done, and the expense shall be charged to the tenant as rent. Nothing larger than the hand, or longer than the finger should be thrown down into the dust-shoots. Tenants are requested to be particularly careful in this respect, as a stoppage in the dust-shoot causes serious inconvenience and expense. The washing-coppers should be kept perfectly dry when not in use, to prevent rust.

' 4. The stairs and passages are to be swept daily, and washed every Saturday by the tenants in turn. Children are not to be allowed to loiter or to make a noise on the stairs or balconies. The roof is intended to be used in common by all the tenants, and the door leading to it must be kept constantly closed, so as to prevent the access of strangers. Clothes-lines must be removed when not in actual use.

' 5. No tenant will be permitted to underlet any of the rooms in his occupation, unless he shall first obtain the permission of the collector in writing.

' 6. Any person neglecting to observe these rules, misusing or improperly occupying these buildings, or causing or creating inconvenience to his neighbours, will be subject to expulsion at the expiration of forty-eight hours' notice in writing, and the forfeiture of all rents paid, without remedy of any kind on account of such expulsion or otherwise, and the company are released from all claims from such tenants for damages arising from such expulsion.'

No very hard terms these for such advantages as the Langbourn Buildings have to offer. The discretionary power given to the collector in Rule 5 is used

in cases where sub-tenancy might be desirable. In
answer to a question put by the writer to Mr. Waterlow, as to the average earnings of the workmen inhabiting his Buildings, he says :—' The tenants of the
improved dwellings are engaged in trades and employments of all kinds, and it would be difficult to
give an accurate estimate of their earnings. The
letter-carrier, with only 18s. a-week, will be found
occupying a set of rooms in the same building with
skilled mechanics earning 2l. or 2l. 2s. The only
difference would be in the number of rooms occupied
by each; the former would be content with two, or
become the under-tenant of the latter, who can afford
to pay for three or four.'

But do even the reduced terms of sub-tenancy
put it within the reach of the *lowest of the poor* to
become inhabitants of such buildings as Mr. Waterlow has erected ? We believe it is generally conceded
that the benefit does not reach them at first-hand ;
but by drafting away from the over-crowded alley or
court, the respectable mechanics and artisans, who, in
virtue of higher wages on the one hand, and better
habits of thrift and economy on the other, are in a
position to appreciate and to use the improved dwellings, space is left for those who occupy a lower grade
in the social scale. With regard to this Mr. Waterlow says, in the letter from which we have already
quoted :—

' If improved dwellings could be provided in sufficient
numbers the denizens of the ' fever dens' would be able to
find better accommodation, *by reason of competition gene-*

rally being lessened. It will not do to provide homes for
the *very* poor at first-hand, as most of this class of people
are dirty and shiftless; but by building homes for those
who appreciate and are able to pay for good accommodation, the pressure on all the classes *beneath* them, in point
of social morals, cleanliness, &c. &c., derive a proportionate
share of the benefits conferred on those who deserve them.'

So far all is satisfactory; but what as to the commercial aspect of the undertaking? Will the Langbourn Buildings stand that crucial test? Competent
judges pronounced that they would do so. The Earl
of Shaftesbury visited them shortly before they were
opened, and declared that a more cheerful and attractive home had been there provided, at a cost of 110*l.*,
than either of the metropolitan associations had produced at a minimum outlay of 180*l.*; and that he had
seen what he had been looking for in vain for many
years,—a clean, healthy, and desirable home for a
mechanic, erected at a price that would *pay a fair
return on the money invested.* A number of noble-
men and gentlemen came together when the first
block was completed to inspect it. Lord Ebury said
on that occasion:—' He did not know whether it was
too early in the day to say that the problem was
solved altogether; but, after having very attentively
perused the document which described the building,
and having now carefully inspected the building itself,
he must say that, taking the figures to be correct,
and that it was capable of producing a rent which
would give a per-centage of 7 *or* 8 *per cent* in the
outlay on its erection, a result had been obtained of

no slight importance, as it solved the difficulty over which previous experimentalists had stumbled, and proved that building enterprises of that nature *could be rendered commercially remunerative.*

The immediate result of Alderman Waterlow's success was the formation of the 'Improved Industrial Dwellings Company, Limited.' This Association is commercial in the strictest sense of the word.   In a letter to the writer Mr. Waterlow says:—' Nearly 100,000*l.* has been expended under my supervision' (he is Deputy-chairman of the Association) ' in the erection of improved dwellings for artisans and others; and as these buildings earn from 5 to 7 per cent annual net-profit rental, I think we are entitled to regard them as successful commercial speculations.'

Since the spring of 1863, twenty-four blocks, on a similar plan to the Langbourn Buildings, comprising in the aggregate 521 tenements and 21 shops, have been erected by this company in various parts of London.   About 3000 persons have been thus provided for, at a cost of some 75,000*l.* to 80,000*l.*   At the fifth half-yearly meeting of the company, recently held in the Mansion House, Alderman Waterlow, who was in the chair, said, that ' out of 1700*l.* they had received in rents since the formation of the company, they had only had 29*s.* of bad debts; a fact which was, he thought, highly creditable to the working classes by whom the buildings were occupied.'

No record of efforts, public or private, to improve the workman's home would be complete without

a mention of the Peabody Fund. Our readers can
hardly need to be told to what we refer; they know
that in 1862 Mr. George Peabody, an eminent
merchant, American by birth, but who had for the
last twenty-five years of his life resided in London,
addressed a letter to Lord Stanley, expressing his
determination to attest his gratitude and attachment
to the people of London by a gift of 150,000*l*. 'to
ameliorate the condition of the poor and needy of
this great metropolis, and to promote their comfort
and happiness.' He placed this sum in the hands
of trustees, leaving them considerable latitude as to
its application, but expressing ' a hope that it would
be so applied that the result would be appreciated,
not only by the present, but by future generations
of the people of London.' He threw out one suggestion for consideration among the many which
would come under their attention, whether it might
not be well 'to apply the fund, or a portion of it, in
the construction of such improved dwellings for the
poor as might combine, in the utmost possible degree,
the essentials of healthfulness, comfort, social enjoyment, and economy.'

We learn from a Report which the Trustees of
the fund published in the *Times*, on the 11th of
January of the present year, that, acting on the
suggestion of the munificent donor, five sites have
already been secured in different parts of London,—
in Spitalfields, Islington, Chelsea, Bermondsey, and
Shadwell; the two first are already built over and
occupied, at rents for each tenement as follows:—

three rooms, 5s. per week; two rooms, 4s. or 3s. 6d.;
and one room, 2s. 6d. per week. The classes of
workpeople accommodated are, as we learn from
the Report, in Spitalfields, 'charwomen, monthly
nurses, basket-makers, butchers, carpenters, firemen,
labourers, porters, omnibus-drivers, sempstresses,
shoemakers, tailors, waiters, warehousemen, &c.' In
the buildings at Islington, among the 674 individuals
now located there, we may include with the foregoing classes persons engaged in trade as watch-
finishers, turners, printers, painters, cabinet-makers,
artificial flower makers, &c. Still, we observe, it is
not the very poorest, but the class immediately
above them, who avail themselves of such improved
accommodation.

The munificence of this princely merchant in
1862 was startling, and might have sufficed for a
lifetime; but 'there is that scattereth and yet
increaseth.' On the 29th of last January (1866) we
find him thus re-opening correspondence with his
Trustees:—

'Gentlemen,—When I made a donation of 150,000l.
for the benefit of the poor of London in March, 1862, it
was my intention, if my life was spared until my retirement from business, and Providence continued me in prosperity, to place in your hands, as Trustees of the charity,
a further gift for the same object. That time has now
arrived.'

The further gift thus modestly introduced was
no less than a second donation of 100,000l. !

His letter dwells upon the hope he entertains, that it will form a fund which prudent investment and judicious management may render so far reproductive that it will be progressive in its usefulness, as applied to the relief of the poor of London. He says:—

'It will act more powerfully in future generations than in the present. It is intended to endure for ever. Should your successors (referring to his Trustees) continue the management of the charity as you have begun it, it is my ardent hope and trust that, within a century, the annual receipts from rents for buildings of this improved class may present such a return that there may not be a poor working man of good character in London who could not obtain comfortable and healthful lodgings for himself and his family at a cost within his means.'

With his eye thus fixed on securing permanent advantages to be reaped by the working classes of future generations, Mr. Peabody anticipates difficulties and emergencies which might hereafter arise in the management of the fund, authorising his Trustees, when sites shall become too dear and scarce within the metropolis itself, to purchase them in any locality within ten miles of the Royal Exchange where salubrity of position, railway accommodation, and proximity to the great centres of labour, shall render them convenient and desirable as homes for workmen. He foresees that, at this distance from London, it might be difficult to procure education for the workman's children, and he provides for the erection and maintenance of schools,

scientific lectures and reading-rooms, in connexion
with future colonies of workmen; and as such
colonies might not be in the neighbourhood of good
markets, he suggests the propriety of providing,
within the buildings or near to them, apartments
in which the tenants may organize co-operative
stores, for supplying themselves with coal and other
necessary articles for their own consumption. Truly
Mr. George Peabody will inherit the blessing pronounced on the man who '*considereth* the poor.'
The *Times* says, with reference to this noble gift
of a quarter of a million of money:—

' He offers to hard-working men exactly that species of
assistance which they can accept without humiliation; and
it is not the condemnation, it is the sanction and practical
approval of his plan, that in doing so the fund does not
disappear. The money which is realized by prudent in-
vestments and judicious management goes to swell the
splendid sum that he has placed to the credit of the poor,
and hence his work of beneficence may be prolonged for
ages. If we are asked whether his scheme, as administered by his Trustees, reaches the very poor of London, we
must still decline to give an affirmative answer; but it
reaches exactly those to whom it is eminently useful, those
whom it enables to live good and respectable lives.
Granted that there are many unfortunate people in London
who cannot afford to pay the rent that is demanded in the
new buildings. It is plain that no individual charity could
have helped *them*. You cannot irrigate Sahara. There
are some wide wastes of misery with which only the State
can deal. That which was possible, and what Mr. Peabody's Trustees have accomplished, was to gift the working
poor—not those who only labour by fits and starts, but

the ordinary toiling poor — with the ability to secure
decent lodgings for a reasonable rent.' *

Such are some of the efforts already made in the
way of wisely-directed commercial enterprise, stimu-
lated by philanthropy, to meet the great social evil
under which our working-classes are labouring,—
over-crowded, insufficient, and unwholesome dwellings. Is this remedy adequate? Will it meet the
emergency? Under ordinary circumstances it might

* Since the above pages were penned, the public has been
gratified by the following graceful acknowledgment from the
Queen of England to Mr. Peabody, for the substantial benefits he
has conferred on her subjects, and by his manly and courteous
answer, in which he confirms our natural impression that the
highest motives have prompted such unparalleled liberality. The
Queen's letter appeared in the *Times*, April 2, and is as follows :—
             ' *Windsor Castle, March 28,* 1866.
  ' The Queen hears that Mr. Peabody intends shortly to return
to America, and she would be sorry that he should leave
England without being assured by herself how deeply she appreciates the noble act of more than princely munificence by
which he has sought to relieve the wants of the poorer class of
her subjects residing in London. It is an act, as the Queen
believes, wholly without parallel, and which will carry its best
reward in the consciousness of having contributed so largely to
the assistance of those who can little help themselves. The
Queen would not, however, have been satisfied without giving
Mr. Peabody some public mark of her sense of his munificence,
and she would have gladly conferred upon him either a Baronetcy
or the Grand Cross of the Order of the Bath, but that she understands Mr. Peabody to feel himself debarred from accepting such
distinctions. It only remains, therefore, for the Queen to give
Mr. Peabody this assurance of her personal feelings, which she
would further wish to mark by asking him to accept a miniature
portrait of herself, which she will desire to have painted for him,
and which, when finished, can either be sent to him to America or
given to him on the return which, she rejoices to hear, he me-
ditates to the country that owes him so much.'

be so; but present circumstances in large towns
generally, and in London especially, are not ordinary. Machinery is being more and more introduced into agriculture, and the number of hand-
workers required for its operations proportionately
lessened. The surplus labour thus set free is
attracted to the metropolis at a time when the
demolition of dwellings for the humbler classes in
London, to make way for great public works, is
advancing with unprecedented rapidity. The ejec-

Mr. Peabody replies :—

The Palace Hotel, Buckingham Gate, London, April 3.

Madame,—I feel sensibly my inability to express in adequate
terms the gratification with which I have read the letter which
your Majesty has done me the high honour of transmitting by the
hands of Earl Russell. On the occasion which has attracted your
Majesty's attention of setting apart a portion of my property to
ameliorate the condition and augment the comforts of the poor of
London, I have been actuated by a deep sense of gratitude to God,
who has blessed me with prosperity, and of attachment to this
great country, where, under your Majesty's benign rule, I have
received so much personal kindness, and enjoyed so many years of
happiness. Next to the approval of my own conscience, I shall
always prize the assurance which your Majesty's letter conveys to
me of the approbation of the Queen of England, whose whole life
has attested that her exalted station has in no degree diminished
her sympathy with the humblest of her subjects. The portrait
which your Majesty is graciously pleased to bestow on me I shall
value as the most precious heir-loom that I can leave in the land
of my birth, where, together with the letter which your Majesty
has addressed to me, it will ever be regarded as an evidence of the
kindly feeling of the Queen of the United Kingdom towards a
citizen of the United States.

'I have the honour to be,
'Your Majesty's most obedient servant,
'GEORGE PEABODY.'

'To her Majesty the Queen.'

124   LENDING A HAND.

tion from their houses of 17,800 of the labouring
poor is involved in the railway extensions projected
in the present year alone. 'In spite of the combined efforts of all the societies,' says the *Daily
Telegraph*, 'during the last twenty-two years, no
more than 9000 or 10,000 have been rescued from
a vast spawn-bed of sickness, suffocation, and
wretchedness.' Where is the power to cope with
the extent of the evil?

Two solutions of the problem have been offered:
on the one hand it is said, Let the working men
take the remedy into their own hands by extensive
co-operation; on the other, Let the State assist with
loans of money at low interest. Let us examine
each in turn.

Mr. Thomas Beggs is the great advocate for co-
operation among the workmen themselves in Building Societies. At a meeting of the Department of
Economy and Trade of the National Social Science
Association, which took place at Adam Street,
Adelphi, on the 22nd of last January, he said, with
reference to freehold land and building societies:—

'I believe that here is the power in an advanced stage
of development that will meet, to a large extent, the evil
of defective dwellings and over-crowding in our large cities.
These societies have originated amongst the people, and to
a considerable extent have been supported, and in some
degree have been managed, by them. They have secured
the confidence of the working classes — a confidence which
is gaining strength year by year.* There are two ways

* 'It is estimated that not less than 12,000,000*l.* of money are
at this moment invested in these societies. About two-thirds of

of helping the working classes : the one is to provide all
sorts of excellent things, according to our own notions of
what is good for them. This plan does not bring much
better fruits than chagrin and disappointment to those who
devise the plans, and to those who are expected to accept
them. The other plan is to stimulate them to exertions
for their own improvement. This does succeed, and freehold land societies are a success, because they have attempted this, and no more. They point out the way by
which the working man can help himself. They greatly
aid the man who is disposed to make the best of circumstances, and incur sacrifices for the attainment of a better
position in society ; but they do not assist the man who
will do nothing to help himself. I wish to see the principle more extensively applied, so as to meet the evils, sanitary and social, to which I have referred ; and I insist that
these societies promise more to that end than any other
scheme which has hitherto been devised. It is quite clear
that benevolent individuals or philanthropic associations
will never be able to provide sufficient house accommodation for all who require it, even if it was wise to rely upon
such exertions as pure benevolence may originate. In-
vestments in this kind of property are not attractive to the
private speculator. I wish to give facilities to all classes
to become proprietors of their own houses — having the
house and the land upon which it stands in one freehold.
I most ardently desire to see every honest and independent
workman able to point to his own house and to say, " This
is mine !" '

Mr. Beggs proceeds to enumerate certain alterations in the law, which he considers would be ne-

that will be the contributions of the working classes, very much of
which has been saved from the channels of waste.'— *Social Science
Journal,* 1866, p. 72.

cessary in order to give fair play to the operations
of Building Societies. It may not be amiss, before
entering upon these, to make sure that we have a
definite understanding as to what Building Societies
are, and what advantages they offer.

'A building society is not,' says Mr. Hole, ' as some
people suppose, a society which undertakes the erection of
buildings. It is a society which consists of lenders and
borrowers conjointly, the one using the society as a savings'
bank, paying in their money by small sums; the other
using it as the means for obtaining the money to buy or
build houses, which they hold, subject to a mortgage to the
society, until they have paid it off by periodical instalments.
To both classes it presents greater advantages than almost
any other form of saving. The interest received by the
lender and paid by the borrower is generally $4\frac{1}{2}$ or 5 per
cent. The payment is usually made in shares, the subscription to which is 2s. 6d. per week, or 10s. per month,
and in some of the best societies a person may take one, two,
three, or four-fifths of a share, involving the payment of
6d., 1s., 1s. 6d., or 2s. per week. Thus a youth may contribute his 6d. per week, and be early induced to form the
habit of saving, both by the practice of taking his contribution and by perceiving how rapidly his little investment,
aided by addition of *compound interest*, soon makes a
respectable amount; and this again stimulates him to take
larger sums to the society, as his wages get higher.
Working men or women, who receive weekly wages, must
possess more than ordinary energy of character and self-
denial to screw themselves up to the point of taking
regularly their little saving to the savings' bank.* But

* Besides that, the rate of interest presents a much stronger
attraction in the Building Society, Mr. James Taylor contrasts
the respective advantages of the two: 2s. 6d. a-week for twelve

the necessity of paying the building society the fixed contribution, under penalty of falling in arrear and rendering
them liable to a fine, just gives their virtue the requisite
fillip at its weakest point.   These advantages are enjoyed
both by the lender and the borrower; but when the latter
borrows from the society for the purpose of buying or
building a house for himself, he redoubles his advantages.
He has an additional motive to use every little saving he
can make to pay off his mortgage.   He acquires a sense of
independence in the knowledge that he is living in his own
house, that every shilling he takes of weekly contribution
to the building society is helping to raise up a better
security between himself and pauperism for days when his
bodily strength will fail.   As his contribution to the
building society is about 5 per cent on the money advanced,
and the ordinary sum he has to pay a landlord is generally
from 8 to 10 per cent, he economises one-half of the very
important item of rent.   The moral effect is also great.
The working man who has acquired a house of his own
will generally gain in self-respect, and often have an impulse given him to raise himself utterly unknown to the
man who becomes indifferent or reckless, because he feels
that he has nothing to lose and little to hope for.' *

We see from the above quotation that the leading
idea of the Building or the Freehold Land Society is
that the working man should become his own landlord, and Mr. Beggs recognizes in this principle a
germ in which lies enfolded an indefinite power of
expansion to meet the present emergency, provided

years in a building society would be 120*l.*; in a savings' bank 92*l.*
The 92*l.* would have to be eleven years to make 120*l.* in the
savings' bank, whereas in the same term of years it would in a
building society be increased to 256*l.*

* *Homes of the Working Classes*, p. 83.

certain restrictions could be removed which at present limit the operations of such societies. For instance: he would confer upon freehold land societies the same powers for acquiring land as are now exercised by railway companies, with this additional advantage, that the freehold land society should not have to bring a separate Bill before Parliament for every projected extension of its operations, but that by a general Act or permissive Bill, any municipal or local authority could take land for the extension of buildings anywhere within the jurisdiction of local Acts, which empower them to pave, light, or drain. He apprehends that the effect of such a permissive Bill would be that any freehold land society or other associated body, or in fact any individual, could, by the instrumentality of the corporation in which they are represented (and which must be best able to decide upon the eligibility of plans submitted to them) obtain sites for building purposes. Mr. Beggs is of opinion that such a permissive Bill ought to stipulate that all houses built under its provisions should be freeholds, and that they should come under the general management of the corporation for all sanitary and public purposes, as well as for all general purposes of town improvements. He would further grant to the corporation the power to enforce the enfranchisement of leaseholds, where such would be required for buildings or extensions of towns.

But the aid Mr. Beggs craves from the Legislature lies chiefly in the *removal of restrictions*, that

the existing agencies in which he has so much confidence may have scope to act; with regard to more
direct aid. He says :—

'I am jealous of Government interference with the daily
life, the trade, and the social arrangements of the people.
The Legislature may assist us by correcting some vicious
clauses in Acts of Parliament, and supplying some omis-
sions, and if they will be pleased to do that, they may safely
leave the matter in the hands of the people themselves.
After removing the restrictions, the best thing they can do
is to stand out of the way.'

Here, then, is the first solution offered to the
problem by those who confide in the power of self-
help and well-directed co-operation which resides in
the working classes themselves. The second, which
we have now to consider, is suggested by those who
consider that the emergency is one which fairly demands that the Government should step in with
State assistance.*

It is urged by such, that the State has a direct
share of responsibility in the injuries which have
been done to the working classes by the development
of the great railway schemes and other large public
improvements in the metropolis, seeing that these
schemes and improvements have been carried out
with the direct sanction of Parliament.

This phase of the subject having engaged the
attention of Alderman Waterlow, he conceived a plan
by which the State might discharge its share of the

* *Journal of the Society of Arts*, p. 177.

responsibility it had incurred. Building schemes such as those in which the Improved Industrial Dwellings Company is concerned, cannot keep pace with the necessities of the times, because capital does not flow in fast enough ; there is a prejudice against house property for the working classes as a troublesome mode of investment; and though the dividend declared by the Company is good, it is not sufficiently high or tempting to overcome the prejudice. On the other hand, unless money could be had at a cheaper rate, the rents demanded from the tenants must continue (in order to pay the present dividend) to be such as practically to exclude the *indigent* classes from immediate advantage in the improved dwellings. *A steady inflow of capital at a cheap rate* is needed, to provide a number of houses at all to be compared with the present overwhelming demand.

Such an inflow Mr. Waterlow hopes to secure, by a proposition which he submitted to the Secretary of the Treasury in April 1865 :—That an Act of Parliament should be passed in the present Session to enable the Public Works Loan Commissioners to advance money to companies, and also to individuals, for the erection of dwellings for the labouring classes; the security for its repayment being a mortgage on the buildings to be erected. The rough draft of the proposition was couched in the following terms :—

‘ That no loan shall exceed in amount three-fifths of the value of the property to be so mortgaged, the value to be determined by the Commissioners.

'That the whole amount of such loan shall, within two years of the grant thereof, be applied, to the satisfaction of the Commissioners, in and towards the erection of other additional dwellings or tenements for the occupation of the industrial classes.

'That the interest to be paid to the Commissioners on account of such loans shall be 3½ *per centum per annum*.

'That the principal and interest thereon shall be repaid to the Commissioners by thirty-five equal annual payments, the amounts of which shall be agreed upon at the time of the granting of the loan.

'That the mortgage shall empower the Commissioners periodically to inspect the mortgaged dwellings (or those erected by means of the loan), with the view to ascertain whether they are kept and maintained in proper repair, and also whether they are occupied solely by persons of the class intended to be benefited by the proposed Act.

'That in the event of the foregoing requirements not being complied with at any time, the Commissioners may, by giving notice to the mortgagers, call in the balance of the loan then remaining unpaid, with interest to the date of its payment; and that the Commissioners may sell the property, failing the repayment of the loan, or compliance with their order, after three months' further notice.'

After some further correspondence between the Secretary and Mr. Waterlow, the Lords of the Treasury consented to apply to Parliament for the purpose of carrying out this Government Loan scheme, on condition that the public bodies, or individuals to whom the State money is lent, shall limit themselves to a maximum profit of 5 per cent, in order 'to distinguish their case from that of ordinary commercial enterprise.' 'The object,' says Mr. Waterlow, when

writing on this point to the Secretary, the Right
Hon. F. Peel, 'should, I think, be, to fix the rate of
interest on the one hand so *low* as to preclude objection that the public funds were being employed for
purposes of private profit; and, on the other, suffi-
·ciently *high* to induce capitalists to embark in
enterprises of this nature.'

In pursuance of the promise of the Lords of the
Treasury, on the 14th of February, 1866, Mr. Childers
introduced the proposed Bill to the House of Commons. It was cordially received and supported, and
there is every reason to hope that the measure .will
shortly be carried, and come into practical efficiency.

By such grants the State would incur no loss;
and a very moderate annual grant would, as Mr. Hole
shows us,* in a few years completely revolutionise
the worst districts of the metropolis and the provinces.
Every year a considerable sum would be repaid to
the Treasury, and the money would be again available
for promoting the same object; and while the State
would not ultimately lose anything by the outlay, it
would have done more to raise the lowest portions of
the population, and to transform them into civilized
human beings, than by almost any measure that could
be devised.

Such is the present history, brought down to the
most recent date, of the treatment of this vexed question in England. We see that public attention is
thoroughly aroused on the subject; and we may con-
fidently hope that the home of the English working

* *Homes of the Working Classes*, p. 105.

man will not much longer be a disgrace to the 'land of homes.' In the following chapter we propose to give an account of the Cités Ouvrières of Mulhouse. The idea developed in them is not indeed unknown, and has not been altogether untried in England. Mr. Edward Akroyd of Copley, and Mr. John Crossley of Halifax, have initiated schemes for the independence and comfort of their workmen's homes which closely resemble those of the large-hearted manufacturers of Mulhouse. For full information with regard to them we refer the reader to Mr. Hole's interesting volume on *The Homes of the Working Classes.* But there is a completeness and finish about the Mulhouse system which tempts us to regard it somewhat as a model to be studied: it has also now stood the test of thirteen years' experience, and every year has added to the proofs already existing of its value and efficiency.

CHAPTER V.

OOD men, benevolent men in England, from our lamented Prince downward, have done well in devising remedies for a great social evil. Have any other men, in any other country, done better? Let us hear and judge. The evil is too pressing; Englishmen are too much in earnest on this subject; they have too much practical good sense and real philanthropy to look coldly on a remedy because it did not originate with themselves.

In the large industrial city of Mulhouse, not far from Basle, the principal manufacturers and employers of labour have for many years been associated in what they have called an Industrial Society. It has for its object the consideration of all industrial schemes, the rewarding and developing of all useful discoveries, and the promotion of every possible improvement in the condition of the workman. This association is based upon the conviction, that a good workman is the principal factor in all questions of national wealth and prosperity; and that an employer who promotes the well-being, both physical and moral, of his workman, has adopted a principle, not more humane and generous than it is sound in economic wisdom.

In 1851 one of its members, M. Jean Zuber, presented to this Society the plan of our own Prince Albert for the model dwellings for the labouring classes which he erected in Hyde Park, and which, in the Great Exhibition of 1851, drew the attention of our distinguished foreign visitors. M. Zuber recommended that the question should be taken up by the Industrial Society, as one eminently important for Mulhouse, where the working population was continually on the increase, and the accommodation neither sufficient nor suitable for the wants of the people.

The idea commended itself at once to the enlightened members of the Association. Mulhouse has been blessed with a succession of capitalists and manufacturers, amongst whom such names as Dollfus, Kœchlin, Schlumberger and Schwartz, stand foremost, who have realized that their workmen are bound to them by other ties than the cold commercial engagement of labour and wages. They have realized that the men, in the sweat of whose brow their speculations have been wrought out and have prospered— by whose toil their large fortunes have been built up, should in some measure share the prosperity to which they have contributed. It was thus they argued about the home of the workman:—

' The comfort and cleanliness of the dwelling has a greater influence than might be at first supposed on the morality and well-being of a family. The man who returns home in the evening to a dirty and disorderly hovel, where the very air that he breathes is unwholesome and polluted, cannot in such a place pass his evening contentedly ; he will be seen to take refuge in the public-house, and spend there most of his available time. As a first consequence, he becomes almost a stranger to his family, and soon contracts fatal habits of self-indulgence, which reduce their resources to a miserable pittance, and lead to swift and sure misery for him and his. Now if we can offer to this same man a clean and inviting dwelling, with a little garden attached, which will furnish him with a pleasant and useful recreation, and which, by its produce, will develope in him that instinct of property, or the love of possessing, which God has placed in human hearts as a motive to industry and good order ; shall we not have resolved in a satisfactory manner one of the most important problems of social economy ? Shall we not have contributed to draw closer the sacred bonds of the family, and have rendered service not only to the workmen in whom we are interested, but to society in general ?'

About nine months were occupied by the Society in collecting information from all who had occupied themselves with the same subject, as to the plans they had adopted in the construction of workmen's houses, and the results, encouraging or otherwise, which had followed. These inquiries were not confined to France. The work of our countryman, Mr. Henry Roberts, on the dwellings of the labouring classes, of which the Prince Louis Napoleon, then President of the Republic, thought so highly that he caused it to be translated and published, furnished many useful hints. After thus collecting and accommodating to their own circumstances the advice of all who had experience on the subject to offer, they took a step in advance by the erection of four houses, to serve as models, in which they placed workmen who might test practically which of them answered best to the daily need of a labourer and his family. This additional experience gained, their plans were ripe, and the founders of the Cité Ouvrière of Mulhouse commenced operations.

Between Mulhouse and Dornach lies a vast plain, watered by the canal which surrounds the city. On either side of the canal, in the fresh country air of the plain, but in close proximity to the most important factories, the ground was purchased, and the limits assigned of the Workman's City.

The Company who undertook to carry out the project consisted at first of twelve shareholders, who took among them 60 shares of 5000 frs. (200l.) each. The Company was formed in June, 1853. They agreed to restrict themselves to an interest of 4 per cent on their money invested, and to forego any other profits that might arise in the course of their operations. The leading idea of the Workman's City of Mulhouse has been, from the first, the advantage of the workman himself.

Very early in their operations a new and important question presented itself:—Should the Company, as had been the general practice of those who had hitherto built workmen's dwellings, retain pos-

session of the houses they constructed, allowing the
workman to occupy them at a moderate rental, or
should they strike out into a new line of action, and
invite him to purchase his house?

It was much to build comfortable and healthy
houses, which they could offer to their tenants at
lower rents than they had hitherto paid for miserable
hovels; but the aim of the Company was still higher,
and showed their intimate acquaintance with the character of the workman, and the motives by which it
is influenced.

Forethought is eminently the result of education: the improvidence of those who live from hand
to mouth is proverbial. 'What do I earn?' says the
Arab.   Say 'a shilling a-day: what does it cost me
to live?—Sixpence.   I am a fool to labour twice as
much as I need; I will sleep half the day and work
the rest.'   Somewhat on the same principle the
French and English artisan will saunter into the
workshop late on the Monday, or even Tuesday, of the
week, reducing his gains to the level of his present
necessities; whereas, by a prudent use of surplus
strength in prosperous times, he would have provided against the three perils of the workman—
illness, scarcity of work, and old age.   How is the
spirit of thrift and wise forethought to be awakened
in him?   M. Jules Simon deals with this question
in his deeply interesting book, *L'Ouvrière*.   He
has been speaking of savings' banks, and he says that
no scheme of usefulness is without its drawbacks;
and the drawback to the savings' bank is this, that

THE WORKMAN'S HOME AT MULHOUSE.   139

while it is excellent for those in whom the tastes of
economy are already formed, it is but a feeble instru-
ment to awaken or call them into existence. For
this he would rather depend on the organ of acquisi-
tiveness, common to human nature. ' If,' says he,
' instead of the pitiful sum deposited in the savings'
bank, to be given back after long years of waiting,
with a small addition in the way of interest—if,
instead of this, the workman could receive as the
reward of his economy the immediate and tangible
enjoyment of a house and a little bit of land—if
such a scheme as this could be realized, it would em-
brace all social reforms in one; for not only would
it develope more than any other known human principle of action, the taste for industry and economy,
but, by directing all the hopes of the workman towards the possession of a home, it would tend
directly to the cultivation of all domestic habits and
virtues.' He proves his position by a striking example:—A stoker in the employment of a wealthy
manufacturer of Roubaix was an excellent workman,
and obtained high wages, but he was an inveterate
drunkard. One day, in leaving the public-house he
made a false step, fell, and broke his leg. He was
a man of superior intelligence when not in liquor,
and scarcely was he stretched on his bed of sickness
and pain, when anxious thoughts as to the future
began to crowd upon him. His employer came in
to the rescue. ' Make yourself easy,' said he; ' I
will charge myself with *your* support at my own
expense; and for your family, they shall draw your

weekly wages as if you were at work. When you
recover you shall repay me by weekly instalments,
kept back from your wages, what I have advanced
for their support.' The cure proved tedious, and it
was a year after the accident before the money advanced had been completely repaid. His wages, as
we have said, were high, and he and his family contrived to live during that time on what remained of
his earnings after deducting the weekly instalment.
These were happy days for the family. The father
lived at home, shunned the public-house, and worked
diligently for their support. At last the loan was
repaid, and the workman's full wages were again
due, but his employer encouraged him to persevere
two years more in his weekly economy. 'You will
then,' he said, 'have saved 1200 frs. (48l.), which is
the price of the house you are renting from me: in
two years you would be a proprietor, with a home of
your own.' The man consented, and the two years
passed happily and quickly; the purchase was concluded, and he was advanced to the dignity of a
house-owner. On the next occasion of receiving his
weekly wages his employer was about to pay him
the full sum he had earned, but was deterred by the
earnest request of his workman. 'Keep it—keep
it,' said he: 'the house next to mine is for sale, in
fifteen months I can save enough to buy it.' In
short, the man is now the owner of three houses, his
wife has opened a little business, and the former
drunkard will soon retire with an honest com-
petence almost amounting to riches—an instance of

what the love of property, wisely directed, can effect.

Considerations such as those put forth by M. Jules Simon, decided the Company to build, in the widest sense of the word, a 'Workman's City;' theirs in possession, as well as theirs for use. We will first describe the city itself, and then explain the plans by which purchase was made easy to ordinary labourers, earning a moderate weekly wage.

The capital invested by the Company amounted at first, as we have said, to 300,000 francs (12,000l.); somewhat later, by the addition of eight more shareholders, and eleven more shares of 200l. each, it was raised to 14,200l. The Emperor considered this philanthropic effort worthy of encouragement, and an agreement was entered into between the State and the Company, in virtue of which the State contributed 12,000l., on condition that the houses to be built should be sold to the workmen at *cost* price, and that none should be let at a higher rate of profit than 8 per cent. The Emperor's munificent donation has been employed exclusively to cover the expenses of what may be termed the public works of the city, such as the laying down of streets and footways, sewers, fountains, plantations of trees, gas-lighting, public buildings, baths, wash-houses, and a general bakehouse and eating-houses. Thus expenses have been met, which must have been shared among the private houses, seriously adding to their cost price.

The selection of a site was guided by several considerations,—the locality must be healthy, ground tolerably cheap, and the distance from the city to the factories not so great as to add seriously to the fatigue of the workmen, who would have to pass over the same ground four times in the day: all these considerations are met in the level plain on which the city, or rather the cities (for they are divided into two by the canal which waters the plain), have been built.

, The first impression of the traveller on arriving at the cities might be that he was entering some public gardens, so pleasantly is each little house bowered in trees. About 120[*] mètres carrés of garden ground are allotted to each house, and in each garden the Company has planted two fruit-trees. The streets, which are straight, and intersect one another at right angles, are airy and broad; the principal one, Rue Napoléon, eleven, the others eight mètres in breadth: they are bordered with lime-trees.

The great aim of the Company was to construct houses on a scale which would enable each family to live apart; the sanctity and privacy of the domestic hearth were, in their eyes, of great price. If the house were too large for the family, the temptation would be strong to sub-let, and this they wished in every way to discountenance. The majority of the houses consist of groups of four, each in its garden, thus: others back to-back, with the gardens in front. For small families there are houses built altogether on the ground-floor, consisting of a kitchen and two other excellent rooms:

* A mètre carré is somewhat more than a square yard.

for larger families the houses have one story, a
kitchen, a living room, and a small bed-room on the
ground-floor; three more bed-rooms overhead. Each
house is built upon a vaulted cellar, which answers
the purpose of storing wood for fuel; the loft is
capacious, and a little bed-room, in case of a very
large family to be accommodated, might well be
contrived there.

Although the cities at Mulhouse have been built
specially with reference to families, there is one building assigned to unmarried men, where a single room
may be engaged for 7 francs (5s. 10d.) a-month, including attendance and the use of house-linen. The
rules are somewhat strict, for the interests of morality and good order were paramount with the Company. An officer superintends this establishment;
the men are required to be in their rooms by ten
o'clock at night, and no woman may set foot in the
building.

The streets are some of them named after the
founders of the city, as 'la Rue Kœchlin,' 'la Rue
Dollfus.' The 'Place Napoléon' occupies the centre
of the town, and on either side of it a public building is conspicuous, the one for public baths and
laundries, the other the city baking-establish-
ment and eating-house. In the laundry, the housewife pays a halfpenny for two hours at the wash-
tub, with free command of hot water, and the use
either of a drying ground or drying cupboard. Over
the bakehouse and cookshop, the first floor is used
for a public library and for a general store, where

the most necessary articles of household and personal consumption are sold for little more than wholesale prices; but it is fair to say that both of these have been somewhat of a failure. The books are not popular, and the workmen have been so long accustomed to the credit system that they continue to supply themselves from shops that give credit, notwithstanding that each article is much dearer.

In France the State charges itself with public education, and schools of primary instruction are established in every commune, and open gratuitously to all: the Company has, therefore, wisely abstained from establishing any separate schools for the children of their workmen, but they have provided an *infant* school (*salle d'asile*), where 250 children, clean, healthy, and decently clothed, are under the careful and willing superintendence of the wives of the principal manufacturers.

Whichever way the visitor may turn his eyes, whether to the interior of the houses, where the housewife will point out with honest pride her well-scrubbed floors and spotless window-curtains, or to the garden, well—nay, even gaily—kept, with its well-selected flowers, and so diligently used that about 40 frs. profit is made in the year by its produce; the visitor, we say, must on all hands receive the impression that the secret has been found at last of raising the workman to a condition of social prosperity and domestic happiness, not by a lavish charity which would in the end only pauperise him and destroy his self-respect, but by awakening in him the instinct of order and economy; by putting a substantial benefit, not into his hands but within his reach, as the reward of patient toil and exertion; by throwing down the obstacles which would have been insuperable, and leaving only those which may stimulate him to exertion and nerve him to self-denial. With head erect and heart buoyant with hope he advances, step by step, towards the coveted advantage; and when it is attained he is not oppressed with the obsequious feelings of one who has received an overwhelming gratuity, for the labour was his, and the prize he has fairly won: but his heart does warm with an impulse of generous gratitude to those who opened for him the way and cheered him on to victory.

We have now to see by what financial arrangements the Company's houses at Mulhouse were brought within the compass of the workman's power to purchase. We must remind the reader of some fundamental principles on which they had agreed. The shareholders would forego any other profit than 4 per cent interest on the capital invested; they would offer their houses for sale to the workman at cost-price, and would allow him a long term of years in which to complete his payment: till houses found purchasers, they should be let on terms bringing in not more than 8 per cent to the Company; the proceeds of the rental pay the 4 per cent interest to which the shareholder is entitled, but any bonus which may be declared over and above this, is set aside for public improvements, or the further extension of the city.

L

M. Jules Simon thus describes the terms offered by the Company to the workman. The Company makes no mystery of the matter; it says to him: ' Here are my houses, all open; enter them; examine them from cellar to garret. The purchase of the ground cost me a shilling the mètre; building, purchase of materials, salary of architect, has brought the price of the smaller houses to 2400 frs. (96*l*.), of the larger to 3000 frs. (120*l*.). I will sell them to you for the same price; I will gain nothing, neither will I lose anything by the transaction. You are not in a position to pay me 120*l*., but I, as a company, can afford to wait. You shall lay down a first instalment of 12*l*. or 16*l*., which will cover the expenses of contract and transfer; you shall then pay me 18 frs. (15*s*.) a-month for a house worth 96*l*., and 23 frs. (19*s*. 2*d*.) a-month for a house worth 120*l*. This will be 4 or 5 frs. more than it would have cost you to rent it. In fourteen years you will have paid up the price of your house, and it will be yours. Not only you will live rent free, but you will leave it to your children, or sell it, or give it away, at your option. The 5 frs. that you have thus economised monthly, and which would, in the savings' bank, have accumulated to something less than 1500 frs. (60*l*.) in fourteen years, have put you in possession of a house worth now 120*l*., but likely in a similar period from this time at least to double in value. And for those fourteen years you will have the comfort of a good roof over your head, you will be subject to no land-

lord's caprices, you will have enjoyed a garden which
will bring you in from 30 to 40 frs. a-year, to say
nothing of the various advantages of residence in
the Workman's City, as compared with your present
quarters in the old town of Mulhouse,—advantages
for which you have been charged nothing in the
price of your house,—such as wide and well-kept
streets, open and airy spaces planted with trees,
infant-school, public baths, and other similar
institutions.'

Palpable as these advantages may appear, they
did not at once convince the workmen of Mulhouse;
at first, purchasers, and even tenants, held back.
This idea of possessing their houses was especially
new to them; they had a lurking suspicion that
they should find themselves brought under vexatious
restrictions and regulations. A Frenchman's passion
for liberty has to brook many restraints during his
hours of labour, for the French Government has its
hand everywhere, and enters into the minutest details.
Mr. Blanchard Jerrold* gives us some curious particulars as to the surveillance to which French
workmen are subjected, and 'honest as well as
dishonest men,' says he, 'chafe under surveillance.'
All work-folk, men, women and children, are bound
by the law to carry a *livret*, and this *livret* is a little
book, on the first pages of which, the laws affecting
the working classes are printed. Then follow the
names, age, birthplace, &c., of the bearer, and the
name of his last employer; every man who gives

* *Children of Lutetia*, vol. ii. p. 12.

him work must inscribe his name in it, and the date
when the work was delivered. Whenever a workman travels, say from the provinces to Paris, he
must repair to the Préfecture of Police to register
his arrival there. Once registered on the books
of the police, he is at liberty to seek work; but
every time he changes his employer he must go to
the Commissary of Police of his neighbourhood to
'legalize' the signature of his late employer in his
livret. Indeed, he must be prepared at any moment
to show his 'papers' to the police. Before he can
move from one town to another these papers must
be in order, and *visé* by the police.

One hardly knows whether these regulations are
more vexatious to the honest man or the rogue;
hurting the self-respect of the former, restricting
his movements, imposing on him endless formalities;
while the latter is kept by them effectually under
the eyes of the authorities. His *livret* he cannot
escape, without incurring fines and imprisonment;
by it he is always to be found, and always kept on
his good behaviour through the police office. It
tends to make the French workman suspicious of
any attempt at organization in his family and private
life. Thus, model lodging-houses in Paris have
proved a failure. The working men say:* 'We are
all day long in severely regulated workshops, under
masters and overseers, where we have to avoid fines
and other punishments, and you wish us, when we
escape in the evening from the workshop, to go to

* *Children of Lutetia*, p. 244.

a home on the door of which you have pasted another
series of regulations which we are bound to obey.
You want to give us another master, to be called
chief of the colony, so that we shall no longer have
authority, even at our own firesides. We have enough
of administrations and regulations, and papers and
livrets, out-of-doors and in the workshop, and at
home we will have none of these. Here we will
continue to enjoy privacy and independence. We
will not inhabit a number in an endless corridor;
we will not enter barracks.'

The Mulhouse workman, therefore, more or less
influenced by the feelings common to his class, did
not at once comprehend the large-hearted and philanthropic object of the Company. With the attractive
little houses of the new city full in sight, he held
back for a time; not for long, however—he soon satisfied himself that comfort was not offered to him at
the price of independence; nay, that as proprietor of
his house he would be, in a new and unaccustomed
sense, a free man. The conditions imposed were so
simple and reasonable as to leave no excuse for suspicion. They were these:—The house and ground
were to be kept up, the garden cultivated, the fencing
kept in good order, the lime-trees bordering the
streets preserved, and, without permission from the
Company, the purchaser of a house for a period of 10
years must neither sell his house nor let off a part to
another family. The Company has, however, always
been ready to grant the requisite permission in circumstances where it was for the advantage of the

owner : as, for instance, in case of a purchaser leaving
Mulhouse and wishing to transfer his property to
another workman ; or in case of a family without
children, where the whole house was larger than the
necessities of the family required.

We have spoken of an instalment of 12*l.* or 16*l.*,
which is credited to the purchaser, and serves to
liquidate the legal expenses of contract.   The sale of
the house is considered merely provisional till this
instalment is paid ; but so careful is the Company to
throw no difficulty in the way of purchase, that a
workman who has no resources to meet the first
instalment may still be put in possession of a house,
provided he can pay a few francs more each month,
till the instalment is paid up.

One condition has been added in the last three
years which might not have been possible at first,
though obviously the advantage of the workman and
his family is the sole object of its imposition,—no
father of a family can now either rent or purchase a
house in the Workman's City at Mulhouse without
entering into an engagement to send his children
to school.

Now let us see how the sale of houses has actually
prospered—how many workmen's families at Mulhouse live in houses of their own.   In June, 1853,
the Company was formed.

In 1854 the number of houses sold amounted to   49
    1855   ,,   ,,   67
    1856   ,,   ,,   72
    1857   ,,   ,,   124

In 1858 the number of houses sold amounted to 234
1859	„	„	294
1860	„	„	364
1861.	„	„	463
1862	„	„	529
1863	„	„	548
1864	„	„	576
1865	„	„	606

besides 8 houses built on a somewhat larger and more expensive scale, for the dwellings of foremen and overseers of the factories.

In all, then, 614 houses in twelve years, from the date of the formation of the Company (these statistics are made up to Aug. 30, 1865); of these 614, the purchase-money for 112 is entirely paid off, and but little remains on those constructed in the earlier years of the Company.

Think of it for a moment,—614 families on whom the magic words, ' my house, my garden,' have acted as a charm to draw the father from the public-house, to introduce a wise economy into the household expenditure, to draw closer the family bond!

' Where does your husband spend his evenings ?' asked a visitor of a workman's wife at Mulhouse.

' With us, since we have had our house,' was the answer. The great philanthropic heart of M. Jules Simon overflows at the sight :—

' All these families withdrawn from unwholesome and noisome streets and alleys, from ruinous tenements where all offends the eye and threatens the health, from scenes of moral contagion where the honest workman is crowded

together with the drunkard, and his wife must mix in
daily with women of doubtful character! And now
his work done, he is not obliged to choose between the
public-house and an offensive garret. Not a public-house
in the town is so gay and attractive as his own little
dwelling. If there are a few minutes to spare before his
dinner he knows what to do with them: a corner of his
garden is waiting to be dug, or a young tree is bending
for want of a stake, or a bed of vegetables has to be sown,
or flowers, dry and thirsty, are appealing to be watered.
Not a member of his family but finds pleasure in the garden; the wife has her hoe and rake, the boys are proud
to fetch and fill the heavy watering-pot. In the summer,
the dinner will be spread in the garden under a bowering
honeysuckle, and a pleasant talk can be held with the
neighbours over the hedge.

'What family consultations are held over projected
improvements—whether a new paper shall be afforded
for a room in the house, whether the ground will bear another fruit-tree, whether a new system of cultivation will
make it more productive! No fear of a landlord coming in
with his veto, for the landlord is the father. How thoroughly, how doubly at home he feels, encircled by his own
family in his own house—their family home! When old
age comes upon him, when his stiffened arms refuse their
daily toil, he will live unblushingly upon the earnings of
his son, because the debt is abundantly repaid in the home
he has provided for the family. He will grow old and die
at home, and his children even, while supporting him, will be
living with him, rather than he with them. He will have
property to leave behind him—perhaps something more
than the house itself, for a habit of economy becomes deeply
rooted in the character in the course of fourteen years, and
he may conclude to lay by, after the purchase is concluded,
the 11*l.* he paid annually towards it. Property! that is
a new-sounding word in a workman's family. His children

succeed him in his property: the garden associated with
the brightest days of their childhood, the domestic hearth
once lighted up with a mother's smile — they have come in
possession of it; they, in their turn, will have a family
history to tell to their children, for he who acquires possession of a freehold is the founder of a family.'

We believe we have given the outline of the system on which the Workmen's Cities at Mulhouse
have been built, and the principles on which their
large-hearted founders have conducted their operations. They have been chiefly gathered from the
work of M. Jules Simon,* and from private correspondence with M. Bernard, père, Director of the cities
of Mulhouse. He kindly furnished the writer with
extracts from the proceedings of the Industrial Society
of Mulhouse, which enter far more fully into details
as to the financial arrangements and the management
of the Workmen's Cities, than the limited space of
the present volume will admit. Among other particulars, full information is given as to the items of
expense in constructing the houses, that strangers
may be in a position to judge whether the work could
be done in their own country for the same money.
Also the laws of the Company on which they bind

* The writer has gratefully to express acknowledgments to
M. Jules Simon for his sympathy in the object of the present
work. In reply to a request to be allowed to borrow freely from the
information contained in *L'Ouvrière*, he says, in a letter dated
17th October, 1865 :—' Il va sans dire que je serai très charmé de
concourir à la réalisation des projets dont vous me parler; on
peut prendre ce qu'on voudra dans mes livres, j'y consens de
grand cœur, et même je m'en trouve très honoré !'

themselves to act, and specimens of their transactions with the workmen in the sale of the houses.

Two or three minor details are of importance, as showing the animus of the whole scheme; namely, a hearty co-operation on the part of the shareholders in anything that can promote the benefit of the workmen. The Company has established a competition for prizes among the householders,—honourable mention and a sum of money are awarded to those who keep their house, their garden, their furniture, their children, in the best condition of cleanliness and good order. Two of the houses of the Company are set apart for a doctor and a deaconess. The ready and efficient help thus provided in times of sickness is greatly appreciated by the workmen. Again, the great factories, by a simple arrangement for discharging their waste hot water outside the building, provide hot water for washing for the women, and for baths; which are so highly approved, that during the summer more than a thousand are taken in a month, at the rate of 5 centimes (one halfpenny) each.

Side-by-side with these instances of kindly forethought on the part of the Company, we may mention a touching proof of good feeling among the workmen themselves. The numbers of the French army are, as our readers are probably aware, kept up by conscription, and the conscript may purchase immunity from the service by paying a certain sum to a returned soldier to take his place and serve for him. Twenty soldiers from Mulhouse, who were returning after a seven-years' absence, took up fresh engagements, and turned their backs again upon home, that with the money thus earned they might purchase and furnish homes for their aged' parents. They felt they could do nothing better for them than to give them a name and a place in the Workmen's Cities.

Some points still remained on which the writer was anxious for more definite information; as, what proportion does the 4 or 5 francs a-week, paid at Mulhouse towards the purchase of a house, bear to the earnings of the workmen?

Are the purchasers of houses usually young unmarried men, or fathers of families?

Has the Workman's City its public-houses, where men assemble to drink? or only shops, where wine and beer are sold?

On these points M. Bernard has kindly supplied the required information; the following is part of a letter dated Mulhouse, 30th October, 1865,—

'Too much cannot be written and said on that capital question—provision of proper lodging for the working classes, who deserve some compensation in their days and hours of repose, for the labours of the workshop.'

In speaking of Mons. Jean Dollfus, Mayor of Mulhouse, and President of the Society, he says:—

'His great aim is to encourage the workman to purchase his own house, by making every arrangement easy, and keeping the price of the house as low as possible. No other motive has been found to work so effectually in

raising his moral tone, and checking vagrant habits, and
the advantages are self-evident which must result to the
workman's family, both in the present and the future.

'England is always ready for good works. In following out the impulses of your own heart, and in endeavouring to give publicity to the thoughts of Jules Simon,
you may lay yet another stone upon the edifice.

'To answer your questions : first, as to the weekly earnings of our work-people, Mons. Dollfus has supplied me
with the following data : The wages of the workmen vary
greatly, according to the nature of their employment. A
labourer employed all the year round in work making no
demand upon skill would receive from 1 fr. 75 c. to 2 frs.
a-day (8s. 9d. to 10s. a-week); a similar workman employed for a shorter time would earn 2 frs. to 2·50 (10s. to
12s. 6d.) weekly. The spinner gains 3 frs. 50 c. to 4 frs.
a-day (17s. 6d. to 19s. 2d. a-week), and this is about the
average for skilled labour—such as the calico-printer, en-
graver, &c. The mechanic may earn a little more;
from 4 to 5 frs. a-day. The women who work in the
factories earn from 1s. 3d. to 1s. 8d. a-day.

'You ask, from what class the purchasers of houses are
drawn ? They are generally either fathers of families from
the surrounding villages, who are glad to settle in the town
in order to avoid for themselves and their children a journey
to and from work in the dark, and in all weathers; or
young married couples; or, again, those who, having a
little sum laid by, appreciate the advantage of spending it
in a way which will free them from the position of mere
tenants, while at the same time it adds to the resources
they hope to leave to their children.

'Artisans and mechanics, very necessary in a little
town of 6000 inhabitants, are also to be found among the
purchasers : I refer to such occupations as tailoring, shoe-
making, baking, and the labours of the forge. The children
of such mechanics often work in the factories.

'The Workman's City has its share of beer and wine-shops, and the baker often adds a wine-shop to his business, which is rather ruinous to the workman.   However, these houses are kept strictly under police regulations; and at least the million of francs deposited in my hands by the purchasers of houses is so much saved from the fire.

'Our population in the Workmen's Cities is chiefly Catholic, and that means *ignorant*.   70 per cent are Catholic, 25 Protestant, and the remaining 5 per cent represent the mixed marriages.   The popular library, however, established by Mons. Dollfus, is beginning at last to find acceptance, and numerous readers now apply for books.

'Pray apply to me without hesitation, if I can be of further use to you.

'BERNARD, père.'

It will be seen from the above letter, that the rate of wages for unskilled labour at Mulhouse is below that earned by the agricultural poor in many rural districts; while the spinner gains at most 19s. 2d. a-week, and his wife or daughter 10s.   Contrast his position as to lodging with that of a London workman who earns 18s. a-week.   A fresh case is just reported, in which Dr. Lankester had to pronounce upon the cause of death, in the case of an infant of five months, whose mother lived in Russell Place, Little Coram Street.   No want of love on the mother's part, no stinting of its natural food quenched the little life; the baby was laid down to sleep, and taken up dead, *because* the poisonous air of the room exhausted its vital power.   The dust-holes in the yard were filled with decayed refuse, the windows were nearly all broken.   The child's father earned

18*s*. a-week, and, doubtless, they got the best lodging
they could afford.   The mother stated that she had
complained to the landlord, who told her that 'if
she did not like it she had better go.'   Go, yes: but
where? landlords know well enough that the ever-
narrowing quarters for the respectable labouring
poor will compel them to accept, aye, and pay high
too, for any quarters, however noisome; and so we
hear of district visitors and humane friends of the
poor, who are at their wits' end what to advise them;
who encourage them in the purchase of filters,
because the nauseous fluid miscalled *water*, with
which their dwellings are scantily supplied on the
ground-floor only, sends their husbands to quench
their thirst at the public-house; who hear, in answer
to their suggestion that the loaf should be put away
in the cupboard, that 'the smell in the cupboard is
that bad, they can't eat anything that has stood
there;' and all for want of a trap, perhaps, which the
landlord has been in vain asked to put in.

In the inquest we have just referred to, the co-
roner made a significant statement as to the absolute
want of accommodation in London for those whose
earnings do not exceed 18*s*. a-week.   'In all the
new model lodging-houses,' he says, 'none are provided for those earning 18*s*. a-week.   The rents he
considered, for those already inhabited, were extremely high.'   The lowest weekly rent, as we have
seen, in the Peabody Buildings, is 2*s*. 6*d*. a-week,
and this is for a single room.

There is certainly no time to lose in making

provision for lodging our London industrial poor.
Mr. Bazalgette, engineer to the Metropolitan Board
of Works, lately presented to the Board a Report
containing important information as to the railway
schemes which were to be brought before Parliament
in this session of 1866. We extract from his Report
the following information. Forty new bills were to
be submitted to Parliament, contemplating the
formation of 104 miles of railway, besides other local
improvements within the metropolitan area, at an
expenditure of twenty-six millions of money, and
power to borrow nineteen millions more.   The effect,
however, as he tell us, of all metropolitan railway
and street improvements, is the destruction of large
masses of houses, by which the occupants of those
houses are driven towards the suburbs, and the area
of London extended. The railway bills of the present
session include within their limits of deviation about
16,000 houses.   If only half this number were actually destroyed, it would still amount to one-sixtieth
part of all the houses in London.   We leave the
reader to judge what will be the distress of the poor,
if eviction is carried on wholesale before any provision has been made for them in the suburbs.

But we venture to press earnestly home upon
capitalists and employers of labour a question with
which we are ourselves incompetent to deal.   Is such
a scheme as that which has prospered at Mulhouse
incapable of transplantation ? Is there no environ of
London, north, south, east, or west, where land could
be purchased on terms sufficiently reasonable to

favour the erection of a workman's city, and of
houses of which the tenants might, in time, become
the purchasers? Not, of course, within walking
distance, but in conjunction with workmen's trains.
If the new railways are to dislodge so many of the
poor, is it more than reasonable that the poor should
reap from them some ultimate advantage? Twenty-
six millions to be spent in facilitating locomotion
within the area of the metropolis, and the whole
capital of the Company at Mulhouse, including the
State assistance, was 26,200l.! Surely, if the money-
holders of the metropolis would consider this question in all its bearings, physical, social, moral,
something analogous to the Workmen's Cities of
Mulhouse, though modified to meet our English
circumstances, would, like the outposts of a *cordon
sanitaire*, dot the Ordnance map round our over-
grown metropolis.

One cannot but be struck, in reviewing the
arrangements of this Workman's City, with the
relation here maintained between the educated and
uneducated, the rich and the poor, the employer
and employed. It is evident that the claims of a
common brotherhood are recognized at Mulhouse.
The rich man is not so selfishly pre-occupied with
making a fortune as to regard his fellow-men merely
as the instruments of his aggrandisement; he does
not use up human bone and muscle with as little
scruple as the fuel consumed in his engine fire, on
the ground that to work out his speculations he
requires a certain proportion of mechanical force,

and a certain other proportion of human intelligence to conduct it.

To the members of this philanthropic Company their labourers are, first and pre-eminently, *men*, then *workmen*. Treating them as men, accountable moral agents, they recognize their own responsibility as employers to use their vantage-ground of superior wealth and education in elaborating a scheme by which their labourers may, at the same time, preserve their independence and raise themselves in the scale of society. They supply a motive which shall prove a powerful stimulus to domestic affection, order, and economy; and thus lay the surest foundation of a social reform.

Compared with this delicate appreciation of the poor man's wants and desires, how easy it is to take out the purse and add a round sum to a subscription list! But in so far as the gift of money is easy, and has made little or no demand on natural selfishness or indolence, in that proportion it is inoperative for the purpose of binding together in any enduring bonds the benefactor and the benefited. Even in this money-getting age, men have not so wholly lost their sense of relative value as to class in the same rank bank-notes and painstaking sympathy. Love is not bought by money, but by love.

M

CHAPTER VI.

THE WORKING MAN'S SUNDAY — HOW TO SPEND IT.

ITH regard to this question, also, it may seem strange that it should be a vexed one in England. Our English Sabbath is proverbial on the Continent, hated by some, sighed after by others.

Yet that the question is vexed was abundantly proved some ten or twelve years back, when the National Sunday League on the one hand, and so-called Sabbatarian ardour on the other, fought the battle as to throwing open the Crystal Palace to the public on Sunday.

We desire to approach the subject in all humility, in the belief that it is not only a vexed, but an extremely difficult question, especially as regards the workmen in our large towns. Let us see what is said by the leaders of public opinion on each side.

To the Sunday-League advocate the day is preeminently one of rest and relaxation; he is the champion of those whose weeks are passed in toil

and drudgery; he taxes with want of sympathy the
well-to-do religious public, who can have any amount
of variety that they please in the week, and whose
rest on Sunday it is to be still; who, if they choose
to take the air, can do so in their quiet garden or
conservatory; if it is their taste to read, have a quiet
study to retire to.

He contrasts with these the hundred thousand
engaged in shops in the metropolis.   Hear what an
able exponent of the views of his party, Mr. Percy
Cruikshank, has to say on the subject.   He writes
in 1854, when the Bill for opening the Crystal
Palace had been thrown out of Parliament:—

' The respectable persons who claim for themselves the
name of the Religious Public have succeeded, by digging
up a clause in a forgotten Act of Parliament, in excluding
all those hardworkers of London who take holiday on Sunday from enjoying walks and rest in the parks, gardens,
and twenty acres of conservatory of the Crystal Palace at
Sydenham.'*

He supports the charge of narrow-minded in-
tolerance by enlarging on the careful regulations
it had been intended to enforce on all Sunday
visitors to the Palace, and further describes from
what classes of society they would have been likely
to be drawn:—

' According to the Reports of the Early-closing Association there are not less than 100,000 souls engaged in
the shops of the metropolis.

* *Sunday Scenes in London and its Suburbs.*

' A hundred thousand souls, who pass from twelve to fourteen, and even sixteen, hours on their feet, in one close atmosphere, contaminated with human breath, thickened with dust, poisoned with gas!

' Day after day, without change and without relaxation of any kind, except what is to be snatched at untimely hours of night or morning, these shop-servers must sleep either in the houses where they work, in dormitories more or less uncomfortable, or in lodgings close at hand. These people have no cosy study to retire to; even in their bed-chambers they are not alone. They have not the advantage of the evening walk or ride to the suburbs, which has become part of the system of the more opulent trading classes of London. They have little chance of the vacation ramble at Margate, Ramsgate, or Brighton; still less a tour through Switzerland, or up the Rhine. A few days' holiday, and one or two pounds to spare, are the utmost they can aspire to; and these are the victims whom a section of the religious public seek to imprison within the circle of the streets of London, and to debar from any other resource than the public-house — the public-house, which is to be found at the corner of every street, from Kensington to Bow.

' Again: beside the hundred thousand who are banded for the boon of closing labour at eight o'clock in winter and ten in summer, there are the numerous tribe of clerks, obliged to keep up a decent appearance on small salaries, in very responsible employments, living in cramped lodgings or miniature cottages, who seldom see their children except on Sundays. There are tens of thousands of mechanics and others, following occupations created by the highly-civilized state of society in which we live, engaged in producing those articles of luxury or comfort which smooth the path of the wealthy.

' For all these town-working people what day of rest is there? What opportunity of exchanging the close air of the City—of seeing grass, and trees, and flowers—of stretching their limbs, and expanding their lungs—of laying in a stock of health for the ensuing week, except on the one day set apart for rest, the Sunday ? It is a libel on the goodness of God to believe that His day was intended as a punishment for the poor, and a luxury for the rich.'

This idea of Sunday turned into a punishment finds place in the work of another popular writer:*—

' It was a Sunday evening in London—gloomy, close, and stale. Maddening church bells of all degrees of dissonance, sharp and flat, cracked and clear, fast and slow, made the brick-and-mortar echoes hideous. Melancholy streets, in a penitential garb of soot, steeped the souls of the people who were condemned to look at them out of windows in dire despondency. In every thoroughfare, up almost every alley, and down almost every turning, some doleful bell was throbbing, jerking, tolling, as if the plague were in the City and the dead-carts going round. Everything was bolted and barred that could by possibility furnish relief to an over-worked people. No pictures, no unfamiliar animals, no rare plants or flowers, no natural or artificial wonders of the ancient world ; all *taboo* with that enlightened strictness that the ugly South Sea gods in the British Museum might have supposed themselves at home. Nothing to see but streets, streets, streets ! nothing to breathe but streets, streets, streets ! Nothing to change the brooding mind or raise it up ! Nothing for the spent toiler to do but to compare the monotony of his seventh day with the monotony of his six days ! think what a weary life he led, and make the best of it, or the worst, according to the probabilities !'

* *Little Dorrit*, p. 21.

We hope that, by keeping chiefly to his own words, we have stated the case fairly for the member of the Sunday League. If we understand him it is this: the man who toils all the week has a right to take his Sunday for amusement and recreation. For this end, museums, public gardens, picture-galleries, and all entertainments where the moral tendency is not pernicious, should be thrown open to the public. Otherwise, the public-house being the workman's only resource, his Sunday, which might have passed innocently and happily at 'the great Intellectual Temperance Garden,' will be disgraced by brawls and drunkenness in the over-crowded beershop. When we demur to this *holiday* notion of the Sabbath, as overriding the *holy* day remembrance handed down to us from our fathers, and enshrined in those tables of the Ten Commandments which are put up in our Christian Churches, very much as if the founders of our National Church wished us to draw the conclusion that in them is contained a code of law and practice binding on Christian men and women —when we demur, he is ready with his answer—'The Sabbath is a Jewish institution; the Fourth Commandment is not binding on Christians.' 'The Sabbath was made for man,' is his watchword; and this is put forward as the modification of the old precept, 'The seventh day is the Sabbath of the Lord thy God.' The ground for Sabbath observance is shifted from duty to expediency; and the expediency relates rather to the welfare of the body than of the soul; rather to things seen, than to things unseen.

If the member of the Sunday League claims the day for the body, and robs the soul, the Sabbath Ritualist, on the other hand, is ready to defraud the body of its lawful share of the day of rest, for the supposed advantage of the soul. *Religious activity,* in contrast to recreation, is the prevailing idea of *his* Sabbath. It has never been denied that, for ultra notions on the subject, we must cross the Tweed. It is there that we hear of parents compelling their children ' to sit in church for three or four hours at a stretch, listening to two tremendously long sermons preached at the same service, in which Christianity is reduced to a system of the driest metaphysics.' * It is there that the Sunday evening is devoted to questioning these self-same children on the Shorter Catechism; so excellent in itself, but so ill-appreciated as an appendix to the sermon, that the children are in danger of learning to hate both the Catechism and the Lord's day.

In direct contrast to Mr. Dickens' lament over the 'penitential look' of the streets, a Highland elder speaks of the awful sight which may be beheld on a Sunday in Edinburgh. 'There,' he said, 'you might see people walking along the street, *smiling as if they were perfectly happy.*'† Had the text dropped out of the worthy elder's Bible,—' This is the day which the Lord hath made; we will rejoice and be glad in it?'

We believe, however, the Sunday-League man

* *Graver Thoughts of a Country Parson,* p. 4.
† Ibid. p. 5.

would let the Ritualist alone, if it were only a question as to the standard of Sabbath observance he chooses to adopt for himself. If, argues his opponent, it is his pleasure to crowd the day with religious engagements, till his heavy eyelids in the evening droop under the spoken, or over the written sermon; if he chooses to incur the risk of mental torpor and spiritual indigestion, it is, after all, an affair of personal taste and discretion: let him cut his own coat as seems him best, only let him abstain from trying to make it fit upon his neighbours. If a week of light and optional occupation leaves him fresh for a day of Sunday labour — no work so enriching — let him labour in it and be thankful; rising earlier, if he will, and later taking rest: but let him not, in thought or word, reproach the man who accepts gratefully the return of that day, when, set free from the compulsory call to early labour, he may give to the body its additional hour of needed rest.

If for one day in the week the Sabbath Ritualist is willing to lighten the labours of his cook, and eat a dinner prepared the day before, it is thoughtful and kind; but the sacrifice to him is very small: it would be very great to the working man, who, on that one day of the week, dines at home with his children.

If, again, he restricts his walk to his garden on the Sunday, because he finds it easier within its walls, and under its shady trees, to shut out week-day life and thoughts, so be it; but let him not frown on hot, dusty pedestrians, who have taken their 'Sabbath-day's journey' to the nearest heath or common, and are walking to or from the stifling room in a crowded court, which is their only home.

In some such language as this we shall hear the Sabbath Ritualist charged by his opponent with want of sympathy, with failing to appreciate that differing circumstances have different wants. In so far as the charge is true it is a grave one, and we are not prepared altogether to repudiate it. We do think that in England, as well as in Scotland, a gloom is often thrown over the day which ought to be the happiest in the week, because one rigid rule is considered as equally applicable to the child in the family, the young son and daughter at home, the unlettered labourer, the toil-worn mechanic, and to the quiet denizen of his study, who finds himself amply provided for profitable enjoyment of the Sabbath, with public services and private reading, or meditation.

There is something curiously conventional, and, we must say it, sometimes strangely inconsistent, about notions of Sabbath observance. To give a few instances, which we believe are not overdrawn: Do not some hold it to be right and profitable to enjoy heart-to-heart intercourse with a present friend, but quite wrong to hold the same intercourse on paper if he were absent? right to sing a hymn, however secular the air may be to which it is adapted — wrong to take part in an anthem? right to enjoy a voluntary on the church organ — wrong to reproduce it on the drawing-room piano? right to go into the garden — wrong to take a walk? right to gather a flower — wrong to

examine its wondrous structure? right to feed pet
animals — wrong to observe, or to be interested with
them? and (though perhaps it is unfair to provoke a
smile at such an institution of English nurseries,
which may really have its value, moreover, in giving
the earliest impression that the day is distinct and
set apart) allowed that an infant-child should set out
the animals of its ark, and gain a patriarchal concep-
tion of Noah with a long beard, but not allowed if
the remote allusion to sacred history should be wanting, and the selected toy should be a doll or a ball?

Inconsistency is always dangerous; children and
young people are quite sharp enough to detect it.
Let the parents — who have always a right to lay
down laws for their own household — say, ' This we
allow, that we forbid;' but let them not say of things
which are really one and the same in principle, ' This
is right, and that is wrong:' let not the conduct of
parents be open to the suspicion that it is to save
themselves trouble they impose Sabbath restrictions
on their children. The game of play with school-
companions is properly suspended, — let it be exchanged for the weekly luxury of a time spent with
their father, who has, perhaps, little opportunity on
other days to make himself the personal friend of his
children. The dinner on Sunday — cooked the day
before, that the cook may get to the morning service—
need not be *all* cold, and, unquestionably, it should
be the best dinner of the week — the dinner in which
the lady-housekeeper, by a little ingenuity and forethought, has contrived some extra-indulgences to keep

up the festival notion which our English Church at-
taches to the Sabbath.   Sunday, be it remembered,
is never a fast day—the forty days of Lent do not
include one Sunday.

Books of study, lesson-books—for this, to children,
is their ' manner of work' — will (probably with their
hearty consent) remain on the shelves from Saturday
to Monday, but other books must be selected with an
eye to their age and tastes.   The highest Lady of the
land does this for her children.   We have been informed, by one who had a right to know, that it is
the practice of the Queen, on Saturday evening, to
make a selection of Sunday reading-books for her
younger children.

The same principle which leads a parent to appreciate the difference between his child's mental
capacity and his own, and to make self-sacrificing
efforts to meet its requirements, will also lead the
enlightened Christian philanthropist to understand
that the same rule and measure cannot be applied to
his own employment of the Sabbath and to that of
the workman; and will lead him also to recognize
that individual, self-denying effort on his part, is called
for, that he may help the workman, as he helps his
child, to a profitable enjoyment of that which is
his inalienable right—a seventh day of rest from
labour.

We say, to help him; because, though the working
classes can point to a goodly and increasing number
of thoughtful and intelligent men in their ranks,
there remain thousands whose highest idea of en-

joyment is confined to animal comforts—a pipe, a
pot of beer, a warm room to drink it in, and boon
companions: beyond these they do not look. It is
extremely difficult to devise any harmless Sunday
occupation for such a class. Some friends of the
writer spent the summer in Blackpool, about an
hour's distance from the busy manufacturing town
of Preston. Into Blackpool Sunday-excursion trains
weekly poured their thousands; but where were they
chiefly to be found? On the sea-shore, drinking in
health and blowing away the noxious fumes and
gas of factory labour? or scattered up and down the
country, enjoying a rural walk and the sight of trees
and hedges? No! the beach and the fields spread
their attractions in vain; for the most part the excursionists took a short course from the railway-
station to neighbouring beer-houses, which on
Sunday were crowded to excess; and 'the day out,'
meant drinking at Blackpool instead of drinking in
Preston, with a deficit in the week's earnings to the
amount of the railway ticket. A gentleman who
had passed the autumn at Brighton, says, 'I made it
my business to make observation with regard to
excursion trains. I found that, so far were the majority of the parties coming to Brighton from seeking
the pure air of the beach, that they spent a great
part of the day in drinking at public-houses.'

Before, however, we can enter upon any questions of detail as to how the workman can be helped
to spend his Sunday with advantage to himself and
his family, it is necessary to come to some sort of

conclusion as to the light in which we regard the observance of the Sabbath.

We have spoken of it as an inalienable right. In what sense? Because it is a gift from God to every man, of which, therefore, no fellow-man has a right to deprive him? or because it is a sacred duty, claimed by God, which it were peril to disobey? or because it is satisfactorily proved by men of science that the physical and mental powers of men require an interval of rest every seventh day to keep them in working order? or because the State has adopted the Sabbath as a civil institution, reckoning it a *dies non*, in which all ordinary matters of business are to be suspended?* Or is it, finally, because Church authority from the earliest ages has pronounced in favour of the observance of the Sabbath, and provided for it in liturgies and forms of worship?

The lowest of these grounds of Sabbath observance has a certain measure of force and value: thus we may say to the workman, as to a brother-man, 'That you may trade well with your sole capital,

* The unbending character of English law in this respect has just been curiously exhibited in the discussion on the sentence of the wretched woman, Charlotte Windsor. The jury sat on Saturday evening, and five minutes before midnight were dismissed by the judge on their statement that they could come to no decision. On any other night they would have been sent back to deliberate, but as no law proceedings could go on on Sunday they could not have announced a verdict till Monday morning, and, as it is well known, must, by the laws which regulate juries, have spent the interval fasting. Therefore, because the Sunday could not be used as an ordinary day, in which ordinary business might proceed, the jury were dismissed and the case re-opened.

which is labour, and by degrees better your condition, you want a healthy mind in a healthy body.
Science has proved, and experience confirms it, that
labour must not be continuous; that you need in seven
days a day of rest. That day, by the laws of the
land, is secured to you; it is your wisdom so to use
it that your body and mind may be recruited, and
prepared to start afresh for another period of six
days' profitable toil. Does it, or does it not, refresh
you to turn into a public-house and spend the day
drinking with your mates? Do you, or do you not,
rise the next morning with a clear head, and courageous mind, and vigorous frame, satisfied with yourself and prepared to set out with renovated powers
as the bread-winner—the prop of your family? Or,
again, you spend your Sunday in an excursion: the
railway ticket is a serious dip into your week's
earnings—*very* serious, if you take your family with
you; for the wife must ' smarten up a bit,' to go out
and see the world. It is not much of country air
you get in the journey, for you like your pipe, and so
do others; and if you left London smoke behind, you
carry tobacco smoke with you. You make a long day
of it: what with a ' bit' here for the children, and a
' drop' there for yourself and wife, money runs fast.
We do not say you will be otherwise than orderly
and well-conducted—you will neither get drunk nor
use bad words; but by the time the day is over,
and you have had your pipe going home, and it
comes to dragging the tired children up the stairs,
we doubt very much whether any one, to look at you,

would say you had laid out your Sunday to the best
advantage for the end you proposed to yourself—
getting strung up for a week's work. We think it
more likely than not, that Sundays so passed are followed by St. Mondays; and, considering how much
you have spent on the day's pleasure, you have not
much need to shorten the next week's earnings.

So we might argue; but does any one who feels
within himself what it is to be a man think that,
when we have said this, we have said all? We are
at issue with the principles of the National Sunday
League, not because it sympathises with the workman, not because it appreciates his circumstances
and cares for his privations, but because its sympathy is so incomplete; it embraces only a part of
his nature, and that the lowest. We are not writing
in an infidel country, or for infidel readers, that we
should be afraid to say, or fear to have our statement
questioned, that man is an immortal being, the son
of a Great Father, who yearns over him with parental
love; that human happiness is wrapped up in this,
to be at peace with God, to know Him, to love Him;
that these deepest laws of our being are, nevertheless, matters of faith, and easily obscured by the
busy concerns of this life, by the scheming, and
planning, and toiling which have reference to earthly
prosperity, in the fraction of an immortal existence
we are destined to spend here; that, *therefore*,
because an immortal spirit tenants our mortal body,
God has given, as an inalienable right, one day in
seven, in which man may rise to his true dignity,

undistracted by the necessity of working to supply
the wants of his lower nature.   The workman is on
the Sabbath God's free man; the day is God's for
him, and his for God; apart from God its glory is
gone; it is a State institution, an expedient device,
whereby our hand-workers are kept in working
order, even as we let our fields lie fallow, or turn
our horses out to grass.

It appears to us, then, that any expedient for
helping our brother-workman to spend the Sunday
is utterly beneath his acceptance which does not
take into account his true dignity, his whole nature,
as a being composed of soul and body.   The body
must not be neglected, but the claim of the soul is
paramount.   On this account, many schemes seem
to us inadmissible for Sunday which would be excellent for a Saturday-afternoon holiday; they provide
for a man's animal and intellectual enjoyment; they
ignore his spiritual necessities; they humanise, they
do not Christianise.   Take, as an example, among
public institutions, the South Kensington Museum.
We walk through it with a throb of pleasure and
exultation that such a school of knowledge and
improvement is open to the workman; we delight
to think that he may spend there holiday-hours with
his family, where everything around him is calculated to dissipate his ignorance, enlarge his ideas,
cultivate his tastes, and wean him from grosser and
more sensual pleasures.   But, even as pleasures of
the mind are higher and nobler than mere sensual
delights, and we should grieve to see our brother-

man neglect the former in the pursuit of the latter; so the joys, and hopes, and aspirations of his immortal spirit are immeasurably higher and nobler than human knowledge or mental cultivation, and we should grieve to lure him from the greater good by offering to him the less. We know it is said, that in enlarging his mind and purifying his tastes we are taking the first steps towards his moral renovation. ' It is taken for granted,' says a modern writer,* ' that architecture, sculpture, and the wonders of nature and art, which such buildings will contain ' (he is speaking of the Crystal Palace), ' have a direct or indirect tendency to lead to true devotion. Only in a very limited degree is there truth in this at all. Christianity will humanise; we are not so sure that humanising will Christianise. Let us be clear upon this subject. Æsthetics are not religion; it is one thing to civilise and polish, it is another thing to Christianise. The worship of the beautiful is not the worship of holiness; nay, I know not whether the one may not have a tendency to disincline from the other: at least, such was the history of ancient Greece.'

One word here may be needful to guard against the idea that the man who has brutalised himself and deadened every moral sensibility by the indulgence of low and sensual vice, is more likely to open his ear to spiritual truth than he will be if,

* Sermons by the late F. W. Robertson. Second Series, p. 190. A book in which truth and error appear to us strangely intermingled.

N

under reforming influences like those on which we
have dwelt, he is reclaimed from social degradation,
regains his self-respect, and becomes an orderly and
well-conducted member of society.   The very reverse
is the case: to have wandered farther from the right
way cannot have diminished the difficulty of return;
to have set human authority at defiance cannot make
it easier to submit to Divine.   The truth which
enlightens and saves is apprehended by that part of
man's nature which thinks and feels; and in proportion as animal propensities have the mastery, the
entrance of truth is made more difficult.

We will not, then, undervalue social reformation,
brought about by civilising influences, but we will
take it for what it is worth; it is likely to replace
certain defences, the loss of which leaves a man very
open to moral assault,—such defences as self-respect,
for instance, or a fair reputation.   Natural affections,
relieved from the incubus of selfish debasement, are
likely to spring up into new life,—the man is a
kinder husband, a wiser father; social virtues are
strengthened,—he becomes a better citizen, a better
subject; his sympathies are now ranged on the side
of law and order,—he has something to lose and
nothing to gain, from anarchy and rebellion.

These are important advantages; and society,
which has to do with man as a social unit, and is ag-
grieved, or otherwise, by his failure in social claims or
his fulfilment of them,—society is satisfied with the
result of the humanising influence she has brought
to bear upon him.   But is the man himself satisfied?

Amid the human claims and natural affections which
he is learning to recognise, and to which he is
beginning to respond, does no consciousness at times
oppress him that a paramount claim on his affections
is disregarded and forgotten? He has been told
that Sunday is the workman's day for holiday and
rest; does the word *rest* never fall upon his ear like
a bitter mockery, because, under all his now decent
exterior, he carries within him a secret source of
unrest, a misgiving that 'acquaintance with God,'
for which, above all other purposes, Sunday was
given to him, is not yet begun? 'I never had my
Sundays!' burst in anguish from the lips of a dying
cabman, when the summons came, which none may
disobey, to call him into the presence of the unknown
God, who might have been his tried and trusted
friend.

We have now regarded the question on its *human*
side, and considering *man*, his interests, his requirements, we contend that the most important use of
the day should not be ignored in any schemes, public
or private, to help the workman to make the most of
his day of rest.

There is another aspect of the question. We have
spoken of man's *interests;* are they met and supported by God's *requirements?* Is there any dictum
in that Book which is the rule of our old English
Constitution, which we put into the hands of our
Sovereign as the guide of her public life and acts,
any direct precept or fair inference, which may be
taken as an expression of the Divine will for us, who

live in this advanced stage of the world's history, when the old religion of types and ceremonies has passed away?

We are told that the Sabbath was a Jewish institution — one among many other observances which served the purpose of keeping the Jew separate from other nations; that it is spoken of indeed as blessed and sanctified at the creation: but no injunctions which have reference to man's observance of the day find place till the Mosaic times, when the reason assigned was in force.

Now it is difficult to see in what sense the day could be sanctified (set apart), unless man were invited to share in the benediction and rest with which God had hallowed the day. Traces do not seem to us so absolutely wanting, that the return of the seventh day was a recognised period in patriarchal times: it was at weekly intervals that the raven and the dove were sent forth from the ark; and we think that any one who will read with an unprejudiced mind the account of the fall of the manna (which was antecedent to the giving of the law, either moral or ceremonial) will allow that the words which occur in Exod. xvi. 23, refer not to the promulgation of a new precept, but to the revival of an old one, which during the long period of bondage in Egypt had fallen into disuse. 'The rest of the holy sabbath' is referred to as something already known and recognised: 'this is that which the Lord *hath said.*'

Besides, until Mosaic times, none of the other moral laws had been collected into a code, or other-

wise written than on men's consciences; yet we never
hear it contended that the 6th or the 7th or the 8th
Commandments are abrogated, because they were
first announced through Moses to the one nation of
the earth who at that time feared God, and professed to take His law as their rule of life.   As soon
as a moral code appears at all, the law of the Sabbath
stands incorporated with it.   As if to mark that its
application, though more immediate to the Israelite,
was designed to take effect on the whole human race,
the reason assigned for the command in the earliest
account (Exod. xx. 11) is universal, and rests on the
creation — the reason assigned in the second account
(Deut. v. 15) is Jewish, and rests on the exodus from
Egypt.   The earliest and most prominent place is
given to that reason in which all mankind have an
equal share.

But, it is argued, when Christ came He announced
a new principle as to the Sabbath,—'The Sabbath is
made for man, and not man for the Sabbath ;' this is
interpreted to mean, that the Sabbath is now handed
over to man to use as he judges most for his advantage; God has relinquished any special claim upon
it; its character is changed from a holy day to a
holiday.

The passage on the authority of which it has been
deemed lawful to pronounce a sentence of reversal on
one of the Ten Commandments, written with the
finger of God on the tables of stone, occurs in the
second chapter of St. Mark, on occasion of a presump-
tuous interference on the part of the Pharisees with

the conduct of the disciples in the presence of their
Master. Supposing Him either culpably unobservant
of the actions of His followers, or culpably lax in His
own notions of what was due to the sanctity of the
day, they remonstrate both with Him and with them.
What was the offence? the disciples were hungry,
and in passing through a cornfield they plucked the
ripe ears, rubbed away the chaff in their hands,
and ate. Not the act itself, for it was allowed in
Jewish law, roused Pharisaical indignation, but their
prejudiced notion that, though lawful on other days,
it was unlawful for the Sabbath, as coming under the
prohibition ' no manner of work.'

The answer of the Lord is twofold, and is directed
against their prejudice on the one hand, and their
presumption on the other. ' You have formed your
own notion of the Sabbath, and would bind all men
to it; as if the Sabbath had been made first, and then
man had been created for the purpose of keeping it :
but the Sabbath was made on account of man (this
is the force of the preposition), not man on account
of the Sabbath.   Again, you insist not on the words
of the law, but on the interpretation you choose to
put upon it : is it seemly to do so in the presence of
the Lawgiver, who must know best the spirit and
force of His own commands ?   That my disciples do
this in my presence, unrebuked by me, should be to
you a sufficient guarantee that such an act in no way
violates my law.' To me, by whom the day was first
set apart, and who am its rightful Lord, you must
look if you would know how to observe it.'

This seems the natural construction to put upon the narrative, and accordingly we watch in the four-fold story of the life of Christ for indications as to how the Sabbaths were spent by Him. Synagogue worship is a prominent feature of them; it was, we are told,* 'His custom;' so also it was His practice to satisfy on that day His own benevolent impulse to relieve suffering by works of healing, and He vindicated such an employment of the day triumphantly against the cavil of the Pharisees.† Intimate social intercourse is also a feature of Christ's Sabbaths. After leaving the synagogue we find Him turning into the house of a friend, a welcome and beloved guest.‡ Days so busily occupied as His, with works of mercy, left little time for seasons of retirement; but these were redeemed from sleep:§ as to recreation and bodily refreshment, the walk through the cornfields was reckoned by Him no desecration of the day; and He was one of the three who enjoyed the Sabbath-evening walk to Emmaus, though he deprecated a journey under any circumstances which would destroy the tranquillity of Sabbath rest. 'Pray ye that your flight be not on the Sabbath-day.'

These few gleanings from the life of Christ, our Example, and the Founder of the Christian dispensation, may serve to show the general principles on which He would have us interpret, 'In it thou shalt do no manner of work.'

We gather—The Sabbath is a day for the direct worship of God and communion with Him, and as

* Luke, iv. 16. † Ibid. vi. 9. ‡ Mark, i. 29. § Ibid. i. 35.

such is called in the latest book of Scripture, 'the Lord's day.' *

It is a day for bodily rest and refreshment, in which the toil should cease by which we win our bread in the week.

It is a day on which all necessary bodily wants may be attended to.

It is a day when the ignorant and the suffering have a special claim upon us.

It is a day for enjoying intercourse with members of our family and intimate friends.

Such relaxation as is needed by body and mind— a walk, for instance, or sacred music, or enjoyment of the beauties of God's work in creation—is not discordant with the observance of the Sabbath.

The writer has felt a real shrinking from going over ground which has exercised so many wiser heads and abler pens; but *some* statement of principle, and the reason on which it is held, seemed necessary, because every suggestion of detail must be modified by it. If the Sabbath is a mere holiday, and my brother-workman has nothing more important to do in it than to amuse and refresh his mind, to rest and recreate his body, then the only problem is, How to provide amusement for *all* without depriving *some* of any rest or interval of labour at all? But if there be truth in the deductions we have drawn, other motives and purposes must be taken into account, and then, in a large town such as London, the question becomes very complex and difficult.

* Matt. xxiv. 20. Rev. i.

We have seen in a former chapter what is too often the workman's home in London—a single room for himself and his family in a crowded court or alley—sounds of profanity and sights of impurity which he cannot shut out—an atmosphere foul, enervating, depressing—green trees and hedge-rows, flowers and singing-birds, are miles away.

He gets up, we will say, later on Sunday—it would be hard to grudge him that, it is a day of rest, and he has had a week of toil; but when he is up there are, perhaps, twelve hours before he will go to bed again: how are they to be used? what facilities are there for his spending the Sunday as we would like him to spend it? If his clothes are very mean and shabby, it will be a hard trial of principle to go to church, for he is very sensitive to slights; and if he sees the rich man handed obsequiously to his cushioned pew, with 'Sit thou here in a good place,' while to him it is said, 'Stand thou there,' if he sees the lady gather up her skirts as she passes him, he will be only too ready to think that he has got into the wrong place, to forget that 'the rich and the poor meet together, but the Lord is the maker of them all.'

We may here suggest a plan which has been tried and found to work well in a church in a populous suburb of London. It is well known how unfairly the free sittings in a church are often occupied by the wealthy, who can spare time to come long before the service begins, and thus appropriate the seats intended for the poor. It is also well

known how a steady church-goer among the working
classes, values 'his own seat,'—cannot feel at ease,
in fact, in any but his accustomed corner. Why
should not every free sitting be numbered, and
tickets with corresponding numbers be given, by
agreement of the clergyman and the churchwardens,
to the district visitors of the parish? They know the
men and women who, by steady habits of church-
going, are best entitled to a ticket; the numbered
seat would then be reserved as scrupulously for the
ticket-holder as the numbered pew for his wealthy
neighbour. The desire to gain, and the fear of
losing a ticket, would foster habits of regular
attendance, and the poor man would take his place
at once without waiting till it is vacated by the
rich.

The following has also been communicated, as
showing the value of providing liberally and judi-
ciously for the accommodation of working men and
their families in our churches:—

'About 1850 or 1851 I visited Boston one Saturday,
and stayed over Sunday, wishing to see its noble church.
The church itself was, indeed, splendid; but the interior
arrangements very bad. About one-half of the floor was
occupied by various piles of green-lined, or red-lined, or
blue-lined, boxes or pews, of various dates, colours, and
sizes. Provision for the poor there was scarcely any.

'Shortly after, Mr. Blenkin was appointed to the
church, and immediately set about a re-pewing. He collected 3500*l.*, turned out all the old green and red pews,
and thoroughly re-pewed the church from end to end with
oaken pews, *without doors.*

'I visited the place again in 1853, and went to the church on Sunday morning. I found the doors, before they were opened, surrounded by poor people. I asked them what brought them there so soon. They answered, that those who got in first got the best seats.

'I found that the whole middle aisle was left unappropriated for the first-comers. Thus the poor had the best places.

'The side-aisles were appropriated to the families of the town. The advantage they had was, that they needed not to come till ·10·55. The poor crowded the doors at 10·30, and then took possession of the middle aisle.'

But to return. At last, perhaps, all the wearers of broad cloth and silk dresses are successfully squeezed into pews, and soon after service has begun a free seat is left for the workman; then, if he has a prayer and hymn-book, and if the service is read with feeling, and if the music and singing are not so highly decorative that he loses his way in them, and if the sermon is a living message and not an intellectual treatise (thank God, in a growing number of churches these *ifs* can be satisfactorily answered), then he has a fair opportunity of gaining the most important advantage the Sunday has in store for him.

His ear is arrested; those great living truths which take no account of his poverty or wealth, of his social meanness or social dignity, but which address him as a man, as a son, as an immortal being, as one loved and cared for—those truths soothe and calm him; they raise him up to the dignity of manhood; he passes from the church door with a half-formed purpose to come again, to come oftener.

So far all is well: but the Sunday is not half
over yet; his mind is not trained to habits of continuous thought; probably the morning service has
used up his power of attention. Now, if he lived in
the country, he might turn into his little plot of
garden-ground, and enjoy the concért God has prepared for him, and teach his children to distinguish
between the notes of the nightingale, and the thrush,
and the warbling blackbird; or he might show them
how the bud of last Sunday has opened into a flower,
and might give, as he plucks up the ill weed which
threatens to choke tender seedlings, a hundred useful,
profitable lessons, from God's great open book of
nature.

But where is our *Town*-worker to take his children?—the quiet, orderly church-goer we have been
describing—who wants to stretch his limbs and get
a breath of pure air, and see something more refreshing than dingy brick houses, but who would
fain keep his children and himself out of harm's
way, Sunday traffic, drinking and swearing, gambling and betting—what outlets of London are there
within a walk where hundreds have not got the start
of him? The Parks are crowded; Primrose Hill
looks like a human ants' nest; Hampstead Heath is
alive with donkey-races; fields and hedge-rows have
had notice to quit, and half-built suburban villas
mark their former place within even a young man's
memory. Where is he to go? He would like a quiet
walk with his family in winter, or to sit out with
them under the trees in summer; he is almost driven

out of his so-called *home*, for the sights, and sounds, and smells of the neighbourhood are not choice or refreshing; but, except some forlorn deserted-looking streets, where is there a chance of a retreat? We have thought whether it would be too great a sacrifice to ask that the gardens of Squares, some of them very large and pleasant, should be reserved on Sunday for workmen of this class, who would really value a quiet retreat within walking-distance of their homes, and do not know where to go for it? We do not propose to admit them indiscriminately; but surely each household in a large Square has, or should have, its visiting-list of humble and deserving friends in the working classes, and each family might admit a certain number of those it has reason to know would not abuse the privilege. Of course it would necessitate keeping the nurse-maids and children of the squares out of the gardens on that day; but it is only one day out of seven, and the sacrifice made by the rich would gladden the heart of his working brother as a practical and living proof of his sympathy.

And what if, on Sunday afternoon in summer, gentlemen of the Square, fathers or sons, should spare an hour from their own ease and Sabbath rest, and turn into the garden with some interesting book in hand, and read it aloud to a group under a tree (good reading and pronunciation have great charm for the working man)? We will venture to say, the effort made would be richly repaid, by the kindly feeling called forth on both sides,

But we are well aware that the class we have been describing hitherto are not those for whom it is most difficult to provide on Sunday; unhappily, it is a mere fraction among the masses of our London workmen who do thus spend the morning at church and the afternoon with their children. ˙Such men are the exception. The rule is, first, to drop out of the calculation altogether that Sunday has anything to do with the needs of man's spirit or his wants beyond the present life; secondly, to sacrifice to pleasure-taking, the needed bodily rest offered by the Sunday. Pleasure-excursions, by rail or boat, are the least objectionable of the ways in which the day is ordinarily spent. Next to these come the frequenters of scenes where excitement and vice are mingled attractions, the *habitués* of Cremorne, Highbury Barn, and such-like places of entertainment. Then, perhaps, lowest of all, the thousands who are too brutalised by drink to care for fun or pleasure; heavy-eyed and leaden-hearted, they turn into public-houses on Sunday as soon as they are opened, with last week's earnings in their pockets. The evening finds them drinking still—excited now, and noisy; at night the miserable wife guides home a drunken sot, whose wages have melted into drink, and who must lose a working day or two in sleeping off the effects of his debauch.

Here is the strong point of the Sunday-League advocate when he argues for Sunday amusements. 'See the effect,' he says, 'of shutting up places of rational amusement—museums, zoological gardens, picture-galleries, and such-like; you leave nothing for the masses but the public-house! You must take things as you find them, and deal with men as they are, not as you could imagine or wish them to be: you cannot infuse into them your ideas of the Sabbath—your taste for church-going; they will not have your religion at any price, but they would spend the day quietly and sensibly at the Crystal Palace or the other public institutions—at once humanising and instructive—from which you exclude them.'

Would they? That is just the question. The better class of excursionists might, who spend the day pleasure-seeking with their families; yet, remembering the excursionists of Blackpool, we cannot feel too sure even of these. But why spend time in conjecture? the experiment is tried weekly. Not twelve hours' distance from London, the most ardent advocate of Sunday-League principles could not desire a fuller catalogue of pleasures and amusements than are open to the public every Sunday in Paris. How does it answer there? Are the public-houses empty, while the masses are informing their minds and refining their tastes in picture-galleries and music-halls? Does Monday morning find them braced up for exertion, ready to do battle manfully, for wife and childrens' sake, with the difficulties and struggles of a workman's life?

Let us take a glance, first, at the bill of fare provided for them in the way of amusement: it is varied enough to suit all tastes:—Versailles, which might

answer to our Sydenham Palace, half-an-hour's distance by train; the exquisite fountains, reserved for
Sunday entertainment; the grounds so large that,
though thousands flock there, the visitor may, if he
chooses, keep apart and find a quiet retreat. The
Champs Elysées, crowded with attractions for all ages
and ranks—billiard-tables for the men, whirligigs
for the active, coquetry for the young, toys for children, dashing equipages for the brilliant and gay.
The streets, sights in themselves, with their glit-
tering shop-windows:—here and there, perhaps, as an
exception, closed shutters, and printed on them in
large characters, ' *Fermé le Dimanche et les Fêtes;*'
but for the most part open, and the scene of busy
traffic. The Theatres—the grand attraction of Paris,
to Parisians as well as strangers—the theatres are
truly in force on Sunday. Dr. Guthrie was there in
February, 1864. We give in a note a list of thirteen
theatres and operas with which he furnishes us, containing the following announcements, to suit the
tastes of all classes of society, on the 28th of that
month.*

Is this amusement enough? At all events if Parisian workmen frequent cabarets, it is not because

---

* At the *Opéra*, ' The Huguenots,' in 5 Acts.
Théâtre Français, ' Une Chaîne,' a Comedy in 5 Acts; and ' The
Young Husband,' a Comedy in 3 Acts.
Opéra Comique, ' The Black Domino.'
Odéon, Representations of ' the Relays' and ' the Will.'
Gymnase, ' Mont Joye,' a Comedy in 5 Acts.
Théâtre Italien, ' Rigoletto,' an Opera in 4 Acts.
Théâtre Lyrique, ' Faust,' an Opera in 5 Acts.

other places are closed to them. Now let M. Jules
Simon speak; his generous sympathies towards the
workmen add weight to his words when he has to
give evidence against them :—' On pay-day the workman receives in a round sum the earnings of the
week or the fortnight; if paid on Saturday, he cannot
wait till the next day to begin his debauch.   By
Saturday night the cabarets are full; they remain so
all Sunday, often all Monday also : a little gambling
serves to pass the time between the cups.   The
pipe never leaves the workman's lips.   Soon the
stifling atmosphere is hardly fit to breathe.   In-
articulate cries, obscene songs, licentious words,
mingle with the rattling of glasses. Money runs fast :
one-third—half, perhaps—of the hardly-earned
wages are gone.   Wives begin to look in—pale and
trembling—remembering the hungry children at
home, and the threatening landlord.   At last nature
asserts itself; the man must sleep somewhere; the
policeman turns him out, and the wretched wife
does her best to guide him home in safety.'*

   Or payment, perhaps, takes place on Sunday—
more usually than not, we believe; for business finds
itself as much at home as pleasure, in a Parisian

Palais Royal, ' La Gannotte.'
Porte Lamartine, ' Faustine.'
Gaité, ' The House of the Bagnio-keeper,'
Théâtre du Châtelet, ' The Shipwreck of the Medusa.
Théâtre de Jeunes Artistes, ' Galatée.'
Variétés, ' Le Petit de la Rue Ponceau,' a Comedy in 2 Acts,
lively and very amusing, preceded by 'The Sister of Jocrice,' and
followed by ' A Trooper who follows the Nursery-Maids.'
   * *L'Ouvrière*, p. 133.

Sunday: in this case, work generally winds up in the forenoon. 'On Sunday morning,' says Mr. Blanchard Jerrold,* 'every workman will be at his bench, hard at his work up to noon, when he will break off, and go forth in holiday attire to enter upon his long span of pleasure. The afternoon of Sunday affords him only a taste of relaxation. St. Monday is his real holiday, and if it leaves him any money unspent on Tuesday morning, he will not be inclined to return to his bench. He is essentially a spendthrift, and wife and children who are dependent on him can have but little hope that he will make any provision for the future.'

With the Parisian example before our eyes, we cannot see that we have any great encouragement to work out the experiment in London, whether Sunday amusements might raise the moral tone of the masses, and draw them away from spending their day of rest in degrading and sensual indulgences. The lever that shall raise them must be stronger in its own nature, and poised on a steadier fulcrum.

It is also reasonable, to say the least, to inquire whether workmen have given any opinion themselves on the subject. They ought to know best their own wants and wishes.

On the 23rd of November, 1865, a deputation of working men of the metropolis waited upon Earl Granville, with reference to the opening of the Kensington Museum and other places on Sunday. Mr. T. Hughes, M.P. for Lambeth, introduced the depu-

* *Children of Lutetia*, vol. ii. p. 100.

tation; and several of the working men addressed
his Lordship on the subject of the agitation by the
National Sunday League for opening public buildings on Sundays. They denied that the working
men of the metropolis *were* anxious to have such
places opened on Sundays, and repudiated the claims
of the National Sunday League to represent the
London operatives.

Mr. Hughes gave subsequently the reasons for
his belief that the deputation which he headed expressed a general feeling among London workmen.
He said the question was raised at every meeting
during his canvass in Lambeth, and invariably
decided *against* opening such places as museums
and galleries on Sunday. He further stated that
various other meetings of special trades, at which
he had presided, had come to a similar conclusion.
They were very anxious for the opening of such places
on the evenings of week-days, and for some short-
ening of the hours of labour; and they deprecated
the Sunday agitation, as tending to diminish their
chance of obtaining these benefits.

The *Times*, in a leading article on the subject,
leaves indeed the theological part of the question
untouched, but expresses its pleasure that the opinions of working men have within the last few
years been taking this direction.

' It may,' says this journal, ' be assumed, that the majority of persons in all classes would be sorry to see the
Sunday deprived of those general characteristics which
have so long marked it among us. How much we all owe

to the observance of Sunday it would be difficult to estimate. In this city, to great numbers of men it is an absolute necessity. It is probably the only institution which
prevents work from becoming continuous. Such are the
daily increasing demands of labour, that to many men,
without this enforced break, life would become one perpetual whirl of occupation. The sudden change of thought,
the pause in every business, afford a refreshment to the
mind, scarcely less than that of sleep to the body, and give
opportunities for family intercourse and for quiet reflection,
which it would be impossible otherwise to obtain. The
artisan, above all, whose business does not follow him to
his home, may spend a quiet day with his family in complete relaxation. We may be allowed to think that the
day has had an influence on our national character, and
contributed a sobriety, a steadiness, and a thoughtfulness
to it, which it would otherwise have wanted. A day of
rest is more than a holiday ; and let us keep Sunday for
the former, and not for the latter. If the working men
are coming to be of this opinion, we congratulate them on
their good sense, and we trust that they will not allow
themselves to be misrepresented. Agitation on this subject has no chance of receiving much attention, except so
far as it is supposed to express the wishes of the working
classes. If they are against such a measure as throwing
open public amusements, no one else is for it.'

Adam Smith, the author of the *Wealth of
Nations*, was not likely to view the question in its
religious aspect, but he comes to the same conclusion as the *Times* about the importance of
repose and rest. A friend of his came to him with
a manuscript he had written, attacking Sabbath observance as practised in this country. 'Put it behind
the fire,' was the advice of the great political econo-

mist. 'If the common notion of the sacredness of
the day secures to the working classes, week by week,
a period of repose and rest, the Sunday, even as a
civil institution, is an invaluable blessing.'

Perhaps, then, we may leave the question of
public amusements. It looked plausible enough as
offering counter-attractions to the beer-shop, but in
a neighbouring country it has on this very point
been tried and found wanting; in our own, it appears
to run counter to the wishes of the very class on
whom it intends to confer a boon.

Another question remains besides Sunday amusements : to pass it over in silence would be cowardly,
for it is confessedly a difficulty. The same leader
in the *Times*, which gives its voice against Sunday
amusements, says, with regard to working men :—
'We would by all means have them get away on
Sundays from the confinement, the bad air, and the
gloom of their narrow courts, into the Parks, and
into the country.'

'Into the Parks!' yes, by all means. We only
wish their size and number corresponded better with
the requirements of the thousands who resort to
them, so that they offered a quieter retreat. But
'into the country!' this involves the whole question
of Sunday travelling. On a superficial view, the
advantage of the workman appears to come into
collision with the integrity of Sabbath observance :
the subject requires to be looked at all round, to
decide that it is not so.

Those in whom sympathy for the workman is

strong and a Sabbath instinct feeble will argue
thus:—' If you shut him out from works of art, at
least make it easy for him to enjoy the beauties of
nature. You have your garden and conservatory,
let him have his cheap run to Kew or Brighton;
you allow, the body as well as the soul has a claim
and part in the day of rest. What refreshment or
bodily strength can he gain pent up in a close
London atmosphere, with nothing to raise his spirits
or brace up his bodily powers? Who can tell what
influences for good sea air and blue sky, and hedge-
rows and green fields, may not exercise? No great
portion of the day need be occupied in the transit
to and fro; he may attend church in the country,
and is likely to do so with far more profit than in
town. Railway servants, indeed, must be employed,
but it is a case in which the few who would suffer
must be sacrificed to the many who will reap advantage.'

Now, in the first place, we are quite ready to
admit that the workman is under unfavourable circumstances, both for soul and body, who has to
spend his Sunday cooped up in a crowded neighbourhood; it is more difficult for him than for an
agricultural labourer to improve the day for the purposes for which it was given—spiritual profit and
bodily rest. Noisy and disorderly neighbours occupying the same house are not helpful to reflection,
dingy brick houses are depressing to the spirits, the
impure atmosphere of a great city is injurious to the
health. They are not imaginary, but *real* evils,

which the steady workman encounters when he re-
solves to renounce the excursion-train and pass the
Sunday in London.

But, on the other hand, are the evils imaginary
which are brought upon workmen, as a class, by
Sunday excursions? If they are fairly compared
with the first-mentioned, which are the worst?

Think of the excursionist himself. It must be
either an expensive or a rather selfish pleasure if he
is a family man. It would be a little hard to leave the
wife at home in her dull room on the day she has been
looking forward to all the week; and if she goes the
children must, or be left to chance it by themselves
about the streets. At the journey's end some place
must be sought to eat and shelter in, for an English
sun is not to be trusted: what place will offer but
the public-house? Will the scenes that go on in
the public room be always those to which a respectable English workman would like to introduce his
wife and young children? Moreover, his railway
ticket is to himself a passport to drink. It has been
decided by the Court of Queen's Bench, that directly
on Sunday a man has purchased a railway ticket he
becomes in the eye of the law a traveller, and may
call for beer or spirits at any public-house in any
place where he may stop; and that, too, in the hours
of Sunday in which, were he to remain at home, he
would find public-houses closed by law. As a traveller, the public-house will be open to him all day;
at home, up to five o'clock in the afternoon, it is
only open two hours—and those hours are from one

to three, when home has a counter-attraction to offer, the Sunday dinner with his family: if he is a man easily led away by drink, such a consideration as this ought to weigh with him, in the question of Sunday travelling.

Again, as to church-going; excursion-trains do not run to quiet country villages, where the door in the rustic church-porch stands open to invite wayfarers to enter, but to attractive watering-places and places of general resort. The excursionist is one of hundreds or thousands whom such a place numbers on Sunday among its visitors. We ask what chance they would have of finding church accommodation, supposing any considerable number of them were inclined to seek it? At home they might not have gone to church or chapel, here they cannot.

Again: the day is one of great fatigue, bustle, and excitement. Let any one who doubts it watch the riotous crowds who flock in to London from the railway stations on Sunday evening: we look in vain for traces that a day of rest and healthful relaxation has been enjoyed; we are compelled to admit that, neither as to his purse, nor as to his family, nor as to his soul, nor even as to his body, has the workman done the best thing for himself, by his Sunday excursion.

But an English workman is open to appeal on other than selfish motives: he may have few sympathies with the classes above him, but he has many with his brother-operatives. It is an honour to humanity to see what generous sacrifices English working men and women will make for each other when occasion calls for it : it is, then, a part of the question from which he will not turn his eyes when it is pointed out to him, that if he is to turn his day of rest into a day of *pleasure*, others must turn theirs into a day of *toil.* Very hard toil, too ; harder than on other days. ' Rest !' said a railway porter on a South London line; 'I do not know what it is to sit down on Sunday.' Another says : — 'I get one clear Sunday in a year.' A passenger-porter says : — 'I work harder on Sundays than on week-days, as there is more passenger traffic.' Another, a railway policeman : — ' On other days I work twelve hours, but on Sunday fifteen ; on Monday, sixteen hours : the work is harder on Sunday and Monday, on account of the excursions.' Again, a London railway servant says :—'I have known as many as 150 trains pass our station on a Sunday. Sunday is the hardest day's work ; guards and policemen get no Sunday in summer, and only one in three in winter. The Sunday labour is very injurious to the characters of young men from the country.'

But, it is said, the disproportion is so great between the few who work, and the many who, by their work, are enabled to take pleasurable recreation, that the end justifies the means. A workman shall answer — a packing-box maker from one of the great industrial centres of the North. ' Grant,' he says, ' that railway labourers form a small portion of the community ; their paucity of numbers is no sufficient reason for disregarding their claim. During a former agitation of the question, shareholders who wished to vote against Sunday trains because the general feeling was against it, were vehemently told that the question was not one of numbers, and that though the parties disposed to travel on Sunday were the smallest fraction of society, they should, and ought to have, the opportunity of spending the Sunday as they thought proper. Now,' said this acute reasoner, 'if this argument be sound, give the railway operatives the benefit of it; whether they be few or many, allow them to keep the Sabbath as they think proper.'

But, in truth, the number is not such a mere fraction who are employed by Sunday travelling: in railways, 100,000; and in omnibuses and cabs, in London alone, 24,000. The workman, who understands better than most men the value of a day of rest, will think twice before he adds another straw to the burden already resting on 124,000 of his mates.

Nor are those connected with conveyance and locomotion the only men who lose their lawful rest. What becomes of the publican's Sunday, while he is attending to his influx of visitors? Nay, he and his servants have more than they can get through — the supply cannot meet the demand; and taverns, public-houses, and cigar-shops, multiply under the fostering wing of Sunday trains.

There are other consequences less evident, because more remote, which have not escaped the notice of intelligent men in the working classes. We quote the words of a gardener: — 'I am informed that the servants of the railway company will now be compelled to work seven days for six days' wages; and if the system is carried out by this Company, it may be carried out in other establishments and works as well. Who can tell where the thing is to end? Employers of other trades may take it up; and, knowing the social position of the working classes, and how many thousands of them, even at the best times, live but from hand to mouth, they may exact that which their workmen have neither the will, nor the strength, nor the power to resist.'

To what conclusion, then, are we to come, as lovers of the working classes? Sunday in the city has its privations, but Sunday in the country, as things are managed at present, has its immediate dangers for the working man himself, its undoubted hardships for a large class of his brother-workmen, and its probable ill-consequences to operatives generally. We honour the man who, in consideration of these things, resists the temptation of a Sunday-excursion ticket; and we think, as he takes his wife and children out for a Sunday-afternoon walk in the streets, if no park or field is within reach, it will be some comfort to him to know that, as far as he is concerned, railway porters, collectors and policemen, might enjoy their Sunday rest.

It is some comfort to know that, much as may be said against London air, London is actually more healthy than the generality of large towns; much, too, of the hardship of remaining in London on Sunday, has arisen from the unsatisfactory state of workmen's homes. To this public attention is at

length effectually roused, and we have reason to
hope that we are on the eve of great and extensive
reformation in this respect.

So, then, with regard to Sunday travelling as
well as to Sunday amusements, after carefully considering this question, and trying to look at it all
round, we seem driven to the conclusion that the
hopes it holds out of improving the workman's Sabbath are fallacious; that it offers no real remedy for
the perverted moral taste which leads him to spend
his Sunday in a beer-house, rather than in seeking
the combined edification and rest for which the day
was given to him.

But have we anything to offer in place of these
remedies? for to reject a proposed remedy is not to
cure the disease.   It is very well to talk of 'edification and rest;' but they are neither secured by shutting up museums and picture-galleries, nor by dis-
couraging Sunday excursions.   Policemen, whose
duty it is to keep the public peace in London on
Sunday, will tell us whether the chosen retreat of
the masses—the public-house at the corner of every
street—looks hopeful either for edification or rest.
There is an old saying in Ireland, that when the devil
finds a man idle he generally puts a job into his
hands.   And London Sabbaths among the working
classes afford abundant proof of it.

There are some, indeed, whose weekly occupation implies severe bodily labour.   When the six days
are over they feel spent with toil, and rest to them
is to spend several extra hours in sleep.   By all

means let them do so; reserving some portion of the day, the part when the body is least likely to act as a clog upon the mind, for that which is the highest end of the Sunday—seeking God—finding rest for the soul in Him as its true centre; then let them sleep as weary men should, and thank Him, by whose provident care the opportunity for doing so is secured to them.

But there are many others whose occupation is sedentary, and, probably, monotonous; occupying their hands, not their heads. Sunday finds them wide awake; ready, to use a popular phrase, for anything that 'turns up,' except church-going; they like to talk politics with their neighbours, or read their Sunday newspaper, or go out with a pleasure-party, or spend the day with their mates at the nearest public-house. If any of their private houses had been fit to sit down in, they would, perhaps, have preferred them; for if men are not far gone in drinking-habits, and if wife and children have still some hold upon them, they have a notion, however feeble and inoperative it may be, that in the public-house they are in harm's way.

Here is our social problem: these men must be got hold of, persuaded to see their own interests, helped to help themselves, led to perceive what they really do want, and how little a day's drinking can supply it; they must be dealt with tenderly, respectfully, discriminately; not in masses, but as individuals, with reference to individual circumstances, character, tastes, perils.

They must be addressed as reasonable men, not in set phrases, which were pregnant with meaning once, but have lost their freshness; like a beautiful flower, which has passed from hand to hand till it is dry and withered. Full credit must be given them · for good sense and intelligence, and the arguments put before them must be forcible and telling.

Now, to what does all this point? Not to Government measures: they are necessarily rigid, inflexible; they act with mechanical force; and what we want is tactile dexterity. It points to a general recognition, on the part of the educated and refined, that they have a work to do for the uneducated on Sunday; what cannot be done by legislation, may be done by the wondrous power of sympathy, translated into action.

But the work is great, and we require the force of united action. There is something for every one to do who can, himself or herself, spend a Sabbath of quiet and refined ease. What if it should be proved after all, that the so-called Sabbatarians have been the men who were ready to make sacrifices of personal ease and indulgence; and to work, not perhaps in always in the wisest way, but with earnestness and zeal, to raise the tone of the workman's Sabbath? What if the over-activity which may have characterised *their* Sabbath should have been in a measure thrust upon them, because they had to do duty for themselves, and their ease-loving neighbours as well?

A book which we all profess to venerate lays

down, as a principle of action,—' Whereunto we have already attained, let us walk by the same rule, let us mind the same thing.' We are speaking to the whole class of educated, kind-hearted, sensible, philanthropic residents in London, and other over-grown towns; where the congregated masses of human beings present a mechanical and moral hindrance to any profitable employment of the workman's Sabbath,—*mechanical*, because he cannot be quiet if he would; *moral*, because evil example is contagious.

Among these educated men and women we may find great variety of opinion as to the true nature of the Sabbath, the demands it makes upon us, the right way of spending it; but all will be agreed, that the workman who drinks up half his week's wages in the public-house is spending it in *the wrong way*, a way which will neither prepare his soul for the other world to which he is hastening, nor instruct or invigorate his mind, nor refresh or recruit his bodily strength.

Yet this wrong way *is* the way chosen Sunday after Sunday by thousands at our very doors. Within a stone's throw of the mansions in our splendid West-end squares, gin-palaces rear their unabashed front, and are lighted as brilliantly as the nobleman's drawing-room; but on what different scenes the gas-jet sheds its brilliance! in the drawing-room, on wealth, refinement, luxury, the gentle courtesies of society; in the gin-palace, on rags and squalor, nauseous fumes of breath vitiated with

spirits, the degrading indulgence which turns men
and women into fiends.

We have said, the drawing-room is within a
stone's throw of the gin-palace; but is it the *exception* or the *rule* that the inhabitant of the one
should concern himself or herself with the frequenter
of the other? These drinking thousands are made
up of individuals; they have each their point of
contact with the classes above them, who employ
their labour or profit by their toil. In many cases
the point of contact is individual and personal;
every family in the upper classes has its own tradesmen, whose shopboys and assistants call at the house
on their daily familiar round; their own laundress,
probably, and charwoman; their poor needlewomen,
their chimney-sweep, postmen, &c.; let us hope, their
little list of pensioners. Here is a direct opening.
These men and women minister to your comfort;
you profit by them; life would have many rough
places for you if they did not smooth them: have
you ever thought whether their being thus brought
into neighbourly connexion with you does not give
them a claim on something more than the hard
cash with which you reward their services? Do
you know anything about their families? Is it to
you they would come as to a sympathizing friend if
trouble pressed sore upon them? Have you ever
asked them how they spend their Sundays? and if
you have reason to think it is this 'wrong way' we
have been talking of, have you in friendly counsel
tried to set them right? Have you let them feel

that you pitied more than you condemned, that you
realized the temptations of their joyless struggling
existence? Have you thought of any substitute to
propose for the fatal dram which is working them so
much woe? Is there not in your beautiful house
some little waiting-room near the door? Could you
not, without exposing your servants to temptation
by having strangers in the kitchen or servants' hall
— could you not tell this poor tempted man to
bring his wife and children some Sunday evening,
and try whether a cup of tea and a cheery fire,
and your pleasant kindness, and a few pictures,
and a little reading, are not better than the gin-
palace? Think what it would be to him to feel
that you cared for him! how it would reflect to
him the patient love of God, and make him strong
in the hope that the remedy lies within his
reach, that he may yet become respected and
respectable!

If each family would thus act as a magnet to
draw up its own immediate dependents, the ranks
of the drinking thousands would soon be thinned.
The same might be urged on employers, the owners
and principals of shops, the masters and mistresses
of workrooms. Sometimes, indeed, they shut their
own mouths by making a common day of the Sabbath themselves. 'I could not stop there,' said a
young dressmaker to the writer; 'Sunday was just
like a week-day.' 'Why, did your employers keep
you at work?' 'No, they could not keep us, but
they worked themselves; when I came home from

P

church they were always at it, and the sewing-
machine going, just like a week-day.'

But those employers who know the value of a
quiet and orderly Sabbath of rest themselves, must
surely feel that it concerns them to inquire whether
those who work for them all the week, and whom
they have associated closely with their interests,
have any settled and regular way of spending their
Sundays; or whether they rank among the idlers
who, according to the Irish proverb, stand ready for
'a devil's job.' Only remember, the employers'
interest and sympathy must be *real;* it must show
itself in something more than advice.   Everybody
knows *that* is cheap; and in these days of independence, advice, however good, must be given
with a great deal of tact and skill not to be resented :
but with these provisoes, and when advice and personal sacrifice go hand-in-hand, it *is* valued, and
often acted on.

We were struck with the graceful tact exercised
on this point by an hotel-keeper in Wales.   Hotel-
keepers are hardly expected to concern themselves
with the religion of their customers; on the contrary,
Sunday visitors and their requirements naturally
tend to reduce to a minimum their own standard of
Sabbath observance.

Some friends of the writer, in spending a Sunday
at Bangor last autumn, were struck with the air of
mourning which seemed to pervade the neighbourhood.   The sermon in the Cathedral, and another
in a principal church, spoke of a serious loss which

society had sustained, by a recent death which had occurred amongst them. Who was it that had so lived as to be thus missed?—The mistress of the George Hotel, Bangor Ferry, who died on the 4th of October, 1865, at the advanced age of 73.

Eleanor Roberts, the daughter of a small farmer at Yspytty, in Denbighshire, became, twenty-three years ago, the proprietress of a small wayside inn near Bangor, in the highroad to Holyhead.

Soon afterwards her house became the resort of engineers engaged in the construction of the tubular bridge over the Menai Straits. From profits made at that time she was enabled to erect additional buildings, until by degrees the little wayside inn could claim rank with first-class hotels; in point of comfort at all events, if not in point of size.

It became a place of favourite resort: among other names in the visitors' book we may read an autograph testimonial from the good old Duke of Wellington, as to the comfort he experienced in taking up his quarters there. The beauty of its site, perhaps, had something to do with its far-spread reputation ; but, doubtless, its chief attraction was owing to her whose genius kept every department under her own personal inspection, and whose consistent Christian character won the respect of all whom she employed.

The servants had an air of quiet responsibility, and showed visitors to their rooms with a respectful solicitude, as if they felt themselves answerable for their comfort.

At every corner of the staircase and corridors

there was some pretty or interesting object to gratify the taste, such as statuettes, pictures, minerals,
aquariums — all such things, in fact, as a lady will
gather round her in her own house, but which she
does not meet with in an hotel, without coming to
the conclusion that its owner must be no ordinary
person.

The arrangements in Miss Roberts' hotel bore,
however, still more legible traces of her character.
On the table of each room there was a Bible and
some other book of devotions, and over the mantel-
piece, instead of a tariff of prices, some texts of
Scripture.

On the Sunday Miss Roberts made a personal
request to all guests staying in the house, that they
would kindly consent to take breakfast at one hour
at the table d'hôte, in order that the servants might
have the privilege of attending public worship. The
same plan was observed about dinner. This request,
proffered with a certain homely dignity, was seldom,
if ever, refused, and by this arrangement the servants
were enabled to observe the Sabbath in as orderly
and regular a manner as they could have done in a
private family.

After breakfast it was announced that carriages
were ready, free of charge, to convey guests to the
Cathedral, or any other church they might wish to
attend.

The drawing-room was filled with attractions on
Sunday for the visitors at the hotel; books carefully
selected on the table, in many of which were in-

scribed expressions of regard from the authors; sacred music, both Welsh and English, were laid on the piano, which was left open for use. The pretty terraced garden, and a conservatory full of well-tended plants, provided for every innocent and pleasant enjoyment in the intervals of public worship.

We do not wonder that the George Hotel prospered, or that, a few months before her death, Miss Roberts refused 50,000*l*. for her business. We have cited her example, as showing that no calling need hinder a personal regard for the Sabbath, and also as a specimen of the delicate tact and painstaking effort, which give efficiency to good advice.

Sometimes, again, the connexion between ourselves and those we seek to influence is *self-made;* that is to say, no other special reason exists why we should put our hand to a work but that confessedly it needs to be done, and no one else comes forward to do it. A case in point occurs to us. The suburb of a populous town had a reputation for its invigorating air, and as such became a frequent sanitorium for invalids. Invalids provide a hopeful source of employment for the owners of donkey-chairs; the suburb in question had its full quota of these conveniences, with a good number besides of saddle-donkeys, for the delight of children who walked up from the town to enjoy the breezes of an ample common.

In direct contradiction to the law, ' In it thou shalt do no manner of work, neither thou, nor thine

ox, *nor thine ass*,' Sunday to these asses and their
drivers was the harvest-day of the week; donkey-
racing was an amusement especially reserved for'
that day, to the exceeding annoyance of affluent
inhabitants, whose country-houses bordered the
common.   In the teeth of the law, and before the
eyes of the magistrates, these donkey-men and boys,
Sunday after Sunday, paid their fines and drove
their obnoxious traffic, fearing neither God nor man.

A lady settled in the neighbourhood, and became
a sharer in its interests.   'Can nothing be done for
these donkey-boys?' was her natural question.   The
smile raised by the inquiry implied, that if she were
not new to the place it would never have been made.
She let it sleep a little, and the donkey-boys ran
riot as before.

Tired of waiting for a more suitable agent, she
determined to begin.   One of · the family sitting-
rooms was made attractive with a glowing fire, and
new reading-books, and appliances for writing, and
the donkey-men were invited to spend an evening
with her.   It seemed to them too strange, incomprehensible; they were not used to sympathy: what
were they to the lady, or the lady to them?   The
hour passed; she waited in vain: not one answered
the summons.   The next week the same experience;
but, at last, the perseverance of their friend roused
the curiosity of the men, and on the third occasion
the room was full.   Unwashed they were, indeed—
unsavoury; scarcely able to command their countenances; yet still living, human souls, brought

within kindly softening influence. She took care
they should not feel they were penned in for a
sermon; except one message from God's Book, and
two or three petitions offered to Him, the evening
(a week-day one) was reserved for teaching them to
read and write. By degrees her guests became too
numerous for the size of her room; clean hands and
faces appeared here and there among the party;
they learned to be diligent and steady. She had an
ear for all their individual concerns, and strange-
enough histories were brought to her.

The week-day class having taken a firm hold,
she has now proposed to them to give up to her a
morning hour of their wild, riotous Sunday; she has
added to the attraction of the Sunday-morning class
by a promise of coffee and biscuit, and has planned
for them a comfortable room, where they can feel
that they are at home. We cannot doubt that the
'nuisance of the neighbourhood' will abate sooner
under this genial influence, than by the most rigidly
imposed fines and legal punishments.

We have not given this as an instance of what
ladies ordinarily could or would do, but to show that
the most wild and reckless are within reach of practical sympathy; and that where points of contact
between ourselves and the working classes do not
already exist, an aggressive benevolence will *make*
them. Direct suggestions as to *what* may be done
and *how* it may be done, are secondary in importance
to arousing the conviction that the remedy for a
great social evil lies in our own hands, and that we

can apply it, not by opening our purses, but our
hearts; by recognising that he who lies there in a
moral slough is yet our human brother, waiting *our*
hand to pull him out, and set him on the *terra firma*
of a hopeful reformation.

It is for this initiatory step that united and
vigorous action is so urgently needed : once allure
the workman away from the tavern, once give
him a pleasant experience of a Sunday otherwise
spent, once reawaken the feelings in him of the
father and the husband, and we shall find we have
given an impetus which he will follow up.   There is
an amount of self-help in the working classes for
which we hardly give them credit.   Let Mrs. Bin-
ley's experience in Kensington prove it.   She gathered round her those whose lives called most loudly
for reform.   She went into the question with them ;
proved that the drink was their enemy ; they wanted
an assembling-place *minus* the drink, a public-
house without the beer : the publican could not
offer it to them, they must have one of their own.
The originating thought was dropped like a living
seed into their minds 'by this true friend of working
men ; she gave the impulse, but it fell into prepared
soil ; conviction ripened into desire, desire was fertile in effort, and the result is, the noble Workman's
Hall in Notting Hill.   A religious service is now
held there one evening in the week, as well as on
Sundays.

Thus it has been proved, that work-people even
in a low neighbourhood can quite well afford to set

up and rent for themselves reading-rooms and a house for their lectures. Probably, if working men can be induced, by the influence brought to bear on them by the classes above them, to exchange their drinking-bouts for a quiet and regular Sunday, it may lead to their opening rooms furnished with books, where they may enjoy the peaceable afternoon of reading or talk with their friends, which is hardly possible in their own crowded dwellings.

Let us now review our position. We invited the general co-operation of all educated and kind-hearted residents in London and large towns; to secure it, we had to lay down the broadest and most general principles of action, namely, a recognition that large masses of our working classes are spending their Sabbath in a wrong and injurious way; that neither Sunday amusements nor excursions offer any effectual remedy for this social evil, and that it is incumbent on the educated classes to exercise, in the varied ways in which it may be open to them to do so, that individual influence which may induce the workman to forsake the beer-house, and spend a quiet and restful day with his family.

This is, perhaps, the highest aim to which we shall secure general agreement, but we are free to confess that we have not *many* expedients to offer, if the aim is to be limited to inducing the workman to make of his Sunday a day of repose. We are free to confess such a day will lack interest, because, while attaining its lower, it will have missed its higher purpose. If this were all that could be offered to the

workman, Mr. Dickens might say with more justice
the words we have already quoted,—' Nothing to
change the brooding mind, or raise it up; nothing for
the spent toiler to do but to compare the monotony
of his seventh day with the monotony of his six
days, and think what a weary life he led.'

But, brother-workman, we appeal to you. Is it
true that the God who gave you the Sabbath offers
to you in it nothing but animal repose? nothing
that can ' change your brooding mind, or raise it
up?' Is there nothing comforting or elevating in
the truths on which a weekly rest from toil gives you
leisure to dwell? nothing comforting in the thought
that you, poor and of little account in society, are of
great price in the sight of God? that your welfare
—yours individually, as one of the human race—
prompted Him to a sacrifice so vast, that parents
who can understand it best, gain but a dim con-
ception of it? Is there nothing comforting in the
belief that your present life of toil and privation
is no proof that God has forgotten you, but rather
that He has planned for you a course of education
and discipline which may, if you will yield to His
hand, and interpret Him aright, prepare you for
honour and dignity, and a royal standing, in the
immortality to which you are hastening?

Brother-workmen, it is better to rest than to
drink; but why be satisfied with resting, when
you may pray? It is better to spend a quiet day
in your own home, than a day of revelling in the
beer-shop; but why be satisfied with that, when

God invites you to *His* house, and will give you such a welcome there as may lead you to say with one of old, 'A day in thy courts is better than a thousand?'

This is the real glory of the workman's Sabbath, but these are principles of action to which comparatively few will subscribe; some will laugh at them as visionary, some will condemn them as exclusive, others will renounce them as incomprehensible, unpractical: the ranks of workers who would combine to rescue Sunday from being a drinking-day, and to establish it as a day of rest, will be greatly thinned when it becomes a question of recognising it as a holy day.

But if few in number, they are firm in purpose, and are animated by motives which admit no relaxation of effort. If on the lower, and more general basis, it was difficult to find expedients whereby to make a day of repose satisfactory and interesting to the workman; on this higher and more restricted basis it is needless to suggest them, so many and varied are the agencies already at work.

To enumerate a few. We have Sunday-schools and classes for all grades among the young; and this is a work in which men of leading talent and position do not disdain to take part. The Attorney-General does not deem that his time is wasted in taking a class in the Sabbath schools of the church which he attends in Langham Place, and we have reason to know that the personal influence exercised by him over his scholars is so strong, that after they

marry and become fathers of families, they still beg
to retain their places as members of his class. Again:
classes are formed for milliners and dressmakers,
for servants, for young women waiting in shops, for
foreigners, and, as we have said, for donkey drivers:
hardly any neglected ones can be named who have
not, somewhere or other, drawn forth efforts of
Christian sympathy and care. City missionaries
visit gas manufactories, cab and omnibus yards,
and other places where the nature of the occupation allows to the labourer no Sabbath of rest.
Similar agents carry the war into the enemy's camp,
follow the drunkard to the tavern, and ply him there
with the good news of Gospel love, and the solemn
importance of eternal realities. We were struck
with the ready tact shown by one of these missionaries but the other day, in a conversation he
related to us, which he had held the Sunday before
in a beer-shop with those assembled to drink.

He entered with a few little books in his pocket,
and taking out one, which was a dialogue, offered
to read it in parts with a man who stood near.

'Oh, yer one of the soul-mongers! Always at it!
talkin' of what yer don't understand. I'd like to
know, *what is a soul?* Come, old fellow, can yer
tell us that?'

Attention was aroused, and the answer to 'Bill's'
question was waited for with some curiosity.

'My friend,' said the missionary, 'a man generally asks a question for one of three reasons: either he
cares to get an answer, or he asks from curiosity, or

he wants to puzzle the man whom he questions.' A
knowing wink from Bill to his mates showed that
the last suggestion had hit the mark. 'Yes, I see,'
said the missionary; 'you want to puzzle me, to show
me up: now, you know, two can play at that game,
and before I answer you, will you be so good as to
tell me what are the component parts of oxygenated
muriatic acid of lime?'

Silence for a moment, then a nudge and a chuckle
on the part of a mate. ' Eh, Bill, he's got yer
there!'

'You can't tell me? Well, at least repeat my
question,—what was it I asked you?'

Bill hardly liked to give in, and turned his head
from side to side in a vain effort to recall the words.

' Can't you say?' inquired the missionary.

' I 'm a thinkin'.'

' Thinking, are you? What with? your finger-
ends? the hair on your head? What is it in you
that thinks?'

' Caught you, Bill! the old fellow's caught you, he
has!' chimed in another neighbour.

' I have *answered* you, my friend: what thinks, is
your soul.'

He then took occasion to speak of its immortality and its redemption, to listeners who were
now all eager in their attention. Such readiness
in turning circumstances to advantage can be
acquired only by experience, but we rejoice to think
how many are thus aggressively Sabbath by Sabbath
seeking out in their own haunts the careless, the

unconcerned, and the morally degraded among our working classes.

It has, however, occurred to us whether the City churches, which present the anomaly of spacious buildings and a clerical staff, for some score or less of worshippers (their natural occupants having drifted away into the suburbs), might not, with consent of their respective incumbents, be utilized for workmen's services, conducted either by the incumbents themselves or by those whose ministrations are proved to be attractive to the working classes. It must be a hard matter to prepare a sermon which shall satisfy the educated, and yet be suitable for the workman; now, here is a case in which the receding tide of civilization has left high and dry churches which only need to be filled : would it not be possible, by some such association as that which organizes theatre services for the 'roughs,' to fill those empty churches with decent workmen and their families, and to provide that they shall receive there teaching suited to their moral wants and intellectual capacity?

We are told, that before many years have passed over us the old barriers will be broken down, and our English Sabbath will be exchanged for a Continental day of work and pleasure. Let philanthropists and religionists combine to avert what both would deplore.

CHAPTER VII.

DOMESTIC SERVANTS — WHAT WE MAY CLAIM FROM
THEM, AND THEY FROM US.

THIS question has long been regarded as vexed. Many a morning-call paid by one lady on another has owed its relish to the zest supplied by this favourite topic; but it was hardly known *how* vexed, till a little passage of arms last autumn between Mr. Ruskin and the Editor of a daily newspaper threw the subject open to public debate. With them the spark originated. *They* represent the flint and the steel, but they were probably scarcely aware themselves how profusely the tinder lay around them.

At all events the subject has been ventilated, and each party has had its say. We have 'done it,' and 'feel better for it,' as the little boy said who revenged an injury by a blow.

Our social storm has cleared the air; we and our servants have alike called upon public opinion to arbitrate in our mutual grievances. Probably re-

action has already set in, and made it easier for the
arbitrator to compose our differences. Probably
the mistress who vented her complaint against 'the
greatest plagues of her life' has since reflected, that
this was rather a hard measure to deal out to those
who are all more or less employed for her comfort
and advantage; and the servant who tossed her head
at her 'one meat-meal a-day and half-pound of
butter a-week,' may have remembered that in her
father's cottage (or room, as the case may be) the
meat-meal is a Sunday treat, and the half-pound of
butter the allowance for the family.

    We can recommend no better cure to the mis-
tress who undervalues her servants than to make
the experiment, just for one day, of serving herself.
We fancy her lighting the kitchen fire, that necessary antecedent to her husband's shaving-water, and
to the morning meal. Well for her if her unaccustomed hands bring up the breakfast-tray in safety.
We excuse her suppressed sigh at the thought that
cups and saucers must be washed and put away,
when they are done with. Then, the bed must be
made. 'Jane' has often had a reproof for spending
too much time over it, yet her own efforts for a
much longer time have left a series of undulations,
strongly suggestive of hills and valleys, but pro-
mising little for the next night's comfort. Let it
be for the moment; she will hear of it again in a
'curtain lecture.' Now time is passing on, and she
must hasten to her cooking. Never having put too
much confidence in Mrs. Ladle, she has been in the

habit of standing by to see things weighed and
mixed — and order and method are strong points
with her: she has been eloquent before now about
' a place for everything, and everything in its place,'
' a time for everything, and everything in its time ;'
so, what with the experience gained by oversight
and her own methodical habits, she feels tolerably
easy as to her success in cooking.   But, alas! theory
is not put in practice at a first attempt.   She gets
bewildered among dishes and basins, jars of stores
and saucepans; she ends with spooning out a liberal
allowance of salt for the custard pudding, and of
dusted sugar for the pickled mackerel.   Let it pass ;
she will hear of *it* again, a few hours earlier than the
bed.   Need we follow her through the day ? or will
the morning glimpse be sufficient to show, that if
servants are plagues, they are something else besides ?

And for the discontented servant also we could
make some suggestions, which may tend to modify
her ideas.   We will suppose that she has a ' day
out,' and that kind feeling leads her to spend it
with her sister the sempstress, who has had to lay
by for a week, because the sharp cold seized her
chest as she turned out of the heated workroom.
' Jane' leaves the fashionable Square where her mistress lives; she has not far to go—Rose Alley turns
out of a Court at the back of the Square, but the
five-minutes' walk on level ground, proves to be a
very steep descent in the social scale.   With visible
disgust on her face, and gathering her skirts as

Q

closely around her as an ample crinoline will admit,
' Jane' picks her way to No. 5, and inquires for
' *Miss* Ellen Mason.'

The laconic and barely intelligible answer, ' Top-
floor back,' directs her to the stairs; the second and
third flights, each narrower and dirtier than the last,
are reached, and ' Jane' has mounted steps enough to
entitle her to an alpenstock, by the time she arrives at
Ellen's garret.   She is a kind sister, and her heart
sickens at the fireless grate, the comfortless bed, the
coarse food untouched; she remembers her last
illness in her place; how kind cook was; what nice
messes she made; how ' mistress' gave orders she was
to have everything she wanted, and came to see her
twice, and sent for the doctor and paid his bill.
' Jane' begins to reflect that it is not for nothing she
has put her time, and strength, and liberty, at her
mistress's disposal.   .

We will then assume that mistresses and servants
are alike forming the wise conclusion, that since
they are really necessary to each other, and domestic
servitude is likely to remain a prominent feature in
social life, it were best to come to some mutual
understanding as to past grievances, remedying such
as admit of remedy, accepting patiently those over
which neither party has any control.

We shall, perhaps, be accused of an overweening
credulity in having taken our text from an anony-
mous newspaper correspondence, and shall be told
that this is not the surest source of information, or
the fairest exponent of public opinion, on a popular

question. But, in truth, it is not because these letters profess to be written some by mistresses, others by servants, that they acquire importance and gain credence with us, but because they do reflect accurately the opinions, the complaints, the phases of domestic life, which may be met with every day. They are true to the life, and, as we sometimes say of a portrait, ' It must be a good likeness,' though we have never seen the original, so are we convinced that originals exist somewhere of these portraits of mistress-and-servant life, and will be identified in many households.

Recognizing the letters, therefore, as reflections of things that are, we shall make frequent reference to them, and shall not hesitate to admit them as evidence in the disputed question with which we have now to deal — namely, the relation which ought to exist between employers and servants.

We confine ourselves chiefly to that part of the subject which concerns the female servant and her mistress, because we believe it is admitted on all hands that masters and their male dependents are less apt to disagree; even if it were otherwise, they could probably best compose their own differences. ·

It may be fair to start with the inquiry, *What is domestic service?* An erroneous impression would give rise to unreasonable expectations on both sides.

In domestic service, women of the working classes do that for money which they would do gratis in homes of their own—those necessary offices which fall to the woman's lot in every household, and which she must either do herself or do by proxy; such as cooking, cleaning, and care of children: these offices working women accept under their employers as their calling in life, their business, and thereby earn their bread as honestly as the cotton-spinner who works a loom. But to the condition of work which is common to them both is added, in the case of the servant, the condition of *servitude;* earning her bread in the family of her employer, she becomes incorporated with it, and is subject to its laws and restrictions. She is not, like the cotton-spinner, her own mistress when the hours of labour are over; on the contrary, the domestic servant is under constant surveillance, and, except as a boon granted by indulgent employers, has no time in the day which she can look upon as her own, or in which she is not liable to be called upon for service.

If we say that domestic service has alike advantages and drawbacks, we do but class it with all other employments. Among the drawbacks, besides loss of personal liberty, we may reckon compulsory association with uncongenial fellow-servants, dependence on the caprices of an employer, and restricted intercourse with family and friends. Among the advantages on the other hand, the domestic servant has no care about provisions and house-rent, no fear while she does her duty of being out of employment, for her work is always 'in season;' she fares better and sleeps softer, is better housed and clothed, than she would be in a lodging of her own; and in proportion as her fidelity and disinterested conduct merit, she is taken into fellowship by those moving in a grade of society above her own. ' *Domestic*,' as we have been reminded, is a word derived from ' *domus*,' and ' *familia*,' or family, meant originally the servants in a family. Among the advantages we must also include the fair and reasonable prospect which the untutored girl has, who leaves her working mother's side to become scullery-maid or maid-of-all-work, of rising by steady diligence one degree after another in the scale of domestic service, till, as house-keeper, she occupies the honourable position of repre-senting her mistress in a large household.

It has always seemed to us, that domestic service might be one of the very happiest ways in which women of the working classes earn their bread; why it so often fails in being so, it will be our present duty to inquire.

We will begin with the raw material, the young girl of twelve or thirteen, who must begin to earn her own bread because the family increases : she is a hungry, growing girl, and her slice off the loaf can ill be spared. If she has hitherto lived with her mother, and the mother has been a decent and respectable woman, she ought to have something more to start with as her capital in trade than youth, strength, and activity; she should have learned habits of punctuality, ready obedience, order, and method, and she should be skilled in such kinds of labour as her home furnishes occasion for : but, as we have seen in a former chapter, more often than not, the house-mother has been drafted away from her family to fill some post of non-domestic labour, and the eldest girl has been left at home in the position of matron—self-taught. In this case she has probably much to unlearn, and has acquired habits of independence which add to her difficulties in her first taste of service in a gentleman's family, where she must begin with being 'servant of servants.'

She is, however, far better off there, as a rule, than if engaged to be 'handy-girl' by small tradespeople just a grade or two above herself. Such are fully alive to their own dignity in 'keeping a servant:' till they took this upward move they worked on contentedly enough—at least, the mother did; the daughters might be more aspiring. Now, by the simple fact that the household includes poor little 'Drudge,' the working wife and daughters become 'mistress and the young ladies.' Very harmonious in their ears are the new titles; the duties they have performed all their lives are henceforth quite beneath their dignity, and the work which had been hitherto shared by all, is now most unreasonably thrown upon one. We quote from an author whose opinions command general respect:*—

'A young girl is hired into a large family, of which the chief burden is at once thrown upon herself alone. Nursing and cleaning, cooking and waiting, perpetual calls and countless errands, all are accumulated upon the one person, who, so far as age and strength, knowledge and experience, are concerned, is the least able to bear them. The condition of many a slave in an American plantation

* Dr. Vaughan's *Plain Words on Christian Living.*

is far, far preferable—outwardly at least—to hers. But just because it is not nominally slavery, just because there is a form of hiring and a. pretence of remuneration, Christian consciences are clear in the matter, and the transaction passes for a religious as well as a legal one. My friends, these things ought not so to be. It is true this young girl has hired herself to your service, but you well know that in that hiring she was scarcely a free agent. She belonged to a family which could not support her. If you cared to know all, you might find that she had a drunken father or a heartless stepmother, who had grudged her, for years past, her poor modicum of education, and who have now turned her out of the family nest to pick up a pittance for herself where she can by service. She has not the knowledge, she has not had the training, for anything better than a place like yours. She must take what she can find, and she has lighted upon you. Now I venture to say, that that servant-girl has a right to your consideration in the assignment of her duties. You must lay no burden upon her which you do not feel and know that she is equal to. Whatever you could allow a daughter of your own to bear or do at her age and in her condition, that, and that only, must you lay upon her. And if you say, that because you pay a servant you have a right to be eased altogether of every inconvenient duty; I reply, that there is a fallacy in such reasoning for which the God of reason and of conscience must call you to a reckoning. Let your children work as well as she. Or else deny yourself something— something of dress, or something of luxury, or something of amusement—and keep two servants where you now keep one. These are plain words—too plain, it may be; but it is in such plainness that Christian morality must express itself, or it will miss altogether the mark of its high and responsible calling.'

We can add nothing to Dr. Vaughan's appeal to

unreasonable employers; but it awakens the question
—Is there not a gap which needs to be filled up in
our philanthropic institutions ? The young girl is
at the mercy of unreasonable employers for two reasons: she is ignorant and unprotected; she has been
hired, not for her own advantage, but to do work
which her employer has either no time or no incli-
nation to do herself. Her ignorance places her at
an immense disadvantage — she is of little use till
she has been taught. We all know the self-denial and
effort it requires to train others to the performance
of duties to which we are accustomed; they appear
so simple to us, it is difficult to believe that repeated
failure does not arise from lack of painstaking. Mistresses among the lower ranks of society, to whom
time is money, are under special temptations to lose
their temper, and speak and act unreasonably towards
the ignorant young girl who, for some time at least
after she enters their service, is rather a hindrance
than a help. Again, the servant-girl is unprotected:
too often the parents care little about her; she is off
their hands, has begun life for herself, and must fight
her own battles—till the case has become very despe-
rate indeed, till she can appeal for protection to the law
(as we read in some recent Police Reports), because
'her person bears marks of brutal violence,' or emaciation confirms her statement, that while 'the daily
meat-meal was served out to the family, her diet
consisted of cold boiled cabbage and potatoes, cooked
in sufficient quantity to last for several days;' — till
abuses like these have taken place, there are none to

-stand between her and her employer, or to extend over her the shield of their protection.

Does not this twofold difficulty under which the young servant labours — want of knowledge and want of protection — point to something like combined effort to establish and increase training-schools, where the duty of teaching may be carried on patiently and efficiently, because it is not complicated with the expectations and requirements of the employer, and where the young girl may acquire friends and protectors to whom she can appeal, when afterwards engaged in actual service? This want is alluded to in very outspoken English terms by one of the correspondents as follows: —

' Now, while we are establishing every kind of school, college, hospital, refuge, home, why don't our philanthropists establish a school for domestic servants? Let them be taught efficiently the simple duties of their calling. It will be a guarantee and a passport into our homes that they have been taught in such an establishment. Brother Bull! as a scheme it will pay, and you are a philanthropist as well! Our high-born and well-born are ever ready by purse and countenance to aid a good work. Do away with these " register offices." I verily believe, within three years, if London were to take the initiative, every town in England, of any magnitude, would be following the example. Undoubtedly, it would require great administrative talent; but give Englishmen the work to do, and Englishmen will do it!'

It has been also pointed out, that nearly all the philanthropic institutions of late years have been

designed for the good of boys. ' Refuges, reformatories, shoe-black societies, &c., are for that class,
and have proved great blessings ; — why, then, should
not one be raised for girls ?' The writer is referring
to the class which is below that from which the present race of domestic servants is usually obtained,
and he says : — ' Let any one go into our courts and
alleys, and there observe the number of girls who
are growing up under influences certainly not favourable to their future respectability and usefulness
in life, and then say whether that is not a fine field
which might be vastly improved by cultivation. It
is not my intention to attempt the sketch of any plan
for the accomplishment of this object. If two or
three benevolent ladies would take up the matter,
and lay their own plans, I believe an Institution
might be provided for the training of such girls,
which would be in part self-supporting, and would
not long want popular support. Much would, of
course, depend on the way in which such an Institution should be conducted. If the "tight rein" and
"strict discipline" system were adopted, I should have
little hope of any great good being done ; but if the
matron would let the girls see that she is their friend,
and is really desirous of raising them in the scale of
society — that she is anxious to see them act in such
a way that they may be able to respect themselves;
if she will also impress upon their minds that nothing
will do so much towards building up a good character,
and making them really happy, as having the love of
God in their hearts, then may we hope to see grand

results.   I have had some experience in similar efforts
among single males of different ages, and feel quite
satisfied that, in order to do much with human nature,
we must trust and respect it.'

We conclude that the writers of these letters are
not ignorant that training-schools for female servants are already in operation, but that they merely
mean to urge that the supply of such Institutions
should be in some better proportion to the number
of young and ignorant girls who begin to earn their
own livelihood at a great disadvantage for want of
such training.   Might not also a great deal of good
be effected in the matter of training young servants,
without waiting for the multiplication of Institutions?   Institutions have always the drawback that
a considerable portion of the money contributed by
the public, must be diverted from its direct object for
the payment of house-rent, officers' salaries, &c.
What training-school can be better than the practical requirements of a well-ordered gentlewoman's
household, if the girl can be entered there as a pupil,
the mistress being indemnified for the expenses of her
board?   A scheme of this kind has already entered
into the fertile mind of Miss Ellen Barlee, authoress
of *Our Homeless Poor*, and Lady-manager of the
Institution for the Employment of Needlewomen at
Hinde Street, Manchester Square.   As the originator
and main-spring of this Institution, Miss Barlee is
familiar with the privations, struggles, and temptations of thousands of workmen's families; and we
may rest assured, that any suggestion coming from

her for extending a helping-hand to their young daughters, will be practical and well-weighed.

In conversation with the writer she explained her plans. A small fund which had been placed at her disposal enabled her to commence it without delay; it was based on the following argument:— Parents of the poorest classes cannot afford to be at any expense for their children longer than is absolutely necessary; as soon as a girl can take the lowest sort of place she must do so; half-fed and half-clothed, with the nourishment provided for her and her pittance of wages, no work that she is likely to have to do in such a place will train her for a gentleman's service—manners and habits will remain uncouth and ill-formed, morals will be little cared for; the girl, scarcely more than a child, and still formed of plastic material, will be cast into a rough mould, and will take its form for life. Here is a want on one side. On the other side many ladies, gentlewomen born and bred, have, from limited means, difficulty in providing servants enough to do the actual necessary work of the household; they would gladly add a girl to their establishment, it would give them pleasure to train her in good habits, but they cannot afford to board her, and they cannot give her wages to purchase her clothing. This is the corresponding want on the other side; nothing, in Miss Barlee's opinion, is needed to fit these two wants to each other but a little money and a little time given to carrying on the necessary correspondence: she proposes to offer to ladies who want another

hand in their household staff, and who would con-
scientiously, either themselves or through their servants, train a girl in good habits, 10*l*. towards her
board for a year; she would also clothe the girl, so
that little or no extra expense would fall upon the
mistress, and her servants would have an equivalent
for the trouble an inexperienced girl might give them
at first starting, by her increasing usefulness as her
training progresses. But, indeed, we should under-
rate the generous motives on which good servants are
ready to act, if we dwelt too much on the idea of
equivalent. Mrs. Sewell, in her suggestive little
book, *Thy Poor Brother*, when speaking on this
very point, the training of a young girl by older
servants, says:*—

' Pity for the destitute is natural, both to servants and
children. They are pleased to have the ministration of
charity pass through their hands; and thus, in some sort,
to become benefactors. This case is the very thing they
can understand and sympathize with. They remember
how it was with themselves in their first service, and they
are more than willing to unite with their mistress to help
this young girl. If they had grown a little negligent in
any of their duties before, at any rate they will teach
"Mary" how to do things as they should be done. They
feel elevated with the power acknowledged in them‘ to
render an unpaid service. They are helpers with their
mistress, and the unselfish points of interest are increased
between them.'

The mechanism of such a plan as Miss Barlee's
is simple in the extreme; girls will apply to her

* *Thy Poor Brother*, p. 65.

who are anxious to be trained for respectable service,
ladies will apply to her who are desirous of adding a
girl to their establishment, and the funds contributed
by benevolent well-wishers will pass at first-hand
from the supporters of the scheme, to those who are
to be benefited by it.   In a private way it has been
done before ; the late Lady Sherborne, a daughter of
the celebrated Lord Stawell, placed the best girls
from her school in private service, paying for their
board and training; the girls so trained mostly did
well, and got into the first families: but a private
effort can of course only operate in a very limited way,
and usually terminates with the life of the individual.   Miss Barlee's idea appeared to the writer
eminently simple and practical, and she had her
free permission to mention it. .

Nor must we ignore the efforts of a Preventive
Mission in Bristol to work up raw material into
efficient servants.   This Mission, with a registra-
tion-office for young girls of the humblest class,
including the much-suffering workhouse-girls, was
started five years ago, under the auspices of Miss
Stephen.   The children were both helped to find
safe situations, and carefully visited while in service.   Clothes of a decent kind were given at a
reduced cost to those whose dress was too poor to
admit of their obtaining employment.   A Sunday-
school was kept by the daughters of the Dean of
Bristol, for such of the workhouse-girls in service
as could be spared by their employers to attend
it.   In the intervals of service the girls were pro-

vided with safe lodgings, and a working school was opened for their instruction. At the close of the first year it was found that 500 girls had obtained the benefits of the Institution, at the cost of about 10s. a-head. At the present time several thousands have been thus guarded and aided, both in Bristol and in four other cities in which Preventive Missions have been established.

We may now pass on to the 'maid-of-all-work;' or, as she prefers to be called, the 'general servant;' who will, perhaps, take rank next to the young servant-girl. Excellent servants are to be met with in this class. To be fit for her place, such a woman must have a practical knowledge of all kinds of work; an orderly mind to plan her time, and make it square with her engagements; and she should have health and strength beyond the average, to meet the demands which will be made upon her. If we may accept her own statement, the writer of a letter signed 'A Drudge,' appears to have been a servant of this stamp. She seems to have been one who acted on the good maxim, 'Drive your work, and do not let your work drive you.' As general servant in a large family there was little time to fold her hands, but she preferred to fold them in the evening rather than in the morning. She rose at four or five; the roughest part of her work was done before the family 'sat down to breakfast;' and by four in the afternoon her clean cap and presentable appearance should have rejoiced the heart of her mistress. But, unhappily, the mistress, instead of commending her

wise distribution of her work, and satisfying herself,
by intelligent observation, that it was not only done,
but well done, rewarded the well-ordered toil for
twelve hours, of her patient 'drudge,' by the insinua-
tion that work 'done so soon' must have been 'done
ill;' and found fresh employment to occupy the
hardly-earned leisure of the evening. We were not
surprised at the servant's confession, 'that, under
such circumstances, her habit of early rising was
abandoned, her energy and spirit failed, and she became more careless every day.'

The lesson is too obvious to need pointing out;
the mistress who, by a baseless suspicion, could dis-
tort the evidence of her servant's good management
into a charge of neglect, is neither worthy to keep
her 'drudge,' nor to get another like-minded to
supply her place.

It may be worth notice, that in the case of 'a
general servant,' a greater degree of sociability is
due from the mistress, than where the establishment
consists of two or more. The lonely position of the
sole occupant of the kitchen must be borne in mind,
and met by a kind readiness to enter into conversation, and meet her at suitable times with something
like companionship and sympathy. Her confidence
must be invited as to those personal interests which
she would naturally share with a fellow-servant, if
she had one.

Having given an example of a 'general servant,'
suffering from an unworthy mistress, fairness demands
that we show a case in which the mistress well ful-

filled her part; but failed, nevertheless, in securing a 'general servant,' whose services were worth retaining. A clergyman's wife, after explaining that her household is a small one, and needs but one servant; and after sundry details as to her domestic arrangements, which need not be repeated, but which show the one servant was by no means oppressed with work, says:—

'I take a kindly interest in the girls' domestic relations, in their joys and sorrows. If friends are living near, they are welcome to take an occasional hour or two to visit them; and if further away, a day's holiday at reasonable intervals. While I never permit waste, there is not a key turned in my house. Wages have never been a stumbling-block with me: indeed, I have often been blamed for giving beyond what is customary. I have no objection to reasonably-timed visits from friends, or even from the "young man;" but in the latter case I must know that an honourable engagement to marry exists, as I set my face against gossiping company and followers sneaking in at back-doors — both of which classes are likely to lead a girl into idleness, vanity, and sin.'

All this sounds both kind and judicious; and it surprises us that the lady in question should have to say,—'I cannot save myself from changing; and that only because I cannot find a servant who will act behind my back as she will before my face.' She enumerates the faults for which she parts with her servants, though informing us that she makes it a principle not to change till she has given 'a fair trial with patient warning.' It would require ac-

quaintance with the circumstances of the case to
know why the principle fails in this instance — that
good mistresses make good servants. The lady herself attributes it to a cause which is a further plea
for training-schools; she says,— 'I do think that
very much of the evil arises from the want of early
training for girls, who need that their minds should
be well regulated, far more than that their heads
should be well crammed.'

Leaving 'general servants,' good and bad, we
now pass on to the establishments which, we imagine,
form the majority in our upper middle classes, where
two, or three, or more servants are kept, according
to the size and requirements of the family. Here
the duties of the mistress become more onerous; she
has to consider her servants' relations to each other,
as well as to herself. She must be not only just, but
impartial. The work to be done by the servants
generally must be so divided, that each shall be responsible for a certain portion assigned to her individually; yet the mistress, as general overlooker,
must reserve to herself the power of varying this
established order when the general good of the
family requires it. *One* servant may take her daily
directions from her mistress, but for the guidance of
several, rules must be laid down and adhered to.

It becomes a much more difficult problem of government, requiring all a woman's tact, and a ready
discrimination of character. Next in order to the
training of her children, a lady ought to care about
the right management of her servants; they are her

individual charge. Generally, in the matter of female servants at least, the joint authority of the heads of the household is delegated to herself alone : her servants are engaged and dismissed by her. She is responsible alike for the comfort of the family, in so far as it depends on their efficient service; and for the happiness of the servants, in so far as it depends on kind, wise, and equitable government.

Where, then, is the limit of her authority? A hue and cry has been raised after the servants of fifty years ago—such subjection! such deference! such a recognition of the impassable social gulf between their own position and ours! Helpless mistresses shake their heads and say, ' The race has died out; we shall never see the like again! ' Now, it is quite true that the servants of the last generation were less given to change, and frequently, from father to son, attached themselves to the families of their employers; the adherent effect of continued service is cumulative, the links strengthen and multiply in an increasing ratio as time passes on, but we demur to the notion that these old family servants were always very respectful or very submissive. Dean Ramsay, in his traits of Scottish character, gives us some curious examples of an opposite kind. Personal attachment, the merging of their own interests in that of their employers, we accord to them, and these are very great virtues, but they are the growth of time. The fact that servants stayed long enough in one place to acquire these excellent qualities, we attribute not so much to their better moral condition as to the comparative difficulties in those days of locomotion. After the fatigue and expense of a two or three days' journey in a cart, over jolting roads, to a new place, it was at least worth while to wait and see whether an unexpected grievance could not be accommodated, whether use and habit would not take off the edge of an annoyance. Thus, a servant who adhered to her place in the first instance from motives of prudence and self-interest, may have remained long enough to take fast hold by the more enduring bonds of affection and mutual regard.

We are confirmed in the idea that it is rather the times than the servants that have changed, because, in the exceptional cases, where servants of the present day *do,* as it were, take root at the foot of the family tree, we find that the adherent and interlacing boughs they put forth of fidelity and devotion take as firm hold as ever : ' Master' is still their ' hero,' and the interests of the family their leading idea. It is perfectly natural that in these days, when change and locomotion are made so simple and easy, servants who partake of the benefit should also share the danger and disadvantage of the new order of things—should become unsettled, and fly off at the smallest grievance to try their fortune elsewhere : the caterpillar makes himself happy on his cabbage-leaf ; the butterfly, with a whole choice of garden-flowers, is always on the wing. But the restless spirit of change, if natural, is none the less to be regretted, because it takes all the poetry out of service, and leaves nothing between servant and employer but the commercial exchange of work and wages.

'But,' we are told, 'the mistress's authority is not only endangered now-a-days by the readiness with which servants give warning; they are also so independent, so spoiled by education, they know as much as their mistresses—know everything, in fact, but how to keep their places and order themselves lowly and reverently to all their betters.' Now, if it were really true that a woman is spoiled for being a servant by acquiring solid and useful information, the case would be very serious, for as surely as the words have come to pass with regard to these latter days, 'Many shall run to and fro,' so surely is the prediction also fulfilled, 'Knowledge shall be increased.' The servant who fifty years ago was innocent of all book-learning, or prided herself on spelling out a verse in the Testament, who on her wedding-day would have put 'her mark' to the parish register, and who kept her reckonings with the tradespeople by chalk-marks on the kitchen wall, *now* spends her evening hour in reading aloud to her fellow-servants the *Leisure Hour*, with its varied and pleasant information, writes letters in a flowing hand and very fairly spelt to her friends or her 'young man,' and reduces her lady's labours to a minimum, by a previous inspection of the tradesmen's books, to ascertain that they are free from error.

Is she necessarily the worse servant for this? Let a case in point be taken for what it is worth.

A clergyman and his wife, in easy circumstances, but without family, employed two female servants. It was the habit of the lady to spare her husband's defective sight by reading aloud to him in the evening. It occurred to them that their servants might as well be partakers of the advantage, and they were invited to bring their work and sit, as listeners, at a little table in the same room. The reading was promiscuous: poetry, history, books of travel, theology, whatever came to hand. A taste for knowledge was soon awakened in the servants; books were borrowed from their employers, and their work was set forward by rising an hour earlier in the morning, so as to secure time to read them. Paley's *Natural Theology* was one of the books borrowed and read through. After a time, serious monetary losses compelled the clergyman to reduce his establishment; he and his wife must henceforward manage with one servant, and she must be of a lower order than those at present in their service. It was hard to come to such a decision, but it was needful; and the servants were made aware of their master's altered circumstances. They received their dismissal in respectful silence, but presently returned, to implore that they might both be allowed to stay for the wages their master could afford to give to one, assuring him that their careful economy and watchful regard to his interests should make it a saving to him to board two instead of one. We do not think these servants were spoiled by education.

All our modern experience will never upset the wisdom of the sacred dictum, 'That the soul be without knowledge is not good;' but there are two conditions to be observed, that the equilibrium of the mistress's authority over her educated servants may not be disturbed: she must not lag behind in the general progress, so as to let her servants overtake her; and the education of the servant must be sound, useful knowledge. Whatever, for instance, gives additional vividness to Scripture narrative or Scripture emblems; such a knowledge of history as will enable them to take an intelligent interest in the events of their own day; some leading principles of mechanics—will a pump-handle be worked less vigorously because the servant knows why it draws water? some idea of the great elementary laws of nature—why should not the housemaid who toils to lift a heavy weight, have the interest of knowing that the law of gravitation is acting against her? why should not the cook when she takes out her spice-box be able to picture the luxuriant Eastern shrubs of which she is using the fruit? Some kinds of knowledge are positively helpful for the work itself; she will be a better nurse who understands something of the principles of health, and the same will apply to the housemaid as to cleanliness and ventilation.

This is the sort of education we would like for servants—that which trains their minds to think, and stores them with facts; not a smattering of drawing and crochet-work, which will neither make better servants now, nor better wives for working men later on.

But there is another condition to be observed: the mistress must not lag behind in the general progress. You ask,—' Can obedience and respect be as readily obtained from an educated as from an ignorant servant?' We would answer the question by another,—' Can you demand implicit obedience from your child of twelve years old as from your child of four?' Undoubtedly, but on rather different grounds; your infant child obeys, because the point has been settled to his satisfaction that you have the upper hand; you are stronger than he. Your older child obeys, not only because there is no appeal from your authority, but because he is learning to appreciate your superiority in the matter of knowledge, and wisdom, and experience; he has daily proofs that you have reason and justice on your side; he recognises that you are fit to guide him; his obedience is unquestioning, as in his infancy, but his reason concurs with it, and it is a higher, a more trustworthy and secure kind of obedience now.

But suppose, as your child grows older, and you become equals in mere physical strength, he should find you deficient in those qualities of wisdom, and judgment, and mental cultivation, which are needful for his guidance: then, we allow, your authority is in peril; he still *ought* to obey, because of the relationship in which he stands to you as your child; but you have made his task difficult.

So with our servants; they *were* in a state of

childish ignorance, with very few notions but that the rich were born to rule and the poor to serve. Now their ideas are enlarged, their minds stored with knowledge, they understand the dignity of labour, the importance of the working classes to the country generally; it is the truth they have got hold of, you can neither alter it nor shut their eyes to it, but act as you do with your child—abandon the infant management and deal with a reasonable being; take the initiative, be beforehand with them, and they will serve you only more heartily and faithfully, for the advances that they have made in intelligence.

Our assertion is confirmed by the experience of a man-servant, who says:—'My present master is absolute master of his own household, all are guided by his will. All his rules are reasonable, and therefore it is not difficult' for a right-minded person to conform to them. By frequent acts of kindness he shows me and my fellow-servants, that although Providence has placed us in a lower social position, he regards us as beings possessing like passions with himself. We render him a willing service of love. It is our constant aim to endeavour to please him by faithfully discharging our respective duties, and I believe we are actuated by something far higher and better than a mercenary feeling. I know well that masters like the one I am happy in serving are, indeed, rare; but I believe that thousands of servants are as good as I and my fellow-servants were when we first came into this household. I fear that there is too prevalent a traditional or hereditary notion of what a servant ought to be. Many people think that servants should not progress with their masters; that they should rest satisfied with the position in which they have been placed by Providence, while all the rest of the. human race is moving onward, and endeavouring to attain something higher and better. Now this is treating them as though they were not free-born sons and daughters of a gloriously free country. Let masters and mistresses acknowledge practically the fact, that their servants are their fellow-countrymen and countrywomen, and then, unless the servants' moral natures are radically bad, they will, as a rule, be served in a satisfactory manner.'

We have thus endeavoured to show that the authority of the mistress need not be compromised because she has now to do with educated servants, who feel their own value in the social scale. Let her rule wisely and well, and in proportion as their obedience is intelligent, it will be cheerfully rendered.

It will be well, however, for the mistress to remember, that her servant being neither her child nor her slave, the authority she is entitled to exercise must be necessarily limited. There are many things in which she lawfully issues her *commands*, others in which she proffers her *counsel*, others which she obtains by *request;* it is in the large margin lying beyond the lawful region of command that opportunity is given both to mistresses and servants to show some of the finest traits of character in their mutual relation.

Let us define: every family has its rules, its laws and customs, which should be explained to the servant when she is engaged. Accepting the place with these conditions, she is undoubtedly *bound* by them. These matters lie well within the region of direct authority; nay, it is said to be a canon law of good housekeepers when engaging a servant, *not to alter such rules* in favour of any applicant who takes exception to them, however desirable she may appear; on the principle that experience having shown to the mistress what rules work well in her family, her wisdom is to hold to them, and fit the servant to the rules, not the rules to the servant.

But what if there should be occasion to add to the existing code of household laws—must the mistress first obtain the consent of the servants then forming her household? Assuredly not! the form of government in a family is parental and autocratic; the mistress combines in herself legislative and executive functions, and she need not obtain ' parliamentary consent' to her measures: when she is convinced of the necessity for a new rule or a new restriction, she will *announce*, not *propose* it, and will see that it is carried out; but in doing so she will act wisely and considerately, especially if her servants are of mature age, if she gives her reasons, and tries to put them in her point of sight.

Generally speaking, the mistress's direct authority extends to all questions which relate to the work assigned to each servant—*what* shall be done, *when* it shall be done, *how* it shall be done. It

also relates to all matters in which the character
and stamp of the household might be compromised
by the servant's conduct. To take a simple instance:
the mistress sees an objectionable book on her
kitchen table; she requires its removal—' I will not
have such books seen in my house.' She is quite
in order in saying so; it might not be within the
limit of her lawful authority to require that the book
should be destroyed.

The debateable ground lies where neither the
performance of the work nor the credit of the household is at stake, but the question relates to the personal welfare and advantage of the servant; if the
better-instructed mind of the mistress sees that a
thing is clearly for her servant's advantage, does she
so far stand to her *in loco parentis* that she can
insist upon it against that servant's will?   We think
not.   In some cases, which involve conscientious
difference of opinion between mistress and servant,
the answer is clearly on the servant's side.   For instance, the lady belongs to the Established Church; it
is quite optional to her to determine, ' I will only have
members of the Church of England in my service.'
It becomes, in such case, a point of stipulation when
she engages her servants, that they shall be Church
and not   Chapel-goers; but if she has engaged
them without such a stipulation, being perhaps at
the time indifferent herself on the subject, the fact
that her own opinions have become more firm and
decided, and that she would now set great value on
her attendance at her church, gives her no right to

require that they should act in conformity with her preferences, and in contradiction to their own nonconformist opinions. She may be so assured it would be for their advantage, and so affectionately desirous for their welfare, as to have very strong *wishes* on the subject, but she can only act by persuasion and counsel: it is not a case for the exercise of authority.

Again: a servant, we will say, earns large wages, and the mistress sees her snare is, not perhaps gaudy, but unnecessarily expensive dress: no money is put away into the savings' bank*—none sent home to her parents: the mistress may counsel affectionately and earnestly, but she has no authority to *require* thrift or generosity: only by request or consent of the servant, can she keep back and lay by for her a part of her wages, however clearly the latter might be the gainer by her doing so. In fact, with grown-up servants as with grown-up children, there are occasions when they will not profit by our experience. Our part is to counsel them, to make it easy for them to do right by removing obstacles as far as possible out of their way; but having done so, we can only leave it with them, the responsibility

---

* A word of caution to mistresses not to conclude too readily that their servants are spending their wages unwisely is suggested by several instances which have recently come to our knowledge, where servants, without a word to their mistresses, or appearing to regard it, when at last it came to their knowledge, as anything but a most natural and obvious duty, charged themselves with the support of aged parents. Such servants, for the best of reasons, could not put by in the savings' bank; but, surely, ' what they have laid out' is in good securities, ' and shall be paid them again.'

and the consequences of rejecting our advice must rest with themselves.

Generally, however, if a mistress has acted so as to gain the respect of her servants, and if she avoids the assumption of authority where she has only the right to counsel, the very fact that it is a matter to which she might be indifferent, as far as her own interests are concerned, and which she takes up from a simple regard to her servant's personal welfare, predisposes the servant to appreciate and follow the counsel offered. ' This is your own concern, therefore I can only advise you; but I *do* advise you, because I care for your welfare.' This language will have weight, because it is unselfish, and love is power.

Once more: the mistress has occasion not only to command and to counsel, but also to *request*. We do not refer merely to courteous forms of speech in requiring and receiving service, but to occasions when she asks services from her dependents, not as a matter of right, but of favour. For instance, one of your servants is absent on her annual holiday; you would like to avoid the expense of a substitute, and the annoyance of having a stranger in the house, and you ask your other servants to parcel out her work between them; it is true their time is yours, but since you engaged them to fill a certain place in your household, and you are now for your own advantage asking them to combine another with it, thus working harder, or leaving their own work to ·mulate, you are asking a favour over and above

stipulated service.   Again, there is sickness in your
house: attendance during the day you may require
from any servant whose duties include personal
waiting; but if an affectionate servant offers to
undertake night-watching, it is something beyond
her duty; when you accept it you accept a favour.
A thousand occasions, far more trivial than those we
have pointed out, may arise to embellish the relationship of mistress and servant in daily life, whereby
the one receives a surplus of loving attention over
and above necessary service, and the other has the
luxury of conferring favours and receiving grateful
acknowledgment.   Sometimes the work itself, which
it was but the servant's duty to do, and to do well,
bears so evidently the tokens of having been done to
please the mistress, and with an eye to her special
tastes, that an expression of gratified feeling from
her is a graceful tribute.

We object to the way in which servants sometimes appropriate to themselves the things of which
they are put in charge—*my* kitchen, *my* furniture,
my plate and glass, *my* children, say respectively the
cook, housemaid, parlour-maid, and nurse.   In their
mistress's presence at least such language is unsuitable, for the only sense in which it is true is, that
she has selected *them* to be caretakers of such and
such portions of her possessions; and the viceroy has
no power in the king's presence.   The mere name
as a figure of speech might be unimportant, but it
has a reflex influence on both parties; it leads the
servant to think that she has fulfilled her duty if

the *things* are attended to without a personal regard
to her mistress's will and satisfaction, and it tends to
lower the mistress's appreciation of good service:
she looks upon it as done by the servant from *esprit
de corps*, and to gain credit in her own department,
rather than from any desire to win her approbation.

Enough has been said to show how far removed
from a mere commercial transaction of work and
wages, is the relationship between a lady and the
working women she has associated with herself.
We cannot forbear from quoting, though at some
length, the experience of one of the recent correspondents on the question of mistresses and servants,
whose theory and practice appear to us alike excellent in her domestic management. She writes
as follows : —

'Sir,— Most of your correspondents on domestic servants have generalised on the subject. Will you bear
with one who, at the risk of egotism, prefers rather to par-
ticularise? I have been a mistress above a quarter of a
century, and cannot, from personal experience, join in the
almost universal complaint against maid-servants. Having
in my youth a wholesome dread of tyrannical cooks, who
never suffer their " missus" in their kitchen — and of those
stately nurses who only allow a young mother to visit her
baby's nursery once a-day, and then not to enter without
knocking — I early tried the experiment of teaching and
training at least one young girl, from fourteen to seventeen. One of these, after nearly seventeen years of good
and faithful service — with, of course, progressive wages
and position — is now leaving to be married. Others have
done very fairly, The present " Bunch" of my household,
after a year's training, improves every day ; for which I

have greatly to thank the excellent housemaid, under whom
" Bunch" is more immediately placed in her novitiate.

' Somewhat elderly now-a-days, and more apt to be
amused than frightened by any amount of servantgalism
—à la Punch—I still like to have young people about
me. My motto, both with children and servants, is,
" Strictness and kindness." On hiring my maids, who,
with the exception of a " Bunch," I prefer to be, on first
coming, between twenty and thirty, care is taken to explain my old-fashioned notions of what the relation between us should be, the exact nature of the work expected
from them, and the rules to which they must conform.
I frankly set before them what they may find disagreeable, as well as what should be the reverse, in my service.
They distinctly understand, before they are hired, that
they must be at their work by six o'clock. The difficulty
of falling into early habits is soon over. They often thank
me for taking the trouble of calling them up, and say they
find the good of it themselves. Of course, they get to bed
by half-past nine every evening, except on occasions; and
if one has to sit up later now and then, she is called proportionably late next morning. I never allow perquisites,
and all applicants for my service are told so.

' When living in London, or other towns, soup was
regularly made in my kitchen for the poor. In the country, the cook brings me the money for any surplus dripping; which money is put aside for charitable purposes.
My servants have always been ready to co-operate with
me in these matters; never objecting to a little extra work
or trouble for the sake of those not so well off as themselves.

' When within a reasonable distance, their parents or
other relations are at liberty to come and see them, always
provided I am duly told of the guest's coming. Equal
permission to visit their friends in moderation is granted to
my servants. They have also time to do their own shop-

ping, and regular afternoons to sew for themselves. But
men-followers in the kitchen, or frequent holidays, I do
not allow. Reasoning thus:—"Young ladies at school,
or as governesses, are never permitted to have gentlemen-
visitors, or frequent holidays out: nay, even in some
schools parents can only see their daughters at stated intervals. Why should more liberty be necessary for you
than for our children and governesses?" When relations
live at a distance I give, once a-year, a holiday, from a
week's to a month's duration, as wished, deducting nothing
from the maid's wages during her absence.

'How this system works is best explained by the fact
that my servants are generally satisfied with their situation, and take an interest in the family. One said to me
lately, "We had far more liberty in our last place, ma'am,
but were not nearly so comfortable." We keep no in-
door men-servants. A "Hooks-and-Eyes" — in other
words, a "Bunch"—can carry up coals as well as any
"Buttons;" while we prefer a neat-handed "Phillis," in
moderate crinoline, snowy cap, cuffs, and muslin apron, to
a "Jeames," in all the glory of red plush, portly calves,
and powdered hair.

'Believing the old adage, that "service is no inherit-
ance," we encourage our maids to lay by a portion of their
wages in the savings' bank, and they rapidly experience
the benefit of any self-denial such a practice may cost them.
The only sumptuary laws I enforce are against feathers,
flounces, double skirts, and an exuberance of crinoline.

'My servants have plenty of work to do, receiving no
help whatever, except the occasional cleaning of the outside of a window by the coachman or under-gardener, both
of whom get their meals in the house. But all have a fair
portion of wholesome recreation. Even in the country
there are Industrial Exhibitions, while innocent merry-
makings are not tabooed. They have books, such as
Uncle Tom's Cabin, or *Robinson Crusoe*, with some of

the best cheap periodicals of the day. The *Daily Telegraph* is not withheld from them, the elder and upper maids being invited to read the leading articles and voluminous correspondence respecting themselves and their employers, though I do not consider " Bunch's " mind matured enough, as yet, to discuss the question.

' They take an interest in the advent of a young calf or brood of chickens, and while modestly sharing our own enthusiasm about horses and meek-eyed cows, they do not despise the humble pigs on the premises. No doubt such simple tastes and pleasures, diversified by gathering in the early fruit of the season, or helping the young ladies to water pet plants, arrange nosegays, or trim off the faded roses, seem vapid and humdrum to the class of servants accustomed to the excitement of casinos, music-halls, and Sunday dances. Poor girls! most of whom are more to be pitied than blamed.

' My younger maids read a little with me on Sundays; all go to church, close at hand, once a-day, and may have a good walk besides. It is a marvel how certain excellent people can see anything sinful in breathing the fresh air of green fields and sheltered lanes on the Lord's day, when they remember Who walked with His disciples through the corn, even on the strict Jewish Sabbath, 1800 years ago.

' For the benefit of those matrons who complain that their domestic grievances are not sympathised in by their husbands, and of those maids who draw invidious comparisons between their master's and their mistress's manner towards them, mode of speaking, &c., I will be yet more egotistical. My husband never finds fault or interferes with the women-servants, but he is extremely particular as to everything being properly done, and naturally expects me, as general officer of the household brigade, to see that everything is properly done. I point out to my staff, that if their work is neglected or slurred over, I, as mistress, am liable to deserved censure from master, and have rarely found this argument to fail in the desired effect.

'I have had some inefficient and indifferent servants, but my experience, on the whole, has been on the bright side. Through frequent illnesses, trials, anxieties, and the anguish attendant on death, these humble friends have shown affection and consideration towards me and mine, and I read with pain of the great gulf which seems to exist between them and their employers at the present day. Sympathy, kindness, and self-respect on the part of mistresses, go a great way towards breaking the ice of distrust and suspicion among servants. Reasonable discipline, a firm, yet gentle exacting of obedience to rules, go far to improve an ignorant mind, and tame an insubordinate spirit.

'Mothers! however blest with worldly riches, train up your daughters to know something of house-management and servant-government. There is too much croquet-playing, devotion to dress, and gadding about, especially among the middle-class young ladies of the day, to give an earnest of having better servants in the next generation. Gentlewomen! study your servants' tempers, so as not to provoke them to wrath. Scold them less and pray for them more. Bear with them if you expect them to bear with you. If we all, whether mistresses or servants, strove to remember and act up to the simple command,—" All things whatsoever ye would that men should do to you, do ye even so to them," there would be fewer heart-burnings, less harping upon grievances, whether real or imagined, and we should, one and all, do far better our " duty in that state of life unto which it hath pleased God to call us."

'I am, Sir, yours, &c.,
'Patiendo Vinces.'

We have transcribed this letter almost without

abridgment, for we believed our readers would thank us for doing so. The recent correspondence would not have been without fruit had it done nothing more than draw forth from the treasure-house of this lady's domestic history, such a compendium of sound principles, tested by the practical experience of a quarter of a century. Her example is specially valuable, as showing that good government must be *painstaking*. She 'that *ruleth*' must do so 'with *diligence*.' Bad servants may like the easy-going mistress, who shuts her eyes to all faults rather than be at the pains of correcting them, but good ones will in their hearts thank and respect the mistress who kindly and firmly keeps them up to their duties. It is, in truth, a very selfish thing to allow habits and practices to go on under our very eyes, which deteriorate the value of our servants as working women, and perhaps even endanger their morals. 'I would rather be cheated out of 400*l*. a-year,' said a lady, 'than be bothered;' but did she remember the price at which she purchased her selfish ease, and that habits of cheating, confirmed under her misrule, might lead her injured servants to a shameful end? It is no light responsibility to be entrusted with the present happiness, the future success in life, and above all, the spiritual welfare of the working women who compose our household staff; they may one day become wives of working men, blessings or curses to their families, according to the habits in which we have trained them.

We are indebted to Mr. Ruskin for a passage he

has translated for us out of Xenophon's *Economics,*
which show that the honourable and responsible
duties of a mistress towards her servants, were understood and recognised in classic times.   He tells
us that he is introducing us to a conversation between a Greek country gentleman and his young
wife (a girl of fifteen only), shortly after their marriage, when 'she had got used to him,' and was not
frightened at being spoken gravely to.   First, they
pray together, and then they have a long, happy talk,
of which this is the close.   The husband is the
narrator :—

   " ' But there is one of the duties belonging to you,' I
said, ' which perhaps will be more painful to you than any
other, namely, the care of your servants when they are
ill.'   ' Nay,' answered my wife; ' that will be the most
pleasing of all my duties to me, if only my servants will
be grateful when I minister rightly to them, and will love
me better.'   And I, pleased with her answer, said, ' Indeed,
lady, it is in some such way as this that the queen of the
hive is so regarded by her bees, that if she leave the hive
none will quit her, but all will follow her.'   Then she
answered, ' I should wonder if this office of leader were not
yours rather than mine; for, truly, my care and distribution
of things would be but a jest, were it not for your inbringing.'
' Yes,' I replied; ' but what a jest would my inbringing
be if there were no one to take care of what I brought!
Do you not know how those are pitied of whom it is fabled
that they have always to pour water into a pierced vessel?'
' Yes, and they are unhappy, if in truth they do it,' said
she.   ' Then, also,' I said, ' remember your other personal
cares.   Will all be sweet to you when, taking one of your
maidens who knows not how to spin, you teach her, and

make her twice the girl she was? or one who has no
method or habit of direction, and you teach her how to
manage a house, and make her faithful and mistress-like,
and every way worthy, and when you have the power of
benefiting those who are orderly and useful in the house,
and of punishing any one who is manifestly disposed to
evil ? But what will be the sweetest of all, if it may come
to pass, will be that you should show yourself better even
to me, and so make me your servant also, so that you need
not fear, in advancing age, to be less honoured in my
house, but may have sure hope that in becoming old, by
how much you have become also a noble fellow-worker
with me, and joint guardian of our children's possessions,
by so much shall you be more honoured in my household.
For what is lovely and good increases for all men, not
through fairness of the body, but through strength and
virtue in things pertaining to life.' And this is what I
remember, chiefly, of what we said in our first talk
together."

Would that in Christian England the first *tête-
à-tête* of all husbands and wives on the subject of
their domestic duties and responsibilities, could bear
comparison with the conversation held by this young
Grecian lady and her bridegroom in heathen times!
Young ladies of the present day, when they become
mistresses and have houses of their own, are ready
enough to admit the dignities of their new position,
and to congratulate themselves, perhaps, on emancipation from the restraints of a parental home; but
if they attempt to enjoy the *honour* of ruling, while
they repudiate its *duties* and its *cares,* they must
pay the penalty of being ill-served: and what is

. worse, the consequences must fall on husband, children, and servants, as well as on themselves.

One more question remains. We have seen the
kind of domestic management which is likely to
develop good qualities in servants and to attach
them to the service of their employers, but we had
also to consider how, when we engage a servant, we
are to escape hiring one of the wrong sort. That
there is a bad class of servants about in the world,
many will be ready to testify. 'I know well,'
says a man-servant, who writes so sensibly that his
opinion is entitled to respect, 'that there are thousands of servants who ought not to be kept in a
respectable establishment for a moment. They have
got into service mostly owing to the laxity of inquiry
on the part of masters and mistresses concerning
their characters and antecedents.' Again, another
says, 'There are many servants so thoroughly corrupt, so dishonest, immodest, and unprincipled, that
an angel himself could make no good impression on
their minds. Should you ever happen to engage
one of these, and you will not be long in discovering
your misfortune, then, without delay, dismiss her.
One bad servant will infect with evil a whole household.'

One correspondent tells us this base coin slipped
into currency because 'masters and mistresses are
not careful enough in inquiring into character.' The
other says, Duty to our household demands that we
should pass it out of our hands immediately. But
are we to commit a fraud upon our neighbour, not

only by leaving him to make the discovery for himself, perhaps with worse results than have befallen us—that it *is* base coin—but also by indorsing it, as if we had found it good? In plain words, are we to give a good character to a bad servant?

In very flagrant cases, we think, a common sense of justice would prevail; we should not pass on, without a word of warning, the thief, the confirmed drunkard, or the profligate: but if the fault has been less glaring, conscience is apt to be very elastic in the matter of giving characters — we become remarkably hopeful all at once, that the servant we are dismissing for bad conduct will take warning, and never fall into the same fault again. ' Her failing spoiled, it is true, the comfort of *our* household, upset our other servants, obliged us to change; but in this *other* household to which she is going it may be different, she may have fewer temptations.' Or again: ' We thought she was the worse for drink the last party we gave, and we could not have a moment's peace in keeping her ourselves; but as we are not quite sure, we will be content with dismissing her, and not mention our suspicion in her character.' Or the elasticity of conscience shows itself thus: ' I am only bound to answer questions; I am asked if this cook—whom I am dismissing for uncleanly habits which might poison us all—is truthful, honest, sober, and a good cook: she is all that; well for me and for her that the inquiries did not include, " Is she clean?" As they did not, I may leave her new mistress to discover that she is incorrigibly dirty.' Not unfre-

quently the falsification of character goes farther, and
the one or two good points (good temper, for instance,
in the servant who is too thoroughly indifferent and
careless to be easily put out, or a certain degree of
cleverness which has shown itself as often in cunning
as in skill) are dwelt upon and enlarged, as if the
lady really had a treasure to recommend; and she
reads over her ingenious deception to the unworthy
servant who has made her bold demand for a written
character, and points out that 'she has said what she
could for her.'

Why do ladies do this? — From fear and from
pity.   From fear lest, if they put down in black and
white their real, honest opinion, the woman they have
dismissed should bring an action for libel against
them: there are plenty of third and fourth-rate
attorneys who are ready enough to get up a case.   It
is desirable, therefore, that the law on the subject
should be well understood.   The *Leisure Hour* for
1865 had a useful series of papers, called 'Hints on
Legal Topics,' in which, among other matters, the
legal basis is examined of the relation between masters and domestic servants.   We there learn that—

'*In the absence of express agreement there is no legal
obligation on any master or mistress to give a servant on
dismissal any character at all, or to give any reason for
refusing to do so.*   In proof of this, in the year 1800, a
Mrs. Carroll being servant in the house of a Mr. Bird, was
dismissed.   After her dismissal she applied for a new place
to a lady named Stewart, who was ready and willing to
have her, if Mr. Bird would give her a satisfactory character.

Mr. Bird, however, wholly refused to give her any character whatever—good or bad. Mrs. Carroll's husband thereupon brought an action against Mr. Bird, alleging that it was the master's duty to have given his wife a character of some sort. Lord Kenyon asked if there was any precedent for such an action. Mr. Gibbs, a very learned counsel, admitted that he had no case; upon which Lord Kenyon said that the action could not be supported by law. " In the case of domestic and menial servants, there was no law to compel the master to give the servant a character; it might be a duty which his feelings might prompt him to perform, but there was no law to enforce the doing of it." '*

Thus we see a mistress may legally·decline to give *any* character; and, certainly, this would be better — more just to society in general, and to mistresses in particular, than to give one which conveys a false impression, if it is not actually couched in false terms. If, however, she intends to act on this principle, she should state to her servants on engaging them, that should she have to dismiss them for bad conduct, she will probably withhold a character altogether.

But a mistress may feel bound in conscience to state what she knows of a servant's character: how far, in this case, does the law protect her?

'The general rule is,' says the article to which we have referred, 'that all words written or spoken defamatory of a person, that is to say, to the injury of his character, are considered malicious and actionable. But there are

* *Leisure Hour for* 1865, p. 685.

certain occasions when malice will not be imputed to you, even if you *do say* what is injurious or to the discredit of a person. The occasion of giving the character of the servant *is one of these.* So that, in giving a servant's character, you will be excused for saying or writing what is unfavourable, if you state in good faith either *what is true* or *what you believe to be true,* even though you should be mistaken. In such case it will be a *privileged communication,* and no action can be maintained upon it. But if you abuse the opportunity, and take advantage of the privilege to say something malicious, something *with intention to injure* the servant, you will be liable to an action.'

Here again it may be well to quote an instance. 'In 1829 a young woman, named Child, had been in the service of a Mr. and Mrs. Affleck, having come with a good character. She left (it does not say how or why), and was afterwards hired by another person, who wrote to Mrs. Affleck for her character. The reply was—' Mrs. A.'s compliments to Mrs. S., and is sorry that, in reply to her inquiries respecting E. Child, nothing can be in justice said in her favour. She lived with Mrs. A. but for a few weeks, in which short time she frequently conducted herself disgracefully; and Mrs. A. is concerned to add she has, since her dismissal, been credibly informed she has been, and now is, a person of loose character in Bury.' In consequence of this letter the servant was dismissed. It seemed that Mrs. Affleck afterwards went to the persons who had recommended the servant to her, and made a similar statement to them. At the trial, no evidence was brought to disprove the statement at the end of the letter; the judge decided that it was a privileged communication. A learned judge in the Court of Queen's Bench said, ' he thought Mrs. Affleck would have fallen short of her duty in withholding the information.'

We may briefly add the opinion of Lord Denman, which arose out of another case where the circumstances differed from the one we have mentioned : ' If I give a good character to a servant, and next day discover that the servant is dishonest, surely in such a case it becomes my duty to communicate my discovery to the person to whom I have given the character.' This opinion was at once confirmed by Mr. Justice Coleridge· in the words, ' Nobody can doubt that.'

So, then, we see that ladies have no ground for being deterred, through fear of legal consequences, from performing a simple act of justice to society, and either refusing a character to an unworthy servant, or stating the truth with regard to her. But perhaps *pity*, more frequently than *fear*, warps a lady's judgment and blinds her conscience in this matter. ' My servant's character,' she will say to herself, ' is her bread ; no mistress will take her without one, no mistress will take her if I tell the unvarnished truth about her;—it is true she is very unworthy, so unworthy that I cannot keep her: but if I give her no character, or a bad one, I shut the door to her of service, which is an honest calling, and leave her no choice but ruin.' Now here we think our guiding principle, 'Whatsoever ye would that men should do unto you, do ye even so to them,' sheds light on the difficulty. Would you feel a lady acted kindly, or justly, or honourably towards you, who palmed off upon you such a piece of spoiled goods as you know this servant to be, coupled with the recommendation of it you are persuading yourself you ought to write? Say it is a flagrant case—a case of vice—of course, if you state it the servant will suffer; sin and suffering are wedded: but who ought to suffer? the guilty servant, or the innocent family to whom your unjustifiable silence as to her real character will admit her? The only thing you can do is to state the case fully, mentioning extenuating circumstances or evidences of repentance, if there are any. And you need not cast her off, or withdraw a helping hand from her, because she is so bad that you have not felt it right to keep her in your own family, or help her into another. Be willing to take some trouble for her; do not let a woman who has stood to you in so near a relation as your domestic servant sink down into the dregs of society, when you might get her into a Reformatory or a Refuge, or some of those merciful Institutions which interpose between transgressors and ruin.

In other cases where the fault is more venial, and you have really done your best to cure it, but because of failure, and because the fault creates too serious a disturbance in your household management to be longer borne with, you feel you must part with your servant ; tell her that, whoever applies to you for her character will hear the truth about her, her good qualities and her bad ones. We believe that, if this were really done, and done by everybody, servants would be the gainers as well as mistresses. Characters now are only half believed, and if the slightest loophole is left for suspicion by silence on one point, or qualified praise on another, it is concluded that more is meant than meets the ear, and the lady concludes to be on the safe side, and declines the bargain. Honesty in this matter would soon sift out the servants who are thoroughly bad or incapable, and for the rest many a kind and considerate mistress would be found to say, 'This servant is no doubt faulty, but these are not faults to which she will be much tempted in my establishment; and since I know them, I can be on my guard against them: I will give her a trial.'

Meanwhile, till a favourable change has taken place in the matter of giving characters, mistresses must be willing to take pains and trouble to avoid being deceived. The advertisement-sheet and the Registry Office should be a last resource, and a personal interview with the former mistress is of great importance, for her recommendation is valuable in proportion to her own character: of this you can judge best by seeing and talking with her. The entrance of a new member into a household, a woman formed and mature in age, habits, and principle, is an event of no light moment; and we venture to say no Christian mistress takes this step without previous prayer that God will guide her to

choose those who may prove blessings and not curses
in her family.

One trait is sometimes sufficient to give an
insight into character; we quote an instance furnished by a friend, of a faithful servant from the
other sex:—

'Many years ago, in New York, our firm was in want
of a porter. A neighbouring merchant recommended a
coloured man, Moses Hunter, who had applied to him.
Among other duties, one which he had required of Moses
was, that he should go to the Post Office on Sunday morning
and bring the letters to his house. Moses, although most
anxious for the place, at once, and most respectfully in his
own way, said, "Sar! I am ready to do all you want of
me on the oder days, but on the Lord's day, 'xcuse me,
sar, I must not work." This did not suit our friend; but
we, viewing the answer in a different light, saw the value
of such a man, and directly engaged him. He served us
faithfully, laboriously, and with scrupulous honesty,
having much entrusted to him, for more than fourteen
years. He seemed, at last, to pine and die of a broken
heart on the breaking up of our establishment. He was a
rare man, Moses, and well known in those days.'

For the servant, too, the question of accepting
employment in a new family, is anxious and mo-
mentous. The Christian servant, no less than the
Christian mistress, will seek for that Parental guidance which is given without respect of persons. In
all lawful ways she will endeavour to ascertain how
the household is regulated, into which she is pro-
posing to enter: not so much whether the heads of
the family make a high religious profession, as

whether their daily life shows that they are guided by religious precepts; that they do 'give unto their servants that which is just and equal; forbearing threatening: remembering that they are themselves servants as well as masters.'

Between employers who act on these principles, and the Christian women who serve them, links of friendship are formed, lasting as eternity. One such case is in our eye at this moment — a loving-hearted woman, who, true to her womanly instincts, was ready to throw her whole heart into her service. For a long term of years she had lived as nurse in a large establishment, and won the regard and esteem of all who had to do with her; a lady heard of her, who had occasion to send a little invalid child from home, and required a confidential person to take charge of him. She undertook the charge, and watched over him in his helpless state of suffering, with a solicitude so truly maternal, that the mother's heart was eased of one of its heaviest cares. After a time, the little one's case was considered hopeless as to cure, and he was allowed to return home. It was now that Christian principle shone out most conspicuously in his devoted attendant. With inimitable tact, she contrived to place herself completely under her mistress's orders; taking upon herself all the burden and the charge, abdicating all the right to judge and decide, she had exercised when alone with the child. Her position towards the other nurses was a delicate one: but her genuine humility and indifference to her own comfort, pro-

T

vided that of her little charge was secured, made it
impossible to quarrel. The child's illness was most
distressing; painful days, wakeful nights, depressing
influences of all kinds. Strangers turned away, but
the heart of his faithful nurse did but wind round
him the more closely. She only waited for his death
to retire from service and live with an aged mother
on her well-earned savings. Yet any accession of
illness, which threatened to snap the feeble thread of
the child's life, pierced to the mother-heart of this
woman. Weary and enfeebled with the demands he
made upon her, nothing could induce her to relax
her exertions. And when the cloud passed by, as it
did again and again, and her charge became less
onerous, she was always urging on her mistress's acceptance some service over and above her immediate
duties; some pleasant token of consideration for her
employer's interests. Her quick eye of ready affection detected symptoms of illness, which escaped
notice from others. And her ready tact was sure to
discover some way — so respectfully urged as to be
irresistible — in which her mistress's cares might be
lightened. What tie is it, short of friendship, which
binds together that lady and her servant? The testimony of a fellow-servant with regard to her was,
'I never saw such a Christian.'

It is hard to calculate where the stream of blessing
may end, which has its fountain-head in the fidelity
and attachment of a Christian servant. We are
reminded of one, who has conferred nothing short
of a national blessing on her country. We speak

the words advisedly, for we can make them good.
Whose is the name which awakens an electric
thrill in the hearts of the working men and women
of England? Who has worked for them with untiring zeal in Parliament, and in Committees, and
on the platform, and in a hundred ways less obvious,
though more laborious? Colliers, operatives in factories, men, wives, daughters, little children, couple
his name, when they hear it, with a fervent benediction. To whom, then, does the noble Earl of Shaftesbury, the workman's friend, trace the earliest im-
planting of principles which have given their stamp
to his whole beneficent life? To a servant—a female
servant. We had heard him mention her worth,
and, anxious for some more definite information, we
sought it from himself. It is by his kindness that
we are furnished with the following particulars: —

'My daughter has asked me to tell you something
about the very dear and blessed old woman (her name
was Maria Millas) who first taught me in my earliest
years to think on God and His truth.

'She had been my mother's maid at Blenheim before
my mother married. After the marriage she became house-
keeper to my father and mother, and, very soon after I was
born, took almost the entire care of me.

'She entered into rest when I was about seven years
old, but the recollection of what she said, and did, and
taught, even to a prayer that I now constantly use, is as
vivid as in the days that I heard her.

'The impression was, and is still, very deep, that she
made upon me; and I must trace, under God, very much,
perhaps all, of the duties of my later life to her precepts
and her prayers.

' I know not where she was buried. She died, I know, in London; and I may safely say that I have ever cherished her memory with the deepest gratitude and affection. She was a "special Providence" to me.'

We heartily thank the noble Earl for affording us this little leaflet out of his childhood's history; because we believe no Christian servant can read it without feeling a holy ambition stirred within her, not only to yield to her employers the services which are bought with their money, but to confer on them that priceless benefit of spiritual vigilance and prayerful interest, which shall turn the *servant* into the *benefactor* and the *friend*.

CHAPTER VIII.

OCK him up,' says English Law. 'Give to him that asketh thee,' says the great Lawgiver. Unless some real harmony can be shown to lie at the foundation of the apparent discrepancy, the question will remain hopelessly vexed, and the line of practical conduct to be pursued a daily-recurring difficulty.

Before the discrepancy can be proved, it must be shown that those whom we have classed together as forming the 'genus Mendicant' are the objects contemplated in the scriptural law as 'him that asketh thee;' it must also be shown that 'giving' means the careless distribution of a few coppers, which by wheedle or menace the mendicant extracts from the pitiful or the timid.

There is a coherence in the Divine law which forbids us to take a single precept and isolate it from the rest. 'This we commanded you, that if

any would not work, neither should he eat,'* and
'An idle soul shall suffer hunger,'† are equally
explicit with 'Give to him that asketh thee;' if practical experience proves that the 'genus Mendicant'
is made up, with few exceptions, of sturdy rogues
who adopt begging as a trade, because they have
neither the honesty nor the industry to pursue a
lawful calling, then English law is giving to the
mendicant what his moral necessities demand, when
it gives him *in charge,* and supplies him with a
term of 'hard labour.'

The demoralizing effect of mendicancy was thus
described to the writer by one who had spent many
years in tracing its effects:—

'There are few things,' said he, 'that so entirely destroy
the moral stamina of honest and truthful manhood. A
man had better be profane; your regular and able-bodied
mendicant is a thief without the thief's courage to steal.
The thief's nefarious calling requires several human and
useful qualifications, as ingenuity, and activity, and
courage; whilst the able-bodied mendicant requires only
idleness, *plus* impudence, *plus* hypocrisy. In seventeen
years' experience, I never knew a case of a mendicant
becoming converted to God. The evils of mendicancy are
incalculable; decent people rarely resort to it, but having
once overstepped the barrier, they still more rarely return
to habits of peaceful industry. But the public are little
aware of this; they know more of the gorilla than of the
beggar at their doors, and by their profuse and indiscriminate charity they unwittingly enhance the evil.'

He had resided for several years in Chelsea, in the

* 2 Thess. iii. 10.   † Prov. xix. 15.

neighbourhood of Belgrave and other large squares, and had had good opportunities of judging of the pauperizing and demoralizing effects arising from shameless beggary and careless charity.

'The first and greatest difficulty,' he says, 'I have had to contend with, is the spirit of beggary that pervades the whole of this district. Lying, as it does, in the immediate vicinity of the rich and great, the people have been accustomed to obtain temporal relief with the greatest facility. They have generally only had to make up a statement of distress, and help has been immediately afforded, frequently without the least inquiry into its truth. I do not know above six persons, or rather families, in the district, except shopkeepers, who do not more or less in the winter receive gifts, either in money or in goods. Some receive as much as two or three pounds at a time; others receive coals and bread, and the giving of these has been so regular that the people very generally depend on them, and expect them as a right, or a kind of natural consequence of their living in the neighbourhood, and invariably become clamorous if they are not satisfied. The effort to relieve the poor has, in a great measure, pauperized them. The people in general depend on it for every season of exigence. The fall of the thermometer ten degrees is sufficient to send a host of them on the search for temporal relief. I have often seen a fall of snow send two or three troops of women from the district begging round the neighbouring squares, and those have been most frequently persons addicted to drink. I have known some of the most worthless get one or two sovereigns, and immediately spend it in drink. The greater portion of the beggars who infest the neighbouring squares come from this locality, and I am told by a detective, whose duty it is to watch them, that what is given is frequently spent directly afterwards in the gin-palace.'

Such is the testimony of one who speaks from lengthened experience. ' I was glad to get away from Chelsea,' he said to the writer; ' the work seemed so hopeless.' Certain it is that a district is always the poorer for indiscriminate charity, for the worst characters are attracted into it, and rooms being much in demand, the rents are proportionately raised.

Perhaps we can best give an idea of the ' genus Mendicant' by showing some of the species into which it is divided.

The best and most moral kind of beggar is the man who adopts a vagrant life from a general instability of character: he can settle to nothing; he has an indomitable love of wandering; he is probably very fond of natural scenery, enjoys his rambles up and down the country, likes anything better than steady hard work : this man is not ruined yet, but he is in a fair way for it.

Next to him we may class the dull, stupid mendicant — a man of very low organization ; he has no idea of comfort, is as easy-tempered as he is idle ; he has been taught no trade, and takes up with begging as the easiest mode of life.

In the third class the evils of mendicancy become more conspicuous, for we have now to speak of the man who, though idle, is intelligent and vicious. He is the writer of begging-letters. One such lived for seven years on a dead horse. His horse died; and a picture of the horse, painted, and put on his mantel-piece, proved a profitable speculation. Pathetic letters drew commiserating persons to the house, and charity flowed freely at the sight of his distress and fidelity to his horse's memory.

Another in Chelsea wrote to the Incumbent of St. Michael's, Pimlico, entreating a call from him at a house which he named in Burton Street, Eaton Square. The respectability of the neighbourhood did not deter the Incumbent, who had been several times victimized by begging-letters, from sending a policeman in plain clothes as his *avant-courier*, to spy out the land. It was a wise step. The policeman found a wretched object lying on the straw in a lower room, whom he recognized as a man to whom the law and its officials had had something to say already. In the upper part of the house two luxuriously-furnished rooms provided a pleasant retreat, where (when the hours had passed by in which charitable donors were likely to call) the mendicant, after shaking himself from his straw, enjoyed an evening bath, and took his meal in comfort on his sofa or ottoman.

Strange chapters in human history are turned up among the begging-letter writers. A City Missionary turned into a low lodging-house in Chelsea, and began to speak to those assembled in the kitchen, or common room. He gained the ear of some, and becoming perhaps a little more elated than the occasion warranted, he was tempted to make capital of a slender amount of Hebrew knowledge, and to insist with regard to a certain expression, that in the original

language its true force was so-and-so. A very dirty
man lying across the table, who had taken no notice
hitherto, turned up a bleared and disfigured face.
' You are wrong: the meaning is correctly rendered
in the common version, for the root is so-and-so;
and it occurs so many times in the Old Testament.'
The Missionary had spoken in the presence of a
savant, once an honoured Rector in the English
Church. Intemperance opened the door to want,
beggary succeeded, and was followed by a thorough
break-down of the whole character, till it was lost
both to shame and hope.

To this class belongs also the song-singer—some
of them make their own songs; the pious hymn-
singer; the street pavement-writer. The broken-down
thief, who has lost courage to steal, sometimes gravi-
tates down to this. A case, now happily reclaimed,
occurred of this kind. The man had had a boarding-
school education, and intelligence without morality
proved his ruin; he had been six times in prison,
and had plundered and destroyed a large amount of
property. Finally, he was reduced to sit on the flags
and trace his appeal to passing charity in the words—
' I am starving !'

In our next class we shall place the *afflicted and
vicious*. It is sad to have to class these together,
but the truth is, that whereas the better sort among
the afflicted learn some trade and eke out a maintenance, the idly-disposed soon find that their affliction
is no unprofitable source of maintenance; it brings
them in more than work, and they give themselves up

to mendicancy: such become eminently profane and
vicious. Painful instances might be given among the
blind, the deaf and dumb, and the crippled. A blind
man at Chelsea, of remarkably respectable appearance,
became absolutely unbearable in his fits of drunken
rage; tables and chairs were broken up by him like
toys: but this man was the pensioner of two or three
societies, and knew well the market-value of his
affliction. He is actually in receipt of a good income, and has been seen with his hand full of
sovereigns.

Parents know how to trade with deformity and
bodily affliction in their children. A friend lamented
to the writer his disappointment in the case of a
crippled girl of thirteen. Backed by the efforts of a
benevolent lady, he procured for her free admission
to the Cripples' Home, and went joyously to the parents to announce his success. 'Let her go in!'
said the father. 'No, Sir, we're too wide awake for
that—that girl's worth 13s. a-week to us.' There is
often a difficulty with parents on this head, nor will
they yield till threatened with the law. It is well
for the poor children's sake that the law should be
remembered. Begging in the streets is illegal, and
a person may be given in charge to a policeman for
it. Selling in the streets (the slight pretext under
which begging is often carried on) is illegal, unless
the salesman, woman, or child, has upon his person a
license, which must be renewed every six months, at
a cost of half-a-guinea.

Besides the really afflicted, there are plenty be-

longing to this class who feign it ; we shall not expect
to find them better than the others. A curious case
was communicated lately to the Editor of the *Times*,
as to a beggar in the streets of London :—

'There is a middle-aged woman who makes a handsome livelihood by simulating blindness, perambulating the
thoroughfares with eyes shut and hands extended, solicitive
of alms. Notwithstanding that the face of this woman
was positively unctuous with comfortableness and good-
feeding, many a copper I at different times deposited in
her fat hands, and which might else have possibly fallen to
the share of the industrious and ragged, but otherwise
unafflicted crossing-sweeper. Indeed, I should no doubt
have gone on contributing to this hour, had I not happened accidentally, when walking one day in a back street,
to meet her with her eyes open, and evidently seeing perfectly. The next time I found her begging I could not
restrain my indignation. " You old humbug !" I said;
"you know you are no more blind than I am !" Her
answer was perfect (with a sardonic grin),—" Well, sir,
and ain't that a blessing to be very thankful for ?" I was
speechless. The argument and the audacity were alike
confounding.

'On asking a neighbouring policeman why she was not
locked up, he explained that she often had been, but that
she made herself so unbearable when under restraint, that
the police were not anxious to have more to do with her
than they could help. The moment she was brought into
gaol she always proceeded with the utmost celerity to
reduce herself " to a classical style of dress which does not
much tax the sewing-machine." This woman may be
seen almost any day in the thoroughfares of London,
plying her trade unchecked.'

Somewhat after the same fashion a Yorkshireman

traded with the facility with which he counterfeited
the agony of a cripple : neither asking nor begging,
but walking with slow, and apparently painful steps,
his body bent forward, and his hands clasped behind
his back.   Passers-by felt their compassion excited
as he approached; when he had gone by it was irresistible to drop a copper into the clasped hands:
before the deliberate movement was effected by
which he turned round to thank them, they were
gone.

Mental misery is often successfully simulated;
and it, too, has its market value.   'The broken-
down gentleman' almost deserves a place to himself
in our classification, so often is he met with : a black
suit and a white tie are his stock-in-trade, and though
his haunt is commonly a low lodging-house, he keeps
them as decent as he can.   This man stands speechless and heartbroken, till the very silence of his woe
moves the onlooker to make a dive in his pocket,
and produce, not a copper (who would dare console a
' gentleman' with a copper?) but some more worthy
coin, accompanied with delicately-worded sympathy.

Among the many readers of the painfully interesting book, *Female Life in a Prison*, there may
be some who remember the case of ' Alice Grey.'
Such will be interested in the following circumstances :—A lady-friend of the writer had taken the
omnibus to Clapham, where her mother resided.   No
better place for study of character than an omnibus
with its shifting occupants; here business, there pleasure ; here sorrow, there joy ; and now and then peace

and sweet content, have stamped the impress of a life
on human faces.

On this occasion a lady, who was indeed past the
age for youthful beauty, but whose countenance and
figure were graceful and refined to a degree that irre-
sistibly pleased the onlooker, arrested the attention ·
of our friend by a visible discrepancy between herself
and her attire: she was every inch the lady—her
clothing mean and rusty.

Involuntary glances were turned into the concerned gaze of compassion when, as the omnibus was
about to stop, our friend saw the stranger apparently
on the point of fainting. No one more ready than
she to do a kind turn; and in this case general
kindness had been quickened into sympathy, by the
interest with which the stranger's appearance inspired
her.

She stepped forward to assist, supported her in
alighting from the omnibus, and proposed to take her
into a chemist's shop for a restorative.

The offer, which appeared to rouse her, was rather
curtly declined; but she gave an address, whither,
she said, she was bound, in Clapham, and asked her
new friend to inquire the way to it, while she waited
at a stationer's opposite.

The lady went, but could gain no light as to the
address. Finally, she invited the stranger to accompany her to her mother's house, and partake ·of a
glass of wine. This she readily consented to do.

By degrees her reserve vanished, and she became
communicative as to her troubles: she had escaped

from home, though entitled to a considerable fortune, because her father, who had been married again to a Roman Catholic, was becoming bigoted on the subject of religion, and wished to place her in a nunnery.

To inquiries as to how she was maintaining herself, she said she taught a few poor children in her one room in the Waterloo Road; it was rather a starving than a living, for she only charged them a penny a-week each : but then she had the comfort of knowing she was doing some good in the world, by instilling into their infant minds a knowledge of God's truth.

Her story was told with touching simplicity, and her grace and refinement well corroborated the statement as to her family and fortune.

The lady became extremely interested in her *protégée;* and, after setting refreshment before her, and making her a present in clothing, she sent her home in a cab, meanwhile revolving in her own mind plans of more effectual assistance.

Her husband—an acute member of the legal profession — was pressed into the service, and requested to take up the case of this persecuted lady, and restore her to her rights.   Probably, if the 'persecuted lady' had been aware that she was pouring out her confidences to the wife of a talented lawyer, she would have been less communicative.   She had given references which were carefully sifted : most of the parties had heard of her, but did not know her personally. At length legal acumen traced her to a source of information which gave her a character anything but flattering, based on personal knowledge which had extended over a period of some twenty-two years. We quote from a letter addressed to the much-deceived lawyer's wife, somewhat abbreviating, though in no way altering, her statement : —

'Dear Madam,—I had lost sight of " Matilda" for many years, and imagined her no longer in this world. I have been almost *dreading* her finding me out, at which you will scarcely wonder when I tell you that I do indeed know much of her past history, and know that, if she is accountable for her words and actions, she is the greatest liar, hypocrite, and impostor, that I ever heard of in modern times. I am sorry to feel obliged to use such strong and harsh terms. I have made so many fruitless attempts, in years past, to reclaim and befriend her, that I have long given up the hope of ever seeing her maintain herself in a respectable manner.

'It must be as much as twenty-two years since I first knew Matilda Kellaway ; it would fill a small volume to narrate to you all that I know about her. Her account of herself is an entire fabrication. After some difficulty and inquiries we discovered that her father is a Mr. C. of London, and she an illegitimate child. She must, I think, now be about forty years of age, and it is surprising how she has existed through all the hardships and sufferings to which she has subjected herself. She has been many times in prison, and in different places—generally, I believe, for obtaining money on false pretences, but, I believe, also for theft : the last that I heard of her (three or four years ago) was when in Brixton jail, or penitentiary, she wrote an apparently very penitent, humble letter, to my friends the P.'s of D. which they forwarded to me. I have had innumerable letters from gentlemen and ladies, chaplains of prisons, &c. &c., in different parts of England, inquiring of me respecting this most remarkable impostor. She has assumed various names; in a book entitled *Female Life in Prison* she appears under the name of Alice Grey. She has been sent to Asylums and Refuges, but she never would remain long in any place; having, it would seem, an unconquerable disposition towards roving, romancing, and acting a part. Several times she has been in the Chelsea Union. Her misdeeds have many times appeared in the public papers, under one or other of her various false names. I have helped her again and again, visited her, written to her, but have been so continually deceived and disappointed that it seemed useless to do anything more.

'I am, yours sincerely,   E. P.'

This was, indeed, a check on the kindly intentions of the lawyer's wife. She could have no doubt, in reviewing the circumstances, that the designing woman had noticed her look of interest in the omnibus, and practised upon it by simulating faintness, which she declined to submit to the more practised eye of a chemist.

Who has not met with 'the Manchester operative' come to London in search of employment? The writer speaks feelingly, having been victimised. Such a man wears a white apron and a paper cap; appears to have all the ingrained reluctance of an honest English workman to lower himself by begging: in fact, asks for nothing more at first than that you will recommend him to some gentleman for a job, by which he can earn a few shillings to pay his railway-fare back to his wife and little ones. At this appropriate moment, his lip begins to quiver and your heart to melt. 'How came he to leave

U

them?' you ask. 'Why, work was scarce; he only
got three days a-week, and he heard there was an
opening for full work in London; but he knew
better now; only wished to get home: if it was but
a crust he could help them to, it was better than
nothing.' Such evident feeling, such sensitive
shrinking from appearing to beg! your respect for
the man rises; you begin to consider how he can be
tenderly induced to allow you to help him. He
sees his advantage, talks of his friends in Manchester, the advice he has had from the Reverend
This and the Reverend That—honoured names,
familiar to you from your childhood. You rejoice
to think your new *protégé* can so endorse his claim
on your sympathy. You take him home, set food
before him,—his mental anxiety will not allow him
to eat much. You ransack your stores to provide
him with warm clothing, for the quivering percep-
tible in his countenance may be from cold. Finally,
you make all arrangements about his journey, pay
for it, give him a few loose pence to get a lodging
close to the station, that he may not miss the early
train, give him an envelope directed to yourself, in
which he is to inform you of his safe return and
happy meeting with his family,—and, a few days
after, hear of him as lurking about at neighbouring
beer-houses, ready to repeat his experiment on any
one equally gullible with yourself!

Another case we may mention, where circumstances, real or assumed, are made to serve their
turn in the mendicant trade. Sometimes the eye is

attracted to a woman who is taking a few moments'
repose on a door-step, or on a bench in the Park; it
is *attracted*, we say, for she looks so clean, decent,
and respectable, a picture of a steady working man's
wife, with her tidy gown and white apron, and
interest is excited in her by the babe in each arm,
on whom she looks in such motherly fashion.   This
is 'the clean mother with twins,' a known class
among mendicants: the children may be her own,
or merely borrowed, but she has calculated to a
nicety their value as a source of income: she knows
how passers-by will give her double credit for her
neat appearance, with so heavy a charge on her time
and hands; the babies will be noticed, and the
woman will get more than notice or commendation,
for many will pity the decent working man's wife,
and slip a gratuity into her hand.

Borrowing children to elicit pity is a common
resource among mendicants.   A woman begging
about Marylebone Road lately, with two children,
excited a good deal of compassion there.   'If she
could get a little clothing,' she said, ' so as to appear
respectable, she had a promise of slop-work from a
shop.'   The neighbours, in fact, were getting up a
little subscription; but Mr. Weylland, whom we have
already mentioned, offered to sift her case before
anything was actually done.   He had great difficulty
in tracing her to Flower and Dean Street, E., a
locality haunted by thieves; there the 'distressed
mother,' unencumbered now with children, sat in a
group of some eighteen or twenty beggars, in a low

coffee-house, drinking gin. We leave the reader to imagine how soon the new clothing which charitable friends intended to provide, would have been transmuted into gin. In fact, to give clothing to common mendicants without investigating their cases is simple waste; it does not suit their purpose to be well clad; the articles would be sold directly, and the money drunk up. The gains of mendicants must be great, if we may judge by their spendings; for at morning and evening meals, when they are not likely to be disturbed, they live extravagantly,— far better than a working man can afford to do,— and are still left with a surplus to squander at the public-house.* Their haunts are generally low lodging-houses. Sometimes they have private rooms, but the appearance of such rooms is always desolate; it is to their interest that it should be so.

In classifying mendicants, we have left the children to the last. More than any others they move us to sadness; yet it is a sadness more largely mingled with hope: the children, at least, are not irreclaimable, if philanthropic and Christian friends enough can be found to reach out to them a helping hand.

The children of mendicants ordinarily follow

---

* A beggar in Moorfields used daily to have a penny given him by a merchant on his way to the Exchange. The penny was withheld, and the appearance of the merchant manifested his embarrassment and distress. The beggar at length spoke to him, offered him a loan of 500*l.*, and another of the same sum if it were required. It re-established his affairs.—SOUTHEY, quoted in *Signals of Distress*, p. 37

their parents' mode of life, and mendicant boys
become young thieves; indeed, as we stated at the
outset, the thief is generally of a less degraded type
of character than the mere beggar: it is a distinction on which he prides himself.

At a meeting held some time ago for vagrants
and thieves, Mr. Jackson, a City Missionary very
familiar with both classes, by long years of labour
amongst them, was busily occupied in finding them
places.   A lad showed a determined purpose to sit
on an already crowded bench, whereas seats were to
be had in plenty a little farther on.   Mr. Jackson's
penetration soon discovered the cause.   The half-
filled benches were occupied by vagrants.   He put
to him the usual test, 'Gonof?' (in recognised
thieves' slang, 'Are you a thief?' Gonof being
Hebrew for thief.)—'Yes, Sir, and a respectable
one: I can't sit among such as them *there.*'

If a mendicant gives his children any schooling,
the bent of his mind is still apparent: one will
be sent to the Roman Catholic, another to a Church,
a third to a Dissenting school, in order to found
a claim on each for temporal gain; but more usually
the hapless little ones are sent into the streets on
their degrading business, and beaten when they
return at night, if they bring in less than parental
selfishness expected.   A clergyman, whose arduous
labours in the poorest districts enabled him to speak
from experience, dwelt earnestly, in conversation
with the writer, on the check which he found in his
ministerial work, from the selfish, idle parents, who

followed no regular calling themselves; because
they reckoned on a livelihood, and gained it too,
from sending out their children to beg. Begging,
or stealing, as the case may be, is *required* from
such children as a matter of submission to parental
authority, and a condition of remaining under
parental protection. Mr. Jackson was holding a
meeting in a certain court, when he was appealed
to by a girl of twelve, who said she was starving;
her mother had wanted her to go and steal wood,
and because she would not, had turned her out of
the house. After the meeting, Mr. Jackson himself
took the girl back to her mother, a Roman Catholic.
She allowed the door to stand a-jar, but refused to
open it while he remonstrated with her:—'Your
daughter here says you have turned her out of
doors, and for such and such reasons.' 'So I have,
and I would turn them all out if they would not do
as I told them.' 'Now, my friend, you go to confession; don't have such a tale as this to tell there:
take your child home.' 'No, not for all the con-
fessors in the world would I take her in!' The
mother was inexorable, and the missionary succeeded
in getting the girl into an Institution.

Not unfrequently, the children of mendicant
parents are hunted away from home, and forced by
their parents to sleep in nightly refuges, for the sake
of the supper or breakfast, or both, given with the
night's lodging. The same correspondent, who communicated to the *Times* his discoveries as to the blind
beggar, seems to have fallen in with some curious

specimens of little vagrant children, who founded
their appeal on the need of a night's lodging. He
says :—

' I was ·crossing Leicester Square at about eleven
o'clock at night, when I passed a little bundle of rags and
tatters coiled up under what were formerly the railings
surrounding the Great Globe Exhibition. I suppose I
looked shocked, or particularly " green," for forthwith
another little bundle of tatters (but this time carrying a
broom and walking about), ran up and explained to me
that " He " (pointing to the sleeping figure), " ain't got
anything to get no bed, sir." I inquired the price of a
bed. " Threepence, yer honour." Though somewhat loth
to disturb the poor little fellow, hygienic considerations
determined me; so I shook him up and provided him with
the necessary coin to procure a shake-down elsewhere. I
fancied the boy wakened singularly slowly, and whether it
was owing to this notion, or to a certain melodramatic air
about the whole scene, I took it into my head to see what
would become of my friend; accordingly I crossed over to
the thoroughfare side of the square and watched. In a
few minutes the boy had curled himself up again, and was,
apparently, as fast asleep as ever, the " chorus " still
walking up and down; while at the other end of the railing,
that nearest Piccadilly, I observed a second broom-boy also
composing himself to sleep. This looked suspicious. I
went round and gave the second sleeper " three-pence for a
bed," and returned to my coigne of vantage. In a few
minutes there were no less than five broom-boys all huddled up in different spots under the railings of the " Old
Globe," and, as far as appearances went, as fast as the
" Seven Sleepers." They evidently considered that the
sleeping dodge " paid." '

Those who are familiar with boy nature will

not be surprised that the shifts to which these poor
children are reduced, develope in them no common
amount of cunning. The Master of the Wandsworth Home for Boys, so liberally supported by
Miss Portal, is pretty well versed in the habits of
these children of the streets, having generally 180
at one time under his care. He says of them :—

'Some of them are the most cunning rogues on the face
of the earth. One, a bit of a boy, wanted to have a little
time out, and he proceeded in this way. He fell down in
one of the dormitories, clasped his elbow, and set up a howl
that soon attracted me to the spot. He had, he said, hurt
his arm. Every touch gave him excruciating pain. I
took him next morning to the doctor, who examined the
elbow, which was very red. He said no bone was broken,
but the arm was injured. It was suggested that he had
better go to St. Thomas's Hospital. He returned with his
arm neatly bound in splints (which, it was afterwards discovered, the artful scamp had cut out of two lesson-boards),
and an order duly drawn up that he was to go on the
morrow. This continued for a day or two, and at last he
brought an order in which the arm was described as in a
state of mortification. This aroused my suspicions; but
there was the order on the printed hospital form. I went
to the hospital, and had a sharp interview with the young
dressers. They knew nothing of the case. I returned to
the boy and told him to take his jacket off. He pretended
that it was impossible to move his arm; however, I stood
over him with a rope, and he took it off as well as I could.
There was nothing the matter with his arm. He had contrived this plot in order to spend a day or two with some
friends of his — publicans. He obtained the order by
going to the hospital, getting his blank ticket, and leaving
with it before he reached the surgeon's room. He had

been in prison many times, though he was only fourteen years of age.' *

This boy had probably learnt from his parents to tamper with hospital tickets, which have been grievously abused for purposes of begging. A wife, for instance, persuades her husband, for some trifling cause, to apply at a hospital, and begs an out-patient ticket for him; having got it, she begins her tour among the charitable and the credulous. 'Her husband is ill and out of work, a patient at such and such a hospital; he gets his medicine and attendance free, but the doctor says he must have plenty of nourishing food, and where is *she* to get that?' The hospital ticket endorses the tale, and help is generally freely forthcoming. To such an extent has this system been carried, that several hospitals adopt the plan of printing in red across the hospital form of admission,—'This ticket is not to be used for purposes of begging; any lady or gentleman to whom it is brought for that purpose, is requested to retain it.'

· To return to the child-mendicant. With all his 'cuteness, a little practice detects him. Mr. Jackson, to whom we have several times referred, was appealed to one morning by a lad, who gave himself out as William Jones.

'Where does your father live?'

'H'aint got none, Sir; died two years ago, come Michaelmas.'

* *Signals of Distress*, p. 149.

'And your mother?'

'Never knowed her, Sir; died soon after I was born.'

'Who do you live with?'

'Did live with grandmother, Sir, a bit ago, up Uxbridge way; but didn't see no opening there, so I stepped it.'

'Walked up to London?'

'Yes, Sir, mostly.'

'Well, take a sup of coffee now, and come and speak to me again to-morrow morning.'

'Ah! that's you, *Robinson*,' said Mr. Jackson the next morning, noticing whether the lad was startled by the *alias*.

Not at all—he is used to them, reflected the missionary. Jones is not his name, and probably his parents are living.

'Now then, my lad, sit down and have some breakfast. Here,' calling to his daughter, 'bring him some nice hot coffee.'

The coffee was brought, but, by previous arrangement with the daughter, it was in a pannikin with no handle. Too eager after the fragrant steaming beverage to set it down and wait, Jones, *alias* Robinson, bent his whole soul alternately to sipping his coffee and blowing his fingers.

Now was the time to ply him dexterously with questions.

'Let us see: you said your name was ——?'

'James Carter.'

'And your father and mother live—where?'

'Second turnin' to the left, —— Lane.'

He had committed himself hopelessly.   It was a case of a child absconding from home.

The vagrant disposition does sometimes manifest itself very early, where the parents are not to blame. There is a little thing now in Whitechapel Road, between seven and eight, whose parents, are kind, and its home respectable; yet the policeman is frequently bringing home the little truant, who seems to prefer any stall to sleep under, to its parents' roof.

These are some species contained in the 'genus Mendicant,' but the practical part of the vexed question remains,—'What must we do with him?'   All the instances we have related have tended to prove that charity has been abused; and is likely be so, because the mendicant is too often an ill-disguised rogue.   Is charity, therefore, to be restrained?   Is there no sense in which 'Give to him that asketh thee,' is still binding on Christian men and women? Are we to harden our hearts and say, 'No doubt this beggar is a lying impostor?'

We confess it is not at all in our thoughts to lower the demand on Christian charity, but to ask what it costs far more to give, than a few spare pence.   An example will best illustrate our meaning. 'In the early part of last winter a lady had just left her home on the Sunday morning on her way to church, when she was accosted by a crossing-sweeper, not far from Tottenham Court Road, who was re-

ceiving the coppers of those who patronized her
calling. The lady in question, however, was not
one of those who gave without ascertaining whether,
by so doing, she was relieving the distressed poor or
encouraging the idle and vicious. The girl had a
modest, interesting, and intelligent face, and the
lady determined she would not merely drop her
bounty and pass on, as many had done before her.
She stopped and spoke to the girl, inquiring where
she lived, and what were the circumstances which led
her to begin the life of a crossing-sweeper, one of
the most dangerous that a girl could follow. The
particulars she heard were as follows:—The father
was a carpenter; and a few years ago he and his
wife and three children went, to better their circumstances, to Canada. Before long his wife died;
this determined him to return to England. This girl
and a boy accompanied him; another girl was left
behind in service. More than a year ago the father
died, and the girl subsequently obtained a small
place at Norwood, where she remained until her
mistress left the neighbourhood. The mistress advised her to return to London: this advice was followed, and on her arrival in town she inquired for
and obtained a lodging with a poor but respectable
woman, until her money and clothes, except those
she wore, were gone. Not succeeding in procuring a
situation, she was compelled to leave that lodging.
An Irishwoman, who rented a cellar in Church Lane,
St. Giles's (one of the worst places in London for
vice and immorality), took compassion on her, and

allowed her for sixpence a-week to occupy a corner
of the cellar. Her appearance was now against her
getting another situation; her clothes were all gone;
those she wore were getting worse every day; neighbours advised her to buy a broom and take to a
crossing. It was a hard trial of feeling, but more
than that, where was money to come from to buy the
broom? The Irishwoman befriended her by advancing it, and the poor shame-faced girl took her
stand in the public street, and soon earned enough
to pay for the broom, comforting herself over her
uncongenial employment by saying,— 'Better this
than starve—far better than to beg or steal.' She
had now worked at the crossing nearly a week.

Such was her story. Now, what was this lady's
method of *giving*? She paid a visit in person to
Church Lane, St. Giles's, undaunted by its ill repute,
verified the girl's story, and found the cellar of
which she occupied a corner in a state words cannot
describe : such places must be seen to be believed.
Suffice it to say, that though the lady procured her
a place, and suitable clothing to appear in it as a
respectable servant, her short residence in the cellar
necessitated a long quarantine in a Refuge before she
could be sent to a clean and respectable family. She
is now well and strong, an intelligent, kind-hearted
girl, and truly valued in her excellent place. We
ask the reader to compare the careless dole of a few
coppers with this well-considered, self-denying aid,
and to say which best comes up to the spirit of the
precept — ' Give to him that asketh thee.'

We are well aware, however, that the cases are very limited in which the benevolent could thus sift, by personal investigation, the tale which is so ready in the mouth of the casual street-beggar. But do they know that that which they have neither leisure nor opportunity to do in person, they may do through the medium of a great and beneficent society, established in 1818—the Society for the Suppression of Mendicity? This Society issues to subscribers, tickets expressly intended for street beggars, whose cases on presentation of their tickets at the premises of the Society in Red Lion Square are examined into and tested. To every beggar the Society offers food and work.

We shall select from the interesting information on the Mendicity Society, furnished by Mr. Blanchard Jerrold,* such particulars as may satisfy the benevolent that through this medium they may safely gratify the impulse of their heart, to ‘ Give to him that asketh.’

The Society was set on foot to check public mendicity, with all its degrading results on the character of the beggar—by, on the one hand, putting the law in force against impostors who adopt begging as a trade, and, on the other, affording prompt and effectual assistance to those whom sudden calamity and unaffected distress may cast, in want and misery, upon public charity. It wages war against the rogue and vagabond, it gives to the deserving poor :—

* *Signals of Distress*, ch. iv.

' The house in Red Lion Square is a large and old-
fashioned one ; on the ground floor are the offices; behind
a covered yard, in which, on crowded days, applicants
wait; and at hand is the constables'. room. The constables (seven in number) are very important persons in the
transactions the examining clerks have with their customers. The kitchen department is roomy, and furnished
with long deal tables, at which the rations are distributed
and consumed. From 9 o'clock till 12, and again from 2
till 4, a constant stream of hungry and workless poor,
mixed with lying rascals who are neither very hungry nor
very poor, pours through the yard to the examining clerks'
offices, and thence, if deserving, through the kitchen, and
so on to the stone-yard, the mill, or the oakum-room.'

Care is taken to proportion the work to the
capacity of the applicant. Thus the disabled and
crippled are sent to the corn-mill or to the oakum-
rooms, while the hale and hearty men are sent to
break stones; but these last have, with their hard
work, double rations. The work hours are usually
from nine in the morning till six in the afternoon.

' In the office, where every applicant for relief is search-
ingly examined as to his antecedents and his present condition, are two most experienced gentlemen, one of whom
has been sifting the falsehoods of vagrants for the last
thirty years. Before him is a library of some thousand
volumes or more, in which the cases of begging impositions
and of apprehensions by the Society's constables are kept
and indexed—a veritable biographical encyclopædia of
beggary and imposture. When the applicant for relief
enters the room, he is asked his name and parish. The
practised hand is not at all embarrassed. If he believes the
old name will be remembered, he will give a fresh one;

but he often in this way overdoes it. When a man's
statement is suspicious, the officers can refer him back
from 10 to 20 years. Their records include (this was in
1863) 60,000 cases of begging impositions, irrespective of
the great begging-letter department.

'The Society is very careful not to meddle with cases
entitled to metropolitan parish relief; their object is not to
do parish work, but to clear the streets. A pauper having
any claim on a London parish is simply referred to the
overseers of that parish. Applicants who have resided for
some time in London, although they may have no claim
on a London parish, receive an order for six days' work.
While at work the pauper receives two meals a-day and
sixpence to provide lodging. A meal a-day is also given
to each member of the family; on Saturday, a shilling and
an extra meal to each. A single meal consists, in winter,
of a pint of nourishing soup with plenty of meat in it, and
a sixth part of a four-pound loaf of bread; in summer, of
the same quantity of bread and a quarter of a pound of
cheese (double Gloucester). When a man applies for relief with his wife and family, they are all put to work and
have all equal rations, so that they have often more than
they can eat. There is no end to the subtleties of vagrants.
The managers are compelled, when serving out rations to
a family of six, to cut the quartern loaf into six parts
before yielding it up, because, when they give a whole loaf
to a family, the parents would make off and sell it from
their children, probably to buy beer or gin.

'We have said, the ticket is given for six days' work.
On application at the end of the week, the order for work
is renewed; but at the termination of a month's employment the applicant is dismissed, unless the sitting manager
considers further relief necessary, when the case is laid
before the Committee, who renew the order, or give such
other relief as is most necessary to prevent the necessity of
street-begging. Tramps passing through London on their

way to the country have one ration given to them, and are
sent off. Should they return on the morrow they are set
to work before they are relieved. They cannot have a
second dip into the hundred-gallon cauldron of soup that is
boiling by steam below, before they have been to the stone-
yard or to the mill.'

The labour test is an invaluable feature in the
operations of the Mendicity Society, because it sifts
out the idle from the simply needy. As winter
comes on, hundreds of country people deliberately
crowd to the metropolis, with the idea of abusing
the charities of London. Flitting from Refuge to
Refuge, from Soup-kitchen to Soup-kitchen, they
contrive to live in idleness throughout the winter.
Here at last, in this old house in Red Lion Square,
the chain of imposture is broken, and the impostor
stands a very good chance of finding himself committed to prison as a rogue and vagabond.

Surely such an agency as is offered in this Mendicity Society goes far to meet our difficulty; by it
we can obey that which is at once a Divine command
and a humane instinct, without the risk of creating
a greater evil than that which we seek to relieve.

On the other hand, where personal investigation
can be made, and relief to cases found deserving
personally given, there is, no doubt, a two-fold advantage both to donor and recipient; we aim at more
than relieving misery, we want both to practise and
to awaken a feeling of human brotherhood: a handsome subscription to the Mendicity Society will put
the first within our reach, the responsive thrill of the

x

second is aroused by the going forth of our own heart to our brother-man, easing him of his burden by taking it in part on ourselves.

We have said that begging children awaken in the philanthropic, at the same time, deeper sadness and stronger hope.

Yes, hope—because they are dissatisfied with their condition and would like to change it. Experience has long proved, that while agencies only work from without on those who are passive and indifferent to their own degradation, little is to be expected; but once rouse in them the sense of shame—the desire for improvement—and they will more than meet you half-way: you have no longer to raise a dead weight, but to guide an impulse.

On the 14th of last February, some 200 of the wild and wandering boys of London were gathered together at the Queen-Street Refuge, by the promise of a supper. The object was to hear their own tale about themselves, and judge what possible steps could be taken for their benefit. Boys who heard of the treat made application for the tickets, and the officials of the various workhouses and night refuges were requested to mention it to boys whom they knew to be 'children of the streets.' The feast had been provided for more than 200, but in some cases, probably, wariness prevailed to keep them away, lest they should be caught and caged. Some did not understand how good the supper was to be, and had pictured to themselves gruel and bread.

A feast it certainly was for these destitute boys,

gathered round in their soiled and uncared-for rags and tatters, rather hanging about than covering their limbs. The general expression of their faces was of sharp curiosity and anxiety, but withal very forlorn and wretched. It had been ascertained that three-fourths of them were, in the strictest sense of the word, destitute. Imagine such seated round hospitable tables, and invited to the unwonted enjoyment of half-a-pound of good roast beef each, with a large roll, a pound of really good plum-pudding, and a pint of coffee!

Visitors found them ready to tell of their own mode of life:—'I sells fuzees and begs.' 'I holds horses.' 'I carry parcels.' 'Oh, I do anything.' 'Have you any parents?' 'No;' or 'Yes, but I don't know where they are.' 'I have a mother, and she drinks; she's on the streets, like me.' 'Where do you sleep?' 'In the workhouse or refuges, when I can — in the streets.'

Their meal being finished, the whole party proceeded upstairs, where a meeting was held. Lord Shaftesbury was in the chair, and addressed the boys thus:—

'My boys, I want to ask you two or three questions. I want to know a good deal about you. In this great town there are hundreds and thousands of boys, to my knowledge, who are wandering about in all directions, who have no houses, no place to sleep in, no father, no mother, many neither father nor mother, in the most miserable condition. We want to know a good deal about you: what you do? what you desire to do? *whether you would like*

to continue as you are, or not?   My belief is, that there is
*not a boy who would not be most glad to get out of it.   Is
that true?*

The chorus of assent was unmistakable, so earnest
was it, and general.

They were then assured that miserable, forlorn,
and neglected as they were, they had friends who
wanted them to do good, if they would only meet
the effort and do a great deal for themselves.   Lord
Shaftesbury put it to them, ' Whether, supposing in
the Thames there was a great ship, large enough for
a thousand of them, they would like to go there to
school to learn trades?'

Here again the responsive assent was general and
eager; but some prudently declined to answer for
their companions who were not present, for they said,
' Thieves, perhaps, would not go there.'

The idea thus thrown out by the noble Earl was
presented to the public five weeks later, in a letter,
signed by himself and Mr. Williams, Secretary to the
Queen-Street Refuge, to the following effect:—

' The information obtained at the supper given in the
Queen-Street Refuge to about two hundred of the wild and
wandering boys of London, on February the 14th, has
determined us to make an appeal to the public sympathy.

' There can be no doubt that the class is numerous, and
made up of lads varying in age from six or seven years up
to sixteen.   It is equally clear that they are the seed-plot
of a large proportion of the crime and violence that disturb
the peace and safety of the metropolis.

' Assuming the individuals assembled at the supper to
be fair samples of the entire body, and having aided our

judgment by the examination of several others, we have
come to the conclusion that a very great number have no
parents at all, that many have lost one parent, that many,
through the desertion or misconduct of their parents, have
practically no home, and that some few are mere truants,
who lead a roving life because they dislike domestic order.

'In any effort that may be made, great care will be
taken to distinguish between the deserving and undeserving
claimants.

'Their education is, of course, very low—amounting, in
truth, to almost nothing at all. The little that any of
them know has been acquired by short and irregular attend-
ances at Ragged Schools.

'Though in tatters and dirty, they enjoy a fund of
physical strength, far exceeding the health of those children
who live perpetually in close and filthy courts, and over-
crowded houses. Their intelligence is remarkable, and, so
far as we can form an opinion from the experience during
five weeks, of some 50 or 60 of these lads, they appear
desirous of instruction, and ready to submit to rule and
discipline if it be administered with kindness.

'We appeal to the public to aid us in a plan for the
recovery year by year of many hundreds of these young
castaways.

'We propose a " Home in the country," near London,
and a ship to be moored in the Thames. The Home in the
country would receive the lads of inferior health and less adventurous dispositions; the ship, those who might be trained
for emigration or a maritime career. By boating, sailing,
and teaching in the various departments of naval industry,
many might be qualified to supply the want of well-prepared
boys so generally felt by the commercial and royal services.*

* We thus learn that the Admiralty will receive into the
service lads trained in these proposed institutions. This is a
privilege from which, by a recent order, boys trained at Red Hill
and Feltham are excluded.

'We have obtained from the Admiralty the promise of a ship, on the condition of undertaking every expense both of adaptation and repair, and we hope to place it under a distinct sub-committee of experienced gentlemen, though directly connected with the Refuge in Great Queen Street.

'The lads would not be taken in at a lower age than ten, nor at a higher age than fifteen. Two years in some cases, and one year in others, of training, would be sufficient.

'The sum required to accomplish these purposes would be 3000*l*. for an outfit and a start in the work, with an annual income of 6000*l*. With this we could safely engage to have 400 boys always under training for service, and to dispose of 200 each year, and thus do something towards the abatement of this deplorable waste of physical and moral energies, and the conversion, God helping us, of what is now a scourge, into a positive blessing.'

To our vexed question, What shall we do with the child-mendicant? here is at least *one* practical suggestion by way of answer. What will the British public say to it? — it would be economical to take it up. An average of 15*l*. a-head is reckoned as the annual expense of each lad in these contemplated Institutions; whereas every professional criminal costs the country over 200*l*. before he is disposed of; to say nothing of the embezzlement of private property, which he cannot make good: 15*l*. for one year, 30*l*. for two, out of the resources of free-handed benevolence; or a charge of 200*l*. on Government; *alias*, an increase to meet it on rates and taxes. Self-interest is supposed to be a principle of very universal operation; may it be carried out in this instance to a legitimate conclusion!

But this is taking very low ground. We should grievously malign the British public if we supposed it incapable of responding to a less interested motive. From *ten to fifteen* these lads are to be admitted; it is the age on which the anxiety of parents in the upper classes is concentrated for their boys. The period of infancy, the sheltered home-life of early childhood, have passed by. There are rough places to be trodden; and the early-instilled principles must endure searching proof in a young boy's school-life. It is the age when character is forming; and the mould into which the mind is cast during those years of formation and growth, will probably shape it for life.

As far as parental love can throw its shield of protection over these dangerous years it will be done. The selection of a school, the choice of companions, the careful maintenance of home influence by a father's counsel, a mother's tenderness, a sister's friendship, all these will be anxiously considered; for the boy is loved and cherished, and should he go wrong, a whole family will mourn.

The child of the hall, and the child of the street, how sharply defined the line which separates them! what contrasts in their present surroundings and future prospects! Yet one common stock of humanity supplies one class and the other. In a national census the aggregate is made up without distinction of these strangely-differing units. Each is the responsible owner of an immortal spirit. All must die — all must live again — all must stand together at a great assize, where the question will not be, 'Rich or poor?' but 'Good or evil?'

We have no wish to obliterate the social distinction between the child of the hall and the child of the street. We do not look higher for the latter, than to see him become an honest working lad. Such an one needs not to hang his head ashamed before the first lord in the land. But give him the chance of becoming honest; do not leave him unheeded, unhelped, till his name turns up in the Police Court for some glaring offence, to which bad companions, or threatened starvation, have driven him.

At the Social Science Congress lately held in Edinburgh, it was stated that sixty per cent of the young London thieves, undergoing imprisonment, are the children of drunkards. Hence, the extreme importance of such plans as those of which we have spoken, and of the Reformatories generally, for withdrawing children from the influence and control of unworthy parents. A bad parent is the child's worst enemy. Mr. Wm. Gilbert * draws our attention to a curious distinction between the prejudicial effect exercised on a child by a drunken father, compared with that of a drunken mother:—

'The drunken father,' he says, 'generally ill-uses his son, frequently beats him brutally. Paternal affection dies within him, and he is totally indifferent to the actions of his child. If he hears he is arrested for a theft, it gives

* ' A Plea for Criminal Boys.'—*Good Words*, April 1866.

him no uneasiness—perhaps induces a feeling of satisfaction, as during the boy's imprisonment he will be relieved from the slight expense he is at in supporting him. He generally attends at the Police Court and gives his son a bad character, as being an incorrigible boy, utterly insensible to all the good advice and kind treatment given to him. Drink appears simply to brutalize man; in hardly any case do we hear of a drunken father encouraging his son to steal, or find him receiving any portion of the profits of his son's crime. He is indifferent to the result of the boy's course of life, but his evil influence is purely of a negative character.

'In the case of the drunken mother, however, it is very different. In woman, intoxication seems to absolutely reverse the natural maternal instincts, and even induces her to take an active part in the demoralization of her child. She generally leads him on, not by threats or compulsion, but by the external appearance of great kindness, till she acquires perfect control over the mind of the child. Unlike the man in his coarse brutality, she takes from the boy the whole of his plunder, repaying him with lavish caresses, sweetmeats, and other childish indulgences. No other plan would succeed. It would be impossible to frighten a boy into the commission of an act of dishonesty; severity would destroy the cool nerve required for its perpetration. This she knows full well, and with a woman's tact adopts the other course. It may be thought that this horrible statement cannot be true, but a visit either to the Middlesex Magistrates' Industrial Schools at Feltham, or to the Philanthropic Society's Farm-Schools at Redhill, would prove that, dreadful as it may appear, the fact is of very common occurrence.'

Mr. Gilbert goes on to describe the conduct of the drunken mother at the Police Court, where her

child is on trial, as the very reverse to that of the
father. ' Where such a woman's son is arrested, she
generally attends; gives him the best of characters,
as being a hard-working, industrious lad; and asserts that if he is sent to prison it will break her
heart. Her tears deceive all but the magistrate,
the policemen, and the reporters, who have looked
on the scene too often to see in it anything remarkable. After the committal of the boy she leaves the
court, and lives as she best can till the time of his
punishment has expired, when she attends to receive
him as he leaves the prison. Every blandishment
and caress is then heaped on him; he is taken
home and petted; and in a short time is again found
practising his former mode of life.'

We are ready to say, ' Can it be that parental
love is ever thus poisoned at its source; retaining the
form and semblance, only the more fatally to allure
and destroy? We would fain hope that the filial
affection for his mother, which is a remarkable characteristic in the young thief, is not thus vitiated,
but remains a simple, natural instinct, or may be
accounted for by the childish yearning to repose
confidence somewhere. Almost with his dying breath
a poor child, who died lately in the Redhill School,
mentioned his mother with intense affection, although
he had been committed nine times for crimes perpe-
trated at her instigation.

Let it be clearly understood, that in speaking of
fathers who are thus indifferent, and mothers who
are worse than indifferent to the moral ruin of their

'children, we are speaking not of parents in general among the poor, but of mendicant, drunken, depraved parents. The self-denying affection of honest working men and women for their children often puts our self-indulgence to shame. How often we are content with the pecuniary sacrifice which provides tutor, and governess, and nurses, and devolves upon others all the duties which call for any real effort! Mrs. Sewell well says : * —

'We make a great mistake if we suppose the daily struggle for daily bread has a natural tendency in itself to harden the heart ; on the contrary, it brings into action some of the finest principles of human nature.   Hard labour may destroy external grace and refinement, but roughness of manner is not synonymous with coarseness of nature ; and perhaps we all know that a base coarseness of nature does not unfrequently exist beneath a fine external polish.   The toil for needful bread is not so likely to harden the heart as the toil to be rich, because one is unselfish and the other selfish.'

Having thus guarded against misconstruction, we must repeat that the depraved parent is the child's worst enemy, the one from whom, above all others, he needs protection, if he is to be trained up to take his place as a useful and respected member of society.

It is, perhaps, not generally known under what conditions the State makes itself the guardian of children who are neglected by their parents ; we

* *Thy Poor Brother*, p. 144.

offer, therefore, some quotations from recent Acts of
Parliament.

The ' Industrial Schools Act of 1861' empowers
justices of the peace to send to any properly-certified
Industrial School, whose managers are willing to
receive it,—

Any child apparently under fourteen found
begging.

*   *   *   *

Any child apparently under fourteen found wandering, and not having any home or settled place of
abode, or any visible means of subsistence, or who
frequents the company of thieves.

*   *   *   *

Any child apparently under twelve who, having
committed an offence* punishable by imprisonment
or less punishment, ought, in the opinion of the
justices, to be sent to an Industrial School.

Any child under fourteen whose parent repre-

---

* 'To the honour of the Middlesex magistrates, they have
obtained a special Act of Parliament, by which young London
thieves can be sent to their Reformatory at Feltham, without
being first committed to prison. It would be impossible to
exaggerate the admirable effect this system has upon dishonest
children. The boy who has been once in prison is a very different
character, and is far more difficult to reform, than the one sent
direct to the Reformatory. It has also another excellent effect.
It prevents the drunken father from assisting in the conviction of
his son. In prison the boy is no expense to his parent, but in the
Reformatory the parent is obliged to contribute something to his
child's support, and he gains nothing by the punishment of the
latter. I am fully convinced, that if this system were practised all
over England, it would facilitate immensely the reformation of a
juvenile offender.'—*A Plea for Criminal Boys.*

sents that he is unable to control him, and who gives an undertaking to the justices, to pay the expenses of the child's maintenance.

* * * *

Children who have been previously convicted of felony are excepted from these provisions of the Act.

Pending the inquiry concerning any child (proposed to be thus dealt with), the justice may send him to the workhouse.

The justice is to specify the religious persuasion to which the child appears to belong.

The justice may make an order on the parent for paying the expenses of the child's maintenance, &c., but not beyond 5s. a-week.

By a subsequent Act, it is enacted that the Act of 1861 shall remain in force until the 1st of January, 1867.

The term of this Act is therefore nearly run out; the probability of its renewal must depend on the beneficial use made of its provisions.

Another Act, passed the following year, 1862 (the 25th & 26th Vict. c. cxliii.), provides for the education and maintenance of pauper children in certain schools and institutions.

It authorises the guardians of any parish to send any poor child to any school (which may be certified as the Act directs) whose managers are willing to receive it, and to pay out of funds in their hands for the maintenance, clothing, and education of the child, to an extent not exceeding the sum which

would have been charged for its maintenance in the
workhouse.

No child can be thus sent unless it is an orphan,
or deserted by both parents, or by its surviving parent,
or one whose parents or surviving parent consent.

No child above fourteen can be kept in the
school against its own consent. Under fourteen, it
cannot be kept there against the consent of its
parents or surviving parent.

No child can be sent to any school conducted on
principles of a religious denomination to which it
does not belong.

Such are some of the conditions under which the
State assumes guardianship over the forlorn and
neglected child, and compels the unworthy parent to
do that to which natural affection should prompt;
namely, to provide for his child till he is of age to
provide for himself.

To the father or mother without natural affection, the child is a simple burden and expense, of
which the selfish parent will rid himself by any
device in his power: thus we hear of infants born in
lying-in hospitals being sold by their unnatural
mothers to lady-visitors, for a consideration of one
or two sovereigns. Mrs. Sewell tells us that a woman
who spent her mornings in begging came to her one
day, and offered her child for acceptance: ' she
wished I would bring him up for my own; she
would not care to see him any more: he was a
beautiful little fellow.'*

* *Thy Poor Brother*, p. 31.

We are ready to welcome any agency, compulsory or voluntary, dependent on Government support or maintained by private benevolence, which rescues the London street-boy from a degraded home and vicious companions.

None of our readers can be ignorant that many such agencies exist; but it would be superfluous to do more than merely catalogue them, because in *Signals of Distress*, to which we have already several times referred, each is minutely described, as to its object, its origin, its mode of operation, and its progressive results, by the graphic pen of Mr. Blanchard Jerrold, after personal inspection and minute inquiry. The Institutions to which he introduces us are :—

The Boys' Home, Euston Road, for unconvicted, destitute boys. Mr. Jerrold's description is very engaging of the truly home-like and simple arrangements which obtain in this unpretentious establishment.

The Boys' Refuge, in Great Queen Street, for houseless boys, and in Broad Street, Bloomsbury, for the same class among girls.

The Boys' Refuge, Commercial Street, Whitechapel, for vicious and destitute boys.

The School of Discipline, Chelsea.

The Boys' Home, at Wandsworth, for criminal boys.

The Middlesex Industrial School, at Feltham, for the same class. Military order and discipline are distinguishing features of the establishment at Feltham.

The Reformatory Ship ' Cornwall,' off Purfleet.

The Industrial School, Constitution Row, Gray's Inn Road; a quiet little place, where no other than moral control is exercised over the boys.

The King Edward Ragged and Industrial Schools, Spitalfields, which hold out a hand to costermongers and weavers in their deep poverty, by providing education, recreation, and clothing for their children.

The Home in the East, at Old Ford, Bow, for criminal boys. It is a small private establishment, but is conducted on the same military system as that pursued at Feltham.

Such are the Homes and Refuges, and the good effected by them proves to demonstration that the moral poison instilled into a child in its earliest years may, by careful treatment, be neutralized. Boys are reclaimable: to use some sacred words, ' He that stole, may learn to steal no more; but to work with his hands, that he may have to give to him that needeth.'

Take one instance of a letter sent from a reformed criminal, who had emigrated, to the Chaplain at Red Hill. It was from a boy who was deemed irreclaimable. He belonged to a town in the midland counties, and had been six times convicted of robbery from the person, some of the cases presenting features of peculiar atrocity. When first sent to Redhill, he appeared as savage a young rascal as could possibly be found. A marked alteration was soon apparent in his behaviour. He became docile and industrious. He was taught the trade of a carpenter, and soon acquired a very considerable amount of skill at it. Last April (1865), the Rev. Mr. Walters received a letter from him. He stated that he liked the country extremely. The situation which had been provided for him he had kept since his arrival, and his master and mistress were both very kind to him, and paid him liberal wages, so much so that he had been able to put fifty pounds in the bank. The letter also contained a ten-pound note. Half the amount he requested might be sent to his sister, who was in bad circumstances, and *the remainder he wished to be spent in decorating the school chapel in which he had learned to be an honest man.'*

Quite the most anxious question which presents itself to devoted chaplains and masters of industrial schools, who have watched with intense interest the work of reformation progressing under their management, is this,—What is to become of their boys when the term of probation is over? The leper is now cleansed, but can he escape if he return to the polluting influences which before surrounded him? can he resist the associates, who are waiting for his term to expire, to welcome him back into the partnership of crime? The question is doubly anxious when it relates to the London boy. Two of the best solutions which seem to have been found, as yet, are —*an honest calling in London,* and *emigration.*

For the first, the Industrial Brigades afford an

---

* *A Plea for Criminal Boys.*

Y

invaluable opening. The Shoeblack Brigade was
the earliest; and the idea of importing to London a
practice already existing in the streets of Paris first
occurred to Mr. J. Macgregor, of the Temple, in the
spring of 1851, as offering a change of employment
during that Exhibition-summer for the boys who
frequented the Ragged Schools, which had been then
seven years in operation. Little did the originator
of the movement think that it would not only continue, but so prosper and increase, that in about ten
years from its commencement the annual earnings of
the Shoeblack Brigade would amount to between four
and five thousand pounds! Mr. Jerrold says truly:—
‘This is a large sum to be collected by blacking
boots in the streets. The dangers of the shoeblack's
calling are obvious. He is sent into the streets with
his brushes and blacking. He is uncontrolled; he
is a loiterer at street corners; his work is light and
fitful; he is his own master. A boy so placed is
likely to fall among bad associates, unless strong
incentives to good conduct are given to him. The
Ragged Shoeblack Society has undertaken to do this
work, and is doing it most successfully. It has
parted the boys into brigades, it has put them under
strong and salutary laws, and it has compelled them
to lay by a share of their daily earnings. A brigade
boy is watched; he must attend school, he must
account for his earnings every evening, and he must
be active at his duties. No boy is admitted who
has not been recommended by the superintendent of
some school in connexion with the Ragged School

Union. The boys are generally drawn from the class of hawkers, char-women, cab-drivers, dock-labourers, bricklayers, &c.'

Four or five shillings are considered a good day's work, but much depends on the station. By the Duke of Wellington's statue, opposite the Royal Exchange, is reckoned the best. Four boys stationed here can earn thirty shillings a-day between them. The three canon laws of the Society are,— 'Bring in all your money—keep to your station—spend Sunday properly.'

Limited space only allows us to mention that, encouraged by the very marked success which has attended the Shoeblack movement, another of a similar nature has been started, called the Rag-collecting Brigade; it commenced its work at the opening of 1862, and gives employment to three classes of boys—collectors, assistants, and sorters. For information as to this intelligent and thrifty scheme, as well as for fuller details of the Shoeblacks, we must again refer the reader to Mr. Jerrold. He thus closes his account of Industrial Brigades:— 'I cannot help thinking that more industrial brigades might be started. Why not news-boy brigades? messenger brigades? and why not a great central agency for the employment of boys?'[*]

A few words on Emigration must close our suggestions as to remedial measures for the child-mendicant and vagrant. Testimonies as to its good

[*] *Signals of Distress,* p. 217.

result, when it follows up a course of reformation
and good training at home, are not far to seek.
With very rare exceptions, boys sent out to the
Colonies from Industrial Schools do well, whereas
twenty-five per cent of those who remain in England
relapse into crime. Mr. Gilbert tells us,.that of fifty
boys, principally from Kent, Sussex, and Hampshire,
who, having passed through a Reformatory, emigrated to Canada and Australia, *not one turned out
badly*. On the contrary, they are much liked by
the settlers for their steady habits and superior
industry. The agent of the Redhill Schools, in
Upper Canada, writes home:—' All the boys you
sent me have turned out well, and are in high
favour; send me fifty more, and I will engage to
find situations for them in a week.'

The experience at the Wandsworth Home is of
the same kind: these reformed boys go out, and fill
with credit and honour responsible posts, as railway
clerks, schoolmasters and artisans. It is a good and
hopeful feature, that they retain a grateful feeling
towards the school or reformatory where they have
been trained in habits of honest industry. 'Most of
them,' says the Wandsworth Master, 'write every
month, and send me papers. They are pretty well
all over the world.'

Our Colonies have had something to bear in
being made the residuum for the depraved adults
of the mother-country; it will be cheering if we can
make it up to them by importations of reformed
boys.

CHAPTER IX.

THE SICK POOR IN LONDON WORKHOUSES * —— WHAT IS
AND WHAT OUGHT TO BE DONE FOR THEM.

F 'the poor shall never cease out of the land',
as we are taught in Scripture to believe,
then is it our bounden duty to provide for
them as best we may.   Under the Jewish dispensation the *duty* of so doing was clearly recognized in
the blessing pronounced on him 'that considereth
the poor:' but Christianity, taking still higher
ground, views it as *a privilege*, remembering His
words who said,—' Inasmuch as ye have done it unto
one of the least of these my brethren, ye have done
it unto me.'

Such a precept obtains peculiar emphasis when
Poverty, as too often is the case, appears with Sickness clinging to her skirts.   Then, indeed, the

---

* This chapter is contributed, at the author's request, by
W. H. Cook, M.D., Medical Officer to Hampstead Parish and
Workhouse.

suffering brother comes before us with an added claim upon our sympathy. We no longer stop to inquire if he be worthy, or what has brought him to this pass. It suffices that the hand of God hath touched him to establish a plea that may not be denied. First, then, let us inquire what is being done for him by those who are constituted by law his guardians: and speak, in the second place, of what ought to be done.

Its aspect, as one of the great questions of the day, cannot be gainsaid when we find peers and prelates united with members of the legislature, and laymen of all classes, under the influence of a common impulse, to investigate this matter, with a view to a remedy for its acknowledged evils. Should the medical profession, to whom, as a class, the evils of the existing system are best known, whose knowledge enables them more than others to appreciate their disastrous influence, and whose experience qualifies them to suggest their remedy, be the last to speak out on this occasion? Surely not, where the question admits of a practical reply.

Much harm has been done to the cause when the public ear has been startled by some complaint, louder than common, which has reached it from time to time, by the endeavour to fasten on some individual the blame which ought rather to be attached to the system itself. This has proved injurious, by diverting public feeling from the channel of reform, where its force was needed to wear

away the obstructing rocks of apathy and prejudice, on which many a useful project has been
wrecked.

The administration of relief to the poor, under
the regulations authorised by the Poor-law Board,
is systematic to a degree. On the first introduction
of this system, indeed, its promoters, as recently
stated by Sir J. K. Shuttleworth, were filled with the
most extravagant notions of the good that it would
accomplish. Thirty years ago he was one of the
Metropolitan Commissioners, and he admitted that
some of them at that time entertained the expectation
that it would almost eradicate pauperism from England.
They did not know, he frankly stated, that they
would have to be taught that generation must succeed
generation; that the question was mixed up with
the questions of public education, sanitary improvement, the general improvement of the condition of
the labouring classes, and many other important
questions, which were all embraced in the one great
subject to which their attention was directed. The
result of their experience may be read in the series
of admirable regulations issued from year to year by
authority of the Poor-law Board, which are no less
remarkable for the precision with which the duty of
each official towards the poor is set forth, and its
limits defined, than for the benevolence which is
inculcated in the carrying out of these instructions.
It is enjoined on all officials, that their conduct
towards the paupers should correspond, not so much
with what the habits and manners of this class ac-

tually are, as with what they ought to be.* Even with
regard to those punishments which the master of a
workhouse is directed to enforce in case of refractory
conduct, we find the same principle of thoughtful
tenderness mingled with severer discipline; as when
it is forbidden to punish a refractory child under
twelve years of age ' by confinement in a dark room,
or *during the night*.'†

' The fundamental principle with respect to the
legal relief of the poor is, that the condition of the
pauper ought to be, on the whole, less eligible than
that of the independent labourer. The equity and
expediency of this principle are equally obvious.
Unless the condition of the pauper is, on the
whole, less eligible than that of the independent labourer, the law destroys the strongest motives to good
conduct, steady industry, providence, and frugality
among the labouring classes, and induces persons,
by idleness and imposture, to throw themselves upon
the poor-rates for support. But if the independent
labourer sees that a recurrence to the poor-rates will,
while it protects him against destitution, place him
in a less eligible position than that which he can
attain to by his own industry, he is left to the undisturbed influence of all those motives which prompt
mankind to exertion, forethought, and self-denial.
On the other hand, the pauper has no just ground
for complaint if, at the same time that his physical
wants are amply provided for, his condition should

* Instr. Letter in Glen's *Consolidated Orders, &c.*, p. 145.
† *Consolidated Order*, Art. 136.

be less eligible than that of the poorest class of those who contribute to his support.'*

The absolute necessity for the maintenance of such principles as are set forth in the preceding paragraph becomes apparent when it is remembered that a very large class of deserving and independent poor can barely afford to pay out of their scanty resources the portion of the rates, trifling though it be, which falls to their share. One of the most painful duties devolving on the local magistracy is that of enforcing summonses upon this class, when professing their inability to meet the strictly legal claim of the collector of the rates. The number of such summonses taken out every year is both sad and startling, and shows, beyond dispute, how many are struggling on from year to year under circumstances of great discouragement, and meeting the privations attendant upon poverty with a noble resolve to do without the parish pay until driven to the last extremity. Those who advocate the amelioration of the condition of the pauper at the expense of the rates, are bound to respect the position of this large and struggling class, and to be very careful lest they impose a burden upon them which they may be unable to bear. Poverty and pauperism are like two adjacent tracts of territory; and those who make the aspect of the latter inviting at the expense of the former may, with the best intentions, defeat their own object, by impelling others over the border line.

* *Report of Poor-law Commissioners on Amendment of the Poor Laws*, p. 45.

Such are the principles which regulate the conduct of Guardians in their administration of local
relief; and it will be found, upon a careful examination of them, that the conscientious discharge of their
accepted function as Guardians of the Rates is not
always, as popularly supposed, inconsistent with their
duty as Guardians of the Poor. I know of at least
one Board where relief with a liberal hand is united
with painstaking discrimination of the merits and
necessities of individual applicants; and charity, in
the just recognition of the principles above set forth,
evinced alike by what is given and withheld. I know
of their large-hearted zeal to promote the comfort
and welfare of the suffering poor, and I have witnessed
their pleasure when these designs have prospered, as
well as their regret when baffled in repeated endeavours to carry out other much-desired reforms within
their house; such as establishing a distinction between
the deserving poor overtaken by misfortune, and the
improvident, if not guilty, inmates: and it is under
strong conviction of the duty of those entrusted with
responsibility in a special department to point out
existing abuses which escape a layman's eye, to those
with whom rests the power to amend them, that I
venture in these pages to record an earnest plea for a
class whose claim for separate consideration I believe
to have been hitherto, to a great extent, overlooked;
and seek to establish their case as exceptional, demanding separate consideration, and capable of
receiving it without infringement of the leading
principles for granting poor-law relief. In support

of these statements I refer, in the first place, to the
published Report of a Commission of Inquiry, promoted by the *Lancet* medical journal, which received
the following notice in a leading article of the *Times*
of 10th July, 1865 : —

' An inquiry is at this moment being conducted by our
contemporary the *Lancet*, which has an interest for a far
wider circle of readers than for the medical profession
alone. The whole public were roused to indignation by
the horrible revelations made in the two recent cases of
Timothy Daly and Richard Gibson. That such treatment of sick paupers should even have been possible was a
disgrace to our poor-law administration, and where the
extreme of mismanagement could reach such a height it
was impossible not to surmise that the ordinary management must be wholly defective. Our contemporary, therefore, was induced to initiate an immediate and independent
investigation, by two physicians, into the state of all the
Workhouse Infirmaries of the country. Their general
Report upon the Infirmaries of the metropolis, by far the
most important part of their subject, is already published.
They appear to have enjoyed every means of making a
satisfactory investigation. They were assisted as far as
possible by the Poor-law Board, they have been admitted
into every workhouse but one—that of the parish of St.
Margaret and St. John, Westminster, which, as might be
expected, bears no good character ; and, to their credit, the
officials of the workhouses have received them willingly,
and have given them every facility for obtaining information.
These advantages appear to have been used in a spirit of
fairness and moderation ; and as a collection of facts, inde-
pendently of the conclusions deduced from them, the Report
cannot fail to be of the greatest value. In some respects
we are glad to say the results of the inquiry are more.

satisfactory than might have been anticipated. Thus, with few exceptions, the quality of the provisions and wines in use is reported to be good ; the diet of the sick has been found on the whole to be liberal, and, in this respect, the Commissioners " have reason to believe that the notorious St. Giles's and Holborn cases are exceptional incidents. With their own eyes they have inspected the medical relief-books, and they can fairly say that the practice of the great hospitals is closely followed in the amount of nourishment and of wines given to the subjects of severe and exhausting disease." The prevalence of epidemic diseases in workhouses is said to be now chiefly a thing of the past, as the practice of sending patients with contagious diseases to special Hospitals is becoming almost universal.

' These, however, are the only favourable features which we can observe in a most moderately-written Report. Everything else is more or less unsatisfactory. Thus we are informed, that only a third of the existing buildings. are fitted either by their site or their construction for the treatment of the sick, and one class out of three " is entirely improper as a residence, either for the sick or even for the able-bodied." In some few of the new houses the construction is said to be satisfactory, but the great majority of the older houses are constructed without any regard to the requirements of the sick. The sick wards are in some cases mixed up with the body of the house ; in other cases they are hot low rooms in the roof. Even the insane are not separated from the other inmates. It is true that acute and chronic cases of lunacy are sent away as soon as possible, but this does not prevent the unfortunate lunatics from being detained in rooms wholly unfitted for them ; and during the few critical hours at the commencement of their malady, in which the possibility of its cure is frequently determined, they are fed with the ordinary rough diet of the house, and are wholly unprovided with the special nutriment required by their position. The wards are almost uniformly insufficient in size, and if the sick ward happens to be above the average the other wards are sure to suffer. In addition to these disadvantages, the infirmary is sometimes surrounded by offensive trades, and in one case, that of the Strand Union, the Guardians have perversely created a nuisance of their own accord. The infirmary is situated in the centre of the grounds, and the Guardians have positively established and carried on for years a large carpet-beating business, which is transacted in the yard immediately below the windows of the sick wards. The business brings in a round sum every year, and for the sake of this the patients are choked with the dust and tortured with the perpetual noise of the carpet-beating. The interior management of the wards is the worst feature of all; and there are facts detailed in this part of the Report more fit for the columns of our contemporary than for our own, which show that the filth and neglect brought to light in the two recent cases are by no means exceptional. In fact, in regard to cleanliness the Commissioners confess themselves "horrified," and any ordinary reader who will peruse this part of the Report will be still more horrified than the Commissioners. Lastly, the miserable system of pauper nursing still prevails to a large extent, though the plan of paid nursing is being "cautiously" adopted.

' In short, it is evident from this Report that, whether as to construction, arrangement, or administration, the infirmaries of many workhouses are absolutely unfitted for the treatment of the sick. Nor is this anything more than might have been anticipated. The treatment of the sick has never been contemplated as a principal feature in the office of a workhouse. The prominent idea has been to provide, at the least possible expense, a bare shelter for idle vagabonds or for the absolutely helpless and infirm.

The sick ward is an addition, and almost an excrescence on the general plan. Nothing can show this more completely than the position of the doctor in a workhouse. He is practically treated as a subordinate official, inferior even in rank to the master, and he receives an almost nominal salary for the performance of duties which it would be impossible for him adequately to discharge, even if he gave up his whole time to them. In infirmaries comparatively well managed, for example, we are told of one surgeon, assisted by one resident junior, being expected, in addition to a private practice, to look after 300 acutely sick and 600 chronic cases; and, again, of one medical officer having to attend to about 130 acute and 200 chronic cases. Their salaries, it must be remembered, are stinted on the express understanding that they may supplement them by private practice; they are still further curtailed by the miserable system of requiring them to provide their own drugs; and, in addition to all this, the surgeons are engaged in a perpetual battle with the prejudices and the selfishness of the Boards of Guardians.

' The Guardians are, in all probability, not the only persons who have hitherto failed to appreciate the extent of the evil involved in such a state of things. There is no one, indeed, with common humanity of feeling who will not be at once grieved and indignant at the ill treatment of the sick poor which we have sketched, but it is not every one who will be aware that by such mismanagement a workhouse is neglecting the most important of its functions. It is, however, a mere fact of statistics, that the treatment of the sick is the principal office which a workhouse has to discharge. The sick and infirm are by far the largest class with which as a rule the workhouses have to deal. In fact, a vast amount of the pauperism of the country is simply so much sickness. When we are startled

to hear that there is one pauper to every twenty of the
population, it should be remembered that perhaps not less
than 3 or 4 per cent of this so-called pauperism is simply
disease. Sickness, in truth, is the poor man's curse. With
the best intentions and the greatest industry he is necessarily in many cases living but just above the world, and
let him only be laid up by sickness for six weeks or two
months, and he is on the verge of pauperism. It will be
evident from this point of view, that in thus neglecting the
sickness of the poor the Guardians are false to their mere
pecuniary interests. In numbers of cases, if the head of a
family were carefully and generously tended in his sickness,
he might recover and support both himself and his family
for the future, whereas if his illness is allowed to become
chronic they become a permanent burden on the rates.
Every workhouse is in fact a hospital, and ought to be
treated as a hospital. If this were recognised we believe
the medical profession, and through them the public at
large, would gain as much as the poor themselves from
having these vast stores of experience placed at the disposal
of medical schools. By such a plan the poor would receive
the same devoted and skilful attention as they receive in
our regular hospitals; such neglect as has recently shocked
us would be absolutely impossible, and the medical profession would be immensely benefited. Such, at all events,
is the prospect suggested by this opportune Report, and
we are satisfied that its suggestions deserve careful consideration.'

The general principles upon which hospitals for
the sick should be constructed and upheld, are set
forth in a lucid statement, on the highest medical
authority, which will be found at page 353. In
contrast to this, the Report of the *Lancet* Sanitary
Commission states that,—

'The present workhouse system is a thing of shreds and patches, which has slowly grown up to its present form, with all manner of miscellaneous additions and alterations from time to time; and the buildings in which the in-door paupers are housed, together with all the arrangements for their care, partake of this patchwork character. Originally, no doubt, the workhouses were designed principally for the custody of sturdy, ne'er-do-well vagrants, whose pauper tendencies required to be discouraged; and the necessity of providing for the genuinely sick and feeble was an afterthought, an appendage to the main scheme (ignoring the leading feature of providing for the sick and infirm poor). But whatever may be the case in some country districts, it is undoubtedly the fact, that in metropolitan workhouses at present the really able-bodied are enormously inferior in numbers to the sick; for the inmates of the sick-wards proper form but a small proportion of the diseased persons in every London workhouse. Multitudes of sufferers from chronic diseases, chiefly those of premature old age, crowd the so-called "infirm" wards of the house, and swell the mortality which is a melancholy characteristic of these establishments. Examples are not uncommon in which the really able-bodied form but a fourth, a sixth, or even an eighth of the total number of inmates. The fate of the "infirm" inmates of crowded workhouses is lamentable in the extreme; they lead a life which would be like that of a vegetable, were it not that it preserves the doubtful privilege of sensibility to pain and mental misery. They are regarded by the officials connected with the establishment as an anomalous but unavoidable nuisance. They get neither the blessings of health nor the immunities and the careful tending which ought to belong to the sick.

'The sooner that we frankly acknowledge that these "infirm" persons are, in the great majority of instances,

patients, demanding a strict attendance, and not a mere
perfunctory medical supervision, the better will it be for
society—yes, and even for the ratepayer's pocket.   If, as
we assert ought to be the case, all the infirm were medically
treated, there would be a very large per-centage of recovery, and, consequently, an important saving of the rates.

'It must be well understood, however, that the existing
medical officers are not responsible for the insufficient care
bestowed upon the less acute cases under their charge.   It
will suffice to point to the numbers of patients nominally
assigned to each workhouse doctor, to make it evident that
the evils we complain of are unavoidable in the present
state of the arrangements.   The contrast between the
working of the hospitals supported by voluntary contributions and that of the workhouse infirmaries suggests the
idea that a *diable boiteux,* who could unroof those cham-
bers of the British heart in which the charitable sympathies
are lodged, would see strange things.   How comes it that
the public (and, for that matter, the profession too) have
nearly ignored these *real hospitals of the land,* while
lavishing princely munificence on the splendid institutions
which ostensibly supply the national hospital requirements ?
There may be all kinds of difficulties in the way of re-
formers who would remove this scandalous inequality in
our treatment of two classes of the sick poor; but they
clearly belong to the difficulties which must be overcome.
We have allowed a number of establishments to grow up
in the external semblance of hospitals for paupers; but in
truth the whose business is a sham, a mere *simulacrum* of
real hospital accommodation.   Our voluntary hospitals can
but lightly touch the surface of the wide field of London
misery.   The eighteen in London provide 3738 beds ; but
the metropolitan workhouses provide beds for 7463 sick,
and nominally for about 7000 "infirm," but in reality to
a much larger number of the latter.   This circumstance is
deeply interesting in more than one aspect.   Not merely are

z

the public, as ratepayers, falsely pretending to supply
proper medical treatment and nursing to a number of persons,
whom, in fact, they neglect and mismanage, but they allow a
mass of most valuable materials for the clinical instruction
of medical students to lie unused. With proper management, what magnificent clinical hospitals might our workhouse infirmaries become! and how greatly would the
patients benefit from the attendance of students, with sharp,
prying eyes! Let us add, that there is one special way in
which the clinical materials of the workhouse infirmaries
might be utilized, with the greatest possible advantage to
science and to the public; namely, by affording opportunities
for the practical study of the chronic forms of insanity :
for these establishments contain an immense number of such
cases, which at present are completely lost to the service of
medical science.'

With reference to the general character of the
buildings containing the sick in the metropolitan workhouse infirmaries, the Report goes on to state:—

'Looking at the infirmaries as vast district hospitals,
we remark, in the first place, that their distribution is in
several instances unnatural and inconvenient, as in the case
of St. Luke's, Middlesex, which is in close proximity with
the Shoreditch house, and Hackney with East London. But
the defects in this respect are as nothing when compared
with the serious evils attendant upon the site and construction of many of them. These evils are often so great
(especially in the older houses, which have, as it were, slowly
grown up to their present state), that we are obliged to
make a preliminary separation into three classes, according
to the degree of these demerits. In the first class we shall
place a certain number of the very worst houses as to situation, construction, &c., which in our opinion are entirely
improper as residences, either for the sick or even for the able-

bodied. In the second we shall enumerate those which might answer the purposes of receptacles for chronic disease and infirmity, after certain necessary improvements. And in the third we shall place those infirmaries which possess a really good situation, and are so far built upon the main principles of scientific hospital construction, that they might be developed into first-rate hospitals, capable of serving all the needs of large districts, for the treatment of the more important and acute diseases, both surgical and medical.

'Perhaps the worst fault in workhouse arrangement for the sick is the practice of mixing up the sick-wards with the body of the house; and where, from the construction of the building, this cannot be helped, such buildings ought to be condemned as regards their use for infirmary purposes. It is this (amidst many other organic defects) which gives the finishing touch to the repulsive picture which Clerkenwell presents to those who visit its wards for the first time. A life more dreary and unhealthy than that of the so-called able-bodied inmates of this house (although they are treated with zealous kindness and care by the officials), it is difficult to imagine; and, on the other hand, there is a total absence of that decent quiet and privacy which any one used to a well-appointed hospital feels to be a first necessary for patients. The evils of narrow, cramped staircases (so built as to admit the minimum of air to the buildings), and of a number of stories piled one above another, are common to nearly all the older houses. These evils exist in St. George's-in-the-East, Charles Street, Old Gravel Lane, where, notwithstanding the fact that there are some excellent wards for old men, there are some extremely objectionable ones for sick and infirm women in the roof, the heat of which during our visit was oppressive. In addition to these evils, the sick and infirm are scattered all over the house. In speaking of "roof-wards," we cannot fail to condemn

several we saw at Greenwich, which with a little expense
might be much improved. One of the most objectionable
features which can distinguish a hospital is the immediate
surrounding, and especially the overlooking of it by houses
of a low class, or by premises where offensive trades are
carried on. St. George the Martyr is surrounded by bone-
boilers, grease and candle manufactories, and—not the least
evil—by a nest of ticket-of-leave-men, whose associations
prove a moral pest. Instances of this fault are also offered
by Clerkenwell, St. James', Westminster, and the Strand.
St. James', Westminster, is a very flagrant offender in
this way. Its premises are closely backed, and in many
cases overlooked, by buildings on nearly their entire
boundary; and, worst of all, the offending structures,
which totally impede any free currents of air through the
area of the workhouse, are in many cases the property of
the parish. But the climax is reached in this respect by
the Strand Union House. Here the premises are closely
environed on three sides by workshops, a timber-yard, and
a range of mews; but inasmuch as the buildings chiefly
occupied by the sick do stand somewhat separated in the
central portion of the grounds, the very demon of mischief
must have put it into the heads of the Guardians to raise
a nuisance of their own to supplement those of the neighbourhood. Accordingly, they have positively established,
and carried on for years, a large carpet-beating business,
which is transacted in the yard, *immediately below the
windows of the sick-wards*. In vain does every sensible
and humane person who hears of this circumstance remonstrate with the Board. That body is deaf to all considerations, except the money value of the trade, which
puts fully 600*l*. a-year into the pockets of the parish: so
the patients continue to be choked with the poisonous dust,
and stunned with the perpetual noise, of this carpet-
beating.

' There are many of the London workhouses which

SICK POOR IN LONDON WORKHOUSES.   341

are liable to much overcrowding, beyond the limits even
of the very moderate allowance of space insisted on by the
Poor-law Board: for instance, the Strand, where (although the two " upper sick-wards" have an allowance of
748 cubic feet to each bed) the general run of infirm and
sick-wards have an average of only 450 cubic feet; and
St. Pancras, where, in winter-time, it has been a common
practice to fill the already too-crowded wards to over-
flowing, by actually putting people to sleep on the floor in
the middle of the room.   And, practically, it is no doubt
the case, that all those workhouses which represent thickly-
populated districts are liable to this abuse.

    ' We turn from one evil to another, and it seems as if
they get worse at each step.   The classification of the
sick in all the workhouse infirmaries belonging to our first
and second classes is most inefficient and improper.   And
here it is not worth while to waste many words in proving
that which a single fact will make abundantly clear and
certain — the fact, namely, that the insane are not separated from the body of the house.   At most there are insane wards; in and out of which, however, the patients
pass, and mingle freely with the general patients.   At
Clerkenwell, indeed, it is true that the male and female
insane are guarded apart in two dismal wards, where, as
far as can be seen, they have no earthly occupation, except
that of moping; but even here the imbeciles pass freely
into the body of the house.   Now it is true that the insane patients in workhouses are for the most part chronic
cases, and that dangerous lunatics are sent away as soon
as possible; but, as a matter of fact, we have ascertained
that a considerable number of cases of acute mania are
retained in the house from four to ten days, owing to
difficulties about the forms of removal.

    ' This was especially noted at Chelsea, where there is
no padded room, nor any provision (beyond the ordinary
receiving-room) for the temporary seclusion of even the

most violent lunatic ; and where there are also about thirty
chronic insane patients, who wander in a melancholy, ob-
jectless manner, about the house and the yards.   The condition of imbeciles in London workhouses is a deeply painful subject, when we think of the great amelioration of
their wretched state, which might be afforded by physicians wielding the resources of a competent establishment.
It is quite an oasis in the desert when, as at Marylebone,
Newington, and some other houses, we find a garden with
swings, bird-cages, and rabbit-hutches, for the amusement
of these poor creatures, and a number of pretty pictures
pasted upon the walls of their day-room.   And to revert
to the acute lunatics who are from time to time admitted,
we must repeat that it is by no means true that they are
all immediately sent away : so far from that, they are often
retained for just those three or four early days in the history of mania, during which the curability or incurability
of the case is so frequently decided.   In the following case
there was too much reason to fear that we witnessed treatment which was almost certain to put recovery out of the
question.   Being shown into the seclusion-room of a workhouse which is, on the whole, rather well-managed, specially medically, we found an unfortunate woman wandering up and down in a state of mingled phrenzy and ex-
haustion, and were told she had been admitted four days
previously, and had certainly had no sleep *since then*.   On
inquiry, we found she had all this time been kept *on the
house diet*.   It is needless to say that, practically, none of
this coarse food had been consumed, or that the absence of
proper and repeated feeding at short intervals was admi-
rably fitted to render such a case hopeless.   So far has the
disdain or neglect of proper classification been carried, that
even contagious fevers of the most dangerous type have in
some houses been freely mixed (till quite lately) with other
patients, in wards containing not more than 500 cubic feet
to each bed.'

The Report next treats of the character of the sick-wards:—

' The first consideration of importance is that of the form of the wards. In this respect there are great variations, but the long rectangular shape prevails, more especially in the older houses ; most of the wards in which contain a considerable number of beds, from fourteen up to twenty-four or thirty, and in a few cases larger numbers than these. Two rows of opposite windows are found in the wards of nearly all the new houses ; and in such wards there is plenty of light, and the opportunity for considerable ventilation. But in many of the older houses there is only one row of windows, and both light and ventilation are therefore interfered with. The basis of good ventilation in hospitals must doubtless always be the provision of sufficient cubic space for each patient ; and this is greatly below the mark in almost every case. No one with any knowledge of hospital requirements as they are now understood, would dream of constructing wards for the treatment of acute disease with a less allowance than 1000 or 1200 cubic feet to each patient ; and for the treatment of fevers it is well known that a much higher proportion of space is requisite. What is the case with regard to our metropolitan workhouse infirmaries ? We turn to Mr. Farnall's Report, and we find that in five infirmaries the allowance of cubic space for the sick, both male and female, is below even the wretched standard hitherto sanctioned by the Poor-law Board, namely, 500 feet ; that in several others the whole average cubic space, either on the men's or the women's side, is below this mark ; and that in all but a small minority, *some* of the wards transgress to this extent the laws of hygiene.

' The practice of painting the wards half-way·up with hideous drab, and finishing them off with glaring whitewash, is still, barbarous though it be, nearly universal ;

and the relief to the eyes and the mind which would be afforded by a few cheap engravings or coloured prints is withheld in all but a few infirmaries. Passing to matters more directly affecting the patients, we have to report that the bedsteads on which they lie are nearly always proper iron ones, and in the great majority of instances they appear to be of sufficient length, *provided that other arrangements correspond.* In the Lewisham house, in many cases the bedsteads are double, with a wooden separation, giving barely two feet in width for each occupant; whilst, as a rule, the beds are but five feet long. In St. Pancras we found that the great majority of the bedsteads were only five feet eight inches long. But these were exceptional instances. It is of little use, however, having the bedstead long enough, if the bed be too short, and we have to mention that in nearly half the infirmaries this was the case. In one house the beds are nearly all of them eighteen inches shorter than the six-feet bedsteads, and nothing surprised us more than the entire unconsciousness displayed by the officials of the great discomfort which such a state of things must cause. But the crucial test, after all, of good ward-management, is the amount of attention bestowed on *cleanliness;* and, on this point, we confess we have been fairly horrified. Some readers will be startled. There is (to the superficial observer) rather a special air of *bescrubbedness,* rather a powerful odour of soap and water, about the wards of workhouse infirmaries. So much for the surface; now for the inside of the cup and platter. In several infirmaries, the nurses of one or more wards admitted, with very little compunction, that the bed-ridden patients habitually washed their hands and faces in improper utensils. Only in one instance, that of Lambeth, did we find a separate hand-bason for each bed-ridden patient; and even here the lavatories for the comparatively convalescent are not what they should be. Only at the new Stepney Workhouse Infirmary, and

one or two others, did we observe proper bath-rooms in
anything like sufficient numbers attached to the sick-
wards. The supply of towels is often most inadequate.
The flock-beds on which the patients lie, in the great
majority of infirmaries, are very unsatisfactory and comfortless. Flock is a nasty material in itself; and we are
informed by the master of the Paddington Workhouse,
that horsehair (which he has introduced at his establishment) is not only more comfortable, but, in the end, more
economical. When a flock-bed is carelessly made up with
too little material, it soon works into a series of uncomfortable knobs. We are glad to notice the liberality which
at Wandsworth and Richmond supplies each patient with
a bed *and mattress.* Pillows should be far more plenti-
fully supplied than is usually the case. Easy chairs for
convalescents are particularly wanted.'

The next feature touched upon claims especial
attention. On the system of nursing which prevails
in these establishments, the Report proceeds thus:—

' On this subject most interesting information has been
supplied by Mr. Farnall's return, which shows the extent
to which the principle of paid nursing has taken root, and
the amount and kind of pauper nursing which supplements
it, or stands instead of it in the various infirmaries. We
regret that we cannot afford space to reprint it at large,
because we have so much to state by way of commentary.
Suffice it to say, that one by one the various Boards of
Guardians are giving a cautious assent to at least a partial
trial of the plan of paid nursing, and that the infirmaries
which are at present supplied with more than one paid
nurse are as follows:—Marylebone (14 nurses, total salaries 250*l.* per annum); St. Pancras (16 nurses, 280*l.*);
St. Margaret and St. John, Westminster (3 nurses, 46*l.*);
Stepney (3 nurses, 85*l.*); Lambeth (4 nurses, 145*l.*);

Paddington (2 nurses, 55*l.*) ; Mile End Old Town (2 nurses, 50*l.*) ; City of London (3 nurses, 83*l.* 8*s.*) ; Bethnal Green (2 nurses, 48*l.*) ; Clerkenwell (2 nurses, 23*l.*) ; Whitechapel (2 nurses, 42*l.* per annum). There are fourteen other houses which employ each one *bonâ fide* paid nurse, besides two or three which employ an assistant matron in that capacity.

'Upon the general question of paid as against pauper nursing, we feel ourselves competent to pronounce a decided opinion. After listening attentively to the most conflicting arguments, not only from laymen, but also, we are bound to say, from workhouse surgeons, we have examined for ourselves the working of the two systems respectively, and we may state that the evidence of facts coincides, in our opinion, very positively with the feeling which is most widely prevalent among those who have had real workhouse experience, that the employment of a full staff of thoroughly trained paid nurses offers the only possibility of a thorough and genuine performance of duties which are at present most perfunctorily discharged. We have no wish to make " sensation" statements against the pauper nurses. But, in the first place, it is notorious that the majority of them are aged and feeble, and past work, or have strong tendencies to drink, and in many cases have otherwise led vicious lives. Even those workhouse officials who on principle oppose the employment of paid nurses, allow that, as a rule, there is no managing pauper nurses, except by confining them strictly to the house— a *régime* which must undermine their health, and unfit them for their work. Secondly, their inefficiency is borne out by the character of their ward work, as to the details of cleanliness, &c., and also by the universal testimony of those benevolent persons who have visited the workhouses in a philanthropic spirit, and have been taken into the confidence of the patients ; which testimony asserts, that in the great majority of cases pauper nurses can only manage their patients by inspiring fear, and that their conduct is consequently often brutal. Their antecedents are such that the patients do not respect them.*

'There is a solution of the difficulty of procuring really good paid nurses, which, however distant, lies plainly before us, and to which we entertain no doubt that the authorities must ultimately resort.   In the district suburban schools, to which the workhouse children are now almost universally drafted off at an early age, there are immense numbers of girls daily growing up to a healthy womanhood, under good physical and moral influences.   What worthier means of completing their emancipation from the inherited curse of pauperism could be devised than the training of them to the respectable and truly dignified calling of skilled nurses?   Surely, by means of the teaching of some of the nursing institutions, these girls might (save for the one pecuniary difficulty of maintaining them during their probation) be readily converted into first-rate nurses, upon condition of their agreeing to serve the infirmaries of the workhouses for a moderate but sufficient stipend.   We may state that this idea originated with Mr. Farnall, who has already made progress—and we may add our earnest wish that he may never let it drop, but persevere amid all difficulties—in bringing it to a successful development in practice.

'There is an aspect of nursing which bears so powerfully on the question of paid *versus* pauper nurses, that we must dwell on it for a moment: we refer to the duty of night-nursing.   It is well known by all hospital physicians and surgeons that it is most difficult to secure the efficient

* The writer is bound to express his conviction of the truth of these statements.   He once visited a workhouse where he found a man ill with fever attended with acute delirium, alone in the ward with two men, placed there to tend him, *both* of whom were *absolutely deaf*.   They had secured their patient with bands to the iron bedstead.

performance of this work, and that nurses of a low *morale* are totally unfit to be trusted with it. At present, the mode of its performance or non-performance in our work-house infirmaries is one of the gravest scandals attaching to these institutions. In our investigations we have almost uniformly failed to obtain any satisfactory account of the behaviour of paupers as night-nurses, while we have re-ceived a great deal of positive evidence of their gross neglect of that sort of duty. If pauper night-nurses are to be employed, nothing short of the perpetual supervision of a vigilant head night-nurse (paid and skilled) could ever keep them up to their work; and nothing will make them quite safe and reliable, especially if they be taken at random for the occasion from the "able-bodied" inmates of the house, since in that case they are nearly always either decrepit or unprincipled.'

Then, as regards provisions and cooking:—

'With regard to the quality of the provisions supplied to the sick paupers we have little to say, and that little is generally satisfactory. The food and drink (except the port wine in some cases) of all kinds appears to be usually of good quality, when expressly ordered for sick persons; and it is only as regards the house diet, which is supplied to the infirm in most cases, that we have to complain at all seriously.'

On the subject of the dietaries established in the workhouse infirmaries, we read:—

'With regard to the diet and extras of the sick, we are free to confess that we cannot perceive any just cause for serious fault-finding on the whole. It is usually the doc-tor's fault if he do not, by vigorous assertion of his own position, obtain any necessary concessions from the guardians; and we have reason to believe that the notorious St. Giles's and Holborn cases are exceptional incidents. With our own eyes we have inspected the medical relief-books, and we can fairly say that the practice of the great hospitals is closely followed in the amount of nourishment and wines given to the subjects of severe and exhausting disease.'

Speaking of the medical officers of the infirmaries, the Report proceeds to say:—

'In the first place, we must declare our opinion, that under the present system the medical officers are habitually placed in an entirely false position, by having twice or three times as many persons under their nominal charge as they can possibly do justice to. We regret to say, also, that the enormous overwork thrown upon the medical men renders it in most cases impossible for them to give their attention to many details of hospital management which every medical officer should study. Taken as a body, the medical officers of the metropolitan workhouse infirmaries apply themselves with a zeal and an amount of success to their disproportioned tasks which are surprising; and it must not be forgotten that they have, in most cases, not only to perform most arduous professional duties and a large amount of desk-work, but that they have to fight the battle of the poor, with terrible earnestness, against the prejudices and gross material interests of the worst members of their boards of guardians. All honour to the more enlightened and disinterested guardians, whose ears are open to truth, and justice, and humanity! But let us try to picture to ourselves a Board of Guardians who allow stonebreaking to be carried on in their workhouse-yards, who could with difficulty be restrained from dressing the unfortunates in their house in a quasi-convict dress of violently contrasted colours, and from setting up beds for

their young, unfallen girls, in close proximity to those
very fallen creatures (so degraded, that it seems there was
no harm in insulting them) ; and whose wilful neglect to
build a properly isolated dead-house for their parish has
long exposed the poor of a crowded district to frightful
sufferings and risks of disease.

'With regard to the remuneration of the medical
officers, we are of opinion that, in the first place, it is in
most cases insufficient, not only for the amount of work
nominally given them to do, but even for a smaller amount
than they can actually execute. The requirement that
drugs shall be found by the surgeon is so gross an abuse,
that we need do no more than emphatically endorse the
general condemnation of it. Were this evil once removed,
it seems to us that the next object which ought to be accomplished is that of raising the respectability and dignity of
the surgeon's office ; for instance, to allow him a proper
dispenser, to relieve him of the mechanical labour of com-
pounding his medicines, and by taking other measures to
inspire in his mind the sense that he is occupying the
gravely responsible post of a hospital medical officer.
These reforms are urgently needed; but Parliament ought,
further, to give the surgeons their appointments for life,
and at a higher money-rate, which should be paid out of
the Consolidated Fund.'

Respecting the prevalence of epidemic disease,
from time to time:—

'The history of the epidemics, which have at times
fastened upon the metropolitan workhouses, would be most
interesting could it be worked out in detail; but it is fair
to say it is now chiefly a thing of the past. The great
curse of workhouses has been the liability to the introduction of typhus-fever from thickly-crowded districts; but
recent events have made the dangers of promiscuous mix-

ture of these cases with other patients so obvious, that the
practice of sending them to the Fever Hospital is becoming
nearly universal.'

On the subject of the mortality, average and
special:—

'The average mortality of the metropolitan workhouses is very high. It is obvious that the enormous
majority of deaths are from causes which induce debility
—such as old age and want (combined often with long-
standing, hopeless disease), the congenital feebleness of
strumous infants, &c. The influence of zymotic disease
upon the mortality is never very large, except from some
special circumstance. Indeed, the only instance in which
it strikes us that the mortality is to any considerable extent preventable is with regard to the infants. It is notorious that an enormously high proportion of infants born
in the workhouse soon die; and we have come to the conclusion that the unhealthy situations of the nurseries, and
the want of supervision of the supplementary food, has
much to do with this. So great is the abuse of arrowroot
and other starchy food in some houses, that we are sure
the greatest harm is done by the use of this improper nutriment for young infants. The extraordinary benefit of
wine also in many infantile cachectic conditions is almost
ignored. Cows' milk is insufficiently supplied.'

The Report concludes as follows:—

'Having regard to the important and difficult character of the problems to be solved in the improvement of
metropolitan workhouse infirmaries, we consider that at
least one medical and one surgical inspector should be immediately appointed by Government, who should make it
their business to inspect and report on the London Infirmaries with regard to their fitness for hospital purposes.

And we think that such Inspectors ought to be instructed
carefully to consider the best way in which—if at some
future time the able-bodied paupers shall be altogether
separated from the sick and infirm, and removed into the
country—the metropolitan workhouses may be best applied to exclusively hospital purposes; carefully distinguishing the sites which are, and those which are not,
fitted for the treatment of acute disease. The Inspectors
should also digest a plan for the organization of proper
hospital medical staffs, by which the pauper in-patients
might receive, in addition to the visits of their present medical attendants, the advantage of advice from consulting
and operating physicians and surgeons.'

Reflection upon the foregoing facts and statements led to the formation of an Association for the
Improvement of the Infirmaries of London Workhouses, which held its first public meeting at Willis's
Rooms, on the 3rd of March, 1866.* The facts and
arguments adduced on this occasion made a profound
impression on those who heard them for the first
time. It was resolved, that such a state of things
as existed in most, though, happily, not in all, of the
metropolitan infirmaries, should no longer be allowed
to continue, but that measures should at once be
taken to bring the subject under the consideration,
in the first instance, of the Poor-law Board, with a
view to the adoption of an efficient remedy.

Accordingly, an influential deputation was or-
ganized, which had an interview with the Right Hon.

* A full report of this important meeting has since been published by Saville and Edwards, Chandos Street, Covent Garden.

C. P. Villiers, M.P., President of the Poor-law Board, at Whitehall, at which the writer was present. Earl Carnarvon introduced the deputation, and in the course of his address presented a statement emanating from the acknowledged heads of the medical profession. This had reference to the principles on which any buildings for the reception of sick paupers should be constructed, and the provisions which, in their opinion, were essential to their comfort and welfare:—

I. That the sick poor should be separated from the able-bodied paupers, and their treatment should be placed under a distinct management.

II. In lieu of sick-wards attached to each workhouse, consolidated infirmaries should be provided, where the following rules of hospital management should be adopted under skilled supervision. They are those generally accepted in this and other European countries :—

    1. The buildings should be specially devised for the purpose, of suitable construction, and on healthy sites. The rules laid down by the Barrack and Hospital Commission may be consulted with advantage on this subject.

    2. Not less than 1000 (and, for particular classes of cases, 1200 to 1500) cubic feet of air should be allowed to each patient.

    3. The nursing should be conducted entirely by a paid staff, and there should be not less than one day-nurse, one night-nurse, and one assistant-nurse, for each fifty patients.

A A

4. There should be resident medical officers in the proportion of not less than one for each 250 patients.

5. The medical officers should not have any pecuniary interest whatever in the medicines supplied, nor should they be charged with the duty of dispensing them.

6. A judicious classification of patients should be observed : the epileptic and imbecile, the acutely sick, and the aged and infirm, being treated in separate wards.

7. The aged and infirm, the chronically sick, and the convalescent, should be provided with day-rooms separate from the dormitories.

This declaration of opinion was signed by Dr. Thomas Watson, President of the College of Physicians; Dr. George Burrows, President of the General Medical Council; Dr. James Clark; Dr. William Jenner; Dr. Edward Sieveking; Sir William Fergusson; and Mr. James Paget.

Mr. Paget supported these opinions by his own experience as surgeon to St. Bartholomew's Hospital, one of the largest in London. He stated that he had there a hundred patients under his special charge. For this number, provision was made of one house-surgeon, five dressers, and sixteen nurses, four of whom were women of superior education, while the remaining twelve were ordinary trained nurses. How significant becomes the contrast with this of the single-handed Union surgeon, with little else, in many cases, to supplement his labours than

pauper help! Nor must it be supposed (Mr. Paget
went on to say) that all the cases in a general
hospital were usually so severe as to require a daily
inspection from the surgeon; for many of them, like
some of the workhouse cases, required only a visit
occasionally as the treatment progressed. With
reference to the amount of cubic space, he admitted
that the Poor-law allowance of 500 feet, if kept
constantly moving, might be salutary; but he knew
of no system of ventilation adequate to produce such
an effect; nor, if such existed, had he found any
staff of ordinary nurses competent so to handle it as
to obtain such a result.   Even in their large and
airy wards, there were times in the day when they
were troubled with foul air; and, therefore, to
recommend less than 1000 cubic feet per bed would
be *simply destructive* to the patients.

The Earl of Shaftesbury alluded to the inquiry
instituted by order of the Poor-law Board, recommending that it should be an open one, conducted
by independent medical inspectors.

Mr. Ernest Hart quoted the authority of Dr.
Parkes, Professor of Hygiene at the Netley Army
Hospital; General Morin, the President of the
Imperial Commission of France on Hygiene and
Ventilation; and Miss Nightingale; to show that
the minimum of space which ought to be allowed
in hospitals was nearly two-thirds more than is given
in almost every London workhouse infirmary.

The Archbishop of York urged that increased
power should be given to the Poor-law Board, to

enable them, not only to recommend needful reforms,
but, if need be, to enforce them.

The President of the Poor-law Board, whose
reply received marked attention, stated that,—

'He was unable to give any definite reply to the propositions laid before him. Lord Carnarvon had appealed
to him as a member of the Government, and as President
of the Poor-law Board; but, looking at the nature of the
case, and the extent of the evils which the Association had
brought under review, and the very comprehensive character of the changes proposed, he could not state what the
Government might think it right to do, or what would be
practicable. But certainly, as President of that Board, he
could say that he felt, and he was sure the public must
feel, deeply indebted to this Association, for the inquiries
which had been instituted, and for the effective manner in
which the results of those inquiries had been made known,
in the effort to reform the system of which they complained.
By bringing such matters forcibly before the public, and
enlisting its sympathies in the cause, the best chance was
afforded of ultimately giving effect to their views. He
felt bound to say that he had seldom known a more
humane and Christian-like labour undertaken than that of
improving the condition of the sick in the workhouse infirmaries of this great city. Many of the things which the
Association had observed had not taken him by surprise,
for cases had often—too often—arisen in these houses, and
come before the Board, showing that the hospital arrangements of the houses were still very defective; and, indeed,
he was not indisposed in consequence to agree substantially
with the terms of the resolution passed at the meeting—
namely, 'That the present management of the sick in the
metropolitan workhouses is unsatisfactory; that the buildings are,' in some cases, 'inadequate, the medical attendance

insufficient, and the nursing merely nominal.' As far as he understood the subject—for to understand it fully almost required a professional knowledge—he believed the resolution to be true; and saying this, it was hardly necessary to add that it was a state of things which ought not, in his opinion, to continue, and in which great change was required. Referring to the statements which had been made with reference to the inquiry instituted by the Board, he assured the deputation that it had been instituted for the purpose of placing the Board in the official possession of facts with regard to London workhouse infirmaries, so as to be prepared to lay them fully before the Government and Legislature if opportunity should offer. The fact that the inquiry was being carried out by Dr. Smith, who was eminent in his profession; and by Mr. H. B. Farnall, the well-known Poor law Inspector for the Metropolis, was a guarantee that the inquiry would be full and impartial. An inquiry had certainly been made, but it was, in one sense, private in its character; he alluded to that instituted by the proprietors of the *Lancet.* He begged to say that he had never questioned the capacity or the good faith of the gentlemen who had made that inquiry, and he had yet to learn that there had been any over-statement in the cases they had apparently established. He feared, however, that the difficulty in the case was not so much in getting at the truth, as in giving effect to the remedy suggested. He was certainly not prepared to dispute the conclusions at which the deputation had arrived, and the remedy proposed was, he understood, that there should be six separate hospitals for the sick at present lodged in the metropolitan workhouse infirmaries. The meeting must not lose sight of the fact, that such a scheme involved a great change in the principle upon which the poor were now maintained in this country. That charge was now local, and the administration of the law was in the hands of those who contributed locally to the fund out of which

the poor were relieved, whereas this scheme would treat
the sick poor as belonging to the whole metropolis; and
the expenses of raising the buildings and maintaining the
hospitals would be charged on the whole property of the
metropolis. He did not say it would be wrong on that account, or that the system of local management, for the purposes of the poor, had been faultless; but the system was one
of which the community was extremely tenacious, and there
would be considerable difficulty in suspending it even in this
city, where the adoption of a more general system would appear to be so reasonable. He did not say that the difficulty
was insuperable, and if it were clearly proved that a change
was essential for the proper treatment of the sick poor, he did
not say that it might not become even popular, especially
if it were proved that the defects under the present system
were irremediable. There had always been a difficulty as
to the hands in which the administration of the Poor-law
should be placed, and the great dread of the Legislature
had been that there would be lax and wasteful expenditure,
injurious to property, and tending to the promotion of pauperism, if the administration was not in the hands of those
directly interested in the economy of the funds, and the
guardians were chosen for this purpose. Some guardians,
he acknowledged, performed their duties with judgment
and humanity, but as the chief duty which they had to
perform was what was termed to keep down the expenditure, it was somewhat of a chance when guardians were
found possessing all the qualities required for a wise administration of the law. The right honourable gentleman
proceeded to deal with the other facts of the case, and said
he thought, that if the House of Commons could be prevailed upon to alter the present system of rating in the
metropolis it would do so for the sick poor, and have a
general rate as in the case of the casual poor. He concluded, amid loud cheers, that, though he could not pledge
the Government in the matter, he could assure the depu-

tation that nothing should be wanting on his part in recommending the propositions for favourable consideration.'*

Limited space precludes me from entering into details of individual infirmaries visited by the Commissioners on the *Lancet* inquiry: their Report, published in the *Lancet*, 1st July, 1866, has already induced several of the Metropolitan Boards of Guardians to take steps to remedy the evils complained of. It may, however, be expected, that some notice of our own Infirmary should be given here, more particularly as their Report upon it has not yet appeared. Suffice it, then, to state that Hampstead (as I was informed when appointed medical officer to the parish and workhouse) is considered at head-quarters somewhat a model workhouse. Without challenging the statement as regards the workhouse proper, which does not fall strictly within the scope of these pages; still less the constitution of our Board, in which thoughtful intelligence and considerate kindness for the poor are largely represented: I must demur to the flattering title being applied to that portion of our establishment devoted to infirmary purposes. Notwithstanding the admirable site on which it is erected (superior, perhaps, to any other Metropolitan Workhouse), from the circumstance of the main features of a building suited to the reception of the sick, being ignored in

* For further particulars, see the *Times*, 16th April, 1866, and *Lancet*, 21st April, 1866, p. 440.

its construction, its accommodation to this purpose is
beset with difficulty. The attention of the Board had
been frequently directed to it, with a view to its en-
largement and better ventilation; and their anxious
care for its improvement was notified to me on taking
office. Nor was this uncalled for. The patients herded
together without proper classification; the plan of
pauper nursing was the only one followed; bedsores
and large sloughing surfaces, frightful to view, were
to be met with; and, rough as were the hands that
tended them, it not unfrequently happened that the
sufferers were exposed to the disadvantages of a
change from bad to worse, owing to their nurses'
suspension for drunkenness or disorderly conduct.
The medicines were located promiscuously on a table
at the end of the ward; the allowance of wine or
spirits usually in the patient's own keeping, or
secreted about the bed. My first care was to
provide proper head-boards and prescription-papers
(hitherto unknown), with a little shelf at the head
of each bed, on which to stand the bottles of medicine, and those containing the wine and spirits.
The latter were four-ounce bottles, of peculiar shape,
holding exactly two glasses (each 'glass' being
understood to mean two ounces), and no corks
allowed in them. The intention of the last proviso
was to secure their always being replaced on the
shelf after taking a portion, so that, in going
through the wards at various times in the day, I
might satisfy myself that the contents were duly and
properly taken. I have appended to this chapter

the form of prescription-paper (reduced in size from
the original) introduced by me for the head of each
patient's bed, which differs in some respects from
those in hospital use, being provided with a fly-leaf,
on which are printed certain questions, which com-
prise the main features of the patient's case when
first admitted to the sick-ward, and furnish a
standard of comparison to note his progress towards
recovery.   This fly-leaf being folded back, is out of
sight; but accessible to observation when required
to refresh the medical officer's memory with the
leading facts of the case.   There is also a blank for
the diet and extras ordered for the patient, by which
the nurse is informed what she is entitled to demand
for that individual.   The face of the paper is left
blank for the prescriptions, which meet the doctor's
eye whenever he visits his patient.   From the advantage we have derived in the methodical treatment
of our sick from the use of this particular form of
prescription-paper I have been led to introduce it
here, in the hope that it may be adopted in
other workhouse infirmaries which are yet unprovided
in this respect.*

My patients were now capable (as in hospitals)
of identification, and though time did not allow of
any lengthened record, yet the facts of each case,
however briefly noted, were valuable for future re-

---

* By forwarding a directed envelope, under cover to the Clerk
to the Board of Guardians at the Workhouse, medical officers
attached to Unions may obtain one as a specimen, to bring under
the notice of their respective Boards.

ference or statistical research.   Classification of the
patients was next attempted, and the various wards
named in accordance therewith.   The Board were
now induced to try the experiment of introducing a
trained nurse into the wards; and though, at first,
the plan encountered some opposition even from those
it was intended to benefit, yet it eventually triumphed
over every obstacle.   The paupers, who at first dis-
liked the strictness with which the nurse put down
the quiet little traffic in wine and extras that existed
formerly from bed to bed, soon came to a sense
of the different way in which they were handled,
and welcomed her entrance into the wards like
a ray of sunshine.   Those gentlemen upon the
Board who were deputed in rotation to visit the
wards, perceived in time the difference in the
aspect of things, and expressed themselves more
than satisfied with the change.   When, after nine
months' faithful service, she exchanged her post for a
private situation, her departure was a matter of
unfeigned regret amongst her poor patients.   One
bedridden woman whispered that she had asked a
relative to bring his horse and cart to fetch away her
things; numbers implored her with tears to stay;
and some actually left the house rather than, by remaining, expose themselves (as they supposed) to a
return to the misery of the old system.   But, with
our Board, *progress* is the word; and through the
kindness of Mrs. Wardroper, lady-superintendent of
the 'Nightingale Fund' for training nurses at St.
Thomas's Hospital, our want has been supplied.   I

cannot omit this opportunity of publicly thanking
this lady for her ready sympathy with the cause in
which we are engaged, and for much trouble undertaken for us under the graceful guise of 'the deep
interest taken by Miss Nightingale in the subject of
improved nursing in Workhouse Infirmaries.'   We
are at present limited to one trained nurse for our fifty
beds, and therefore no adequate provision exists for
night nursing; but this fact is now fairly before the
Board, and I do not despair of securing, after awhile,
the benefits of trained nursing throughout our Infirmary. The nurse herself has not been overlooked by our
Board, who have assigned a separate apartment for
her use, and furnished it in a way conducive to her
comfort, including in the arrangements a small range
by means of which sundry delicacies, such as skilled
nurses know how to prepare, may be concocted out
of the wards; thus sparing the necessity of having
frequent recourse to the distant infirmary kitchen,
where the ordinary meals are prepared.   The ob-
structive frosting on the lower panes of some of our
windows, for the removal of which I pleaded, exists
no longer; so that a cheerful prospect obtains now
from all our infirmary wards—itself a help towards
recovery : and on the suggestion of Mr. Farnall, arm-
chairs were substituted for the wooden benches in use
for convalescent patients.

Yet further to put the infirmary on a hospital footing, the Board placed at my disposal a well-lighted room
on the basement, which could be used as a surgery, and
furnished it with a firm operating table, closets to hold

bandages, testing apparatus, &c., and washstand with
supply of water. Here I summon those patients
who used formerly to slip away to the terraces during
the doctor's visit, lest their unquestionable convales-
cence should imperil their continuance on the extras
list. Here also I am allowed to operate on cases
from the parish, which would sometimes be imprac-
ticable in the dark and wretched courts in which they
reside. If it be asked why I have been thus particular in describing our proceedings, it is that I wish
it to be known that when the foregoing helps to hospital treatment were initiated, we had not heard of
the *Lancet* inquiry, and that they were in active
operation before the first Report of the ' Commission'
appeared. It will, therefore, be understood that the
sweeping censures quoted from that Report do not,
of necessity, apply to every workhouse in this metropolis; nevertheless, we are willing to share the obloquy
if good may arise from the painful exposure, for well
we know that despite our best efforts our cases suffer
from the defective construction of our sick wards —
their wretched ventilation exposes the inmates to the
alternative of being poisoned by foul air on the one
hand, or chilled by down-draughts on the other; and,
beyond controversy, the *overcrowding* which we are
powerless to prevent while the law remains unaltered
which compels us to admit paupers, as long as 500
cubic feet of space remain for each, is, to adopt Mr.
Paget's mournful expression, ' simply destructive to
the patients.'

To close the notice of our proceedings it may

be added that, child-bed fever having occurred in a recent case owing to the small size and defective ventilation of our lying-in ward, the Board have effected an excellent improvement by removing the partition wall which separated this room from an adjoining one. This has not only doubled its size, but greatly improved its lighting and ventilation by allowing a third window, hitherto blocked by the partition, to open into the ward. At the same time two convenient bath-rooms are being constructed in the infirmary—one on the men's side, and another for the women's use. Bedside closets, with a basin, towel, &c., for each patient, have also been introduced into the sick wards.

There is yet, however, a darker side to the picture of the sick pauper's misery—one which has not yet been fairly placed before the public. If the condition of the sick paupers within the Workhouses be so gloomy, what shall be said of those outside their walls? I speak from experience when I say that their state is often incomparably worse. I could point to paupers in this favoured parish who are *never* off my sick list, and who never will be while they are living—I ought rather to say dying—in tenements where they get but 150 to 200 cubic feet to each occupant. To such even the workhouse infirmary proves indeed a boon; but when I urge upon them this advantage, I am foiled again and again by their deep-rooted aversion to enter 'the house.' In vain I expostulate and explain it is the infirmary, not the workhouse, I wish them to enter. They

know that both are under the same roof; they dread
the workhouse officials and the workhouse system;
and they are deterred from advantages which are
their right, and remain from year to year a burden
upon the industry of the community. It cannot be
alleged that in recommending such a course I am
acting contrary to the spirit of the Poor-law (which
defines the objects to be kept in view in the administration of medical relief to the sick poor to be—
1. To provide medical aid for all persons who are
really destitute; 2. To prevent medical relief from
generating or encouraging pauperism),* because they
are admitted to be destitute, and constituted paupers
by virtue of the medical order which they present to
me : nor can it be urged that I wish to get them off
my hands, for in the workhouse they would still remain under my care. But if the advantages of
treatment in the infirmary, where the medical supervision is supplemented by skilled nursing, and the
sick man placed under proper control—if these advantages are such as tend to restore the bread-winner
of the family to health in a shorter period, how
important that the *district* medical officer should be
empowered to order his reception into a parish
infirmary detached from the workhouse, under separate management, and replete with arrangements
conducive to his speedy recovery. Moreover, such a
building would be available for the reception of sick
inmates from the workhouse, whose health it must

* Glen's *Orders of the Poor-law Board*, note to Art. 96.

SICK POOR IN LONDON WORKHOUSES.   367

be remembered, has already broken down under the conditions of space and ventilation in which they reside there, and whom it is unreasonable to expect to recover when merely removed to the sick wards, which are some of the worst rooms in the house in this respect. The number of these broken-down cases might perhaps be lessened if an improved diet for the aged and infirm were established by the central authority, and those only placed on the infirmary lists whose health failed in spite of such additional support. The rational treatment claimed for the *sick* pauper being thus conceded, its exceptional character would be vindicated by his being remitted, on his recovery, to the workhouse.

APPENDIX.

COMMON LODGING-HOUSES.

REGULATIONS for Common Lodging-Houses (under the Common Lodging-House Act, 1851) situate within the Metropolitan Police District.

Number of Lodgers.

1. No keeper of a common lodging-house within the Metropolitan Police District shall admit or suffer to remain in such house, or in any room thereof, a greater number of lodgers or other persons than shall be fixed by the Commissioners of the Police of the Metropolis, as is hereafter mentioned.

2. A ticket, according to the Form A. in the schedule to these Regulations, signed by one of the Commissioners of the Police of the Metropolis, stating the entire number of lodgers allowed to sleep in each such lodging-house, and which number such house is registered to accommodate, will be supplied to the keeper of every common lodging-house; and he is to produce such ticket whenever required by any officer appointed for inspecting common lodging-houses by the Commissioners of Police.

3. The keeper of every common lodging-house shall put up, in a conspicuous place in each room, a ticket, signed by one of the Commissioners of the Police of the

Metropolis, stating the number of lodgers allowed to sleep
in such room, which will be supplied to the keeper of every
common lodging-house; and he shall keep such ticket at
all times visible and legible, which ticket shall be according
to the Form contained in the schedule to these Regulations
marked B.

4. Two children under ten years of age to be counted
as one lodger.

5. Each room occupied as a sleeping-room shall be
furnished with bedsteads and sufficient bedding for the
number of lodgers authorised to be received in such room.

6. Rooms in the basement, or below the level of the
ground, shall not be used as sleeping rooms, unless specially approved of for that purpose by the Commissioners
of the Police of the Metropolis. Such approval, when
given, will state the number of lodgers to be allowed according to the circumstances of such case, to sleep in each
room.

7. Rooms used as kitchen or scullery shall not be occupied as sleeping-rooms.

8. The keeper of every such common lodging-house
shall reduce the number of lodgers, upon receiving notice
to that effect from the Commissioners of Police of the
Metropolis, such notice stating the special cause of the
same being given, and the period during which it shall
continue in force.

Separation of Sexes.

9. Persons of different sexes shall not occupy the same
sleeping-room, except married couples, or parents with
their children under ten years of age, or any children
under ten years of age.

10. More than one married couple shall not occupy
the same sleeping-room, unless the beds are separated by a
partition to secure the privacy of each married couple;
such partition to be of wood or other solid material, and of

B B

such height as shall be fixed in each case by some officer appointed by the Commissioners of Police of the Metropolis for inspecting common lodging-houses.

Keeping Houses clean.

11. The keeper of such lodging-house shall cause the walls and ceilings of every room, and of the staircases and passages of such house, to be thoroughly cleaned and well and sufficiently lime-washed twice (at least) in every year, during the months of October and April, and shall cause the floors of all the rooms, passages, and stairs of such house to be kept at all times clean and washed, and swept as often as necessary; and the blankets, rugs, or covers, and sheets used in such house shall be kept clean, and in a wholesome condition.

Ventilation.

12. The keeper of such lodging-house shall cause every room and the passages in such house to be ventilated, to the satisfaction of the officer appointed by the Commissioners of Police of the Metropolis for inspecting common lodging-houses.

13. The keeper of such lodging-house shall provide such accommodation for washing and such a supply of water for the use of the lodgers as shall be satisfactory to the officer appointed by the Commissioners of Police of the Metropolis for inspecting common lodging-houses.

In case of Fever, &c.

14. The keeper of such lodging-house shall, when a person in such house is ill of fever or any infectious or contagious disease, give immediate notice in writing to the Commissioners of Police of the Metropolis, which notice shall be left at the office of the Commissioners, Great Scotland Yard, or at the nearest police station to such lodging-house.

15. The keeper of such house shall forthwith cause all other lodgers to be removed from the room in which any person is ill of fever, or any infectious or contagious disorder, and shall make such reduction of the number of lodgers in each room of such house as shall be directed by the officer appointed by the Commissioners of Police of the Metropolis for inspecting common lodging-houses.

16. The keeper of such house shall use any disinfecting process which may be directed to be used by the officer appointed by the said Commissioners of Police for inspecting common lodging-houses; and the keeper of such house shall cause the blankets, rugs, and bedding used by any person affected by such fever or disorder to be burnt, or thoroughly fumigated and cleansed, immediately after the removal of the person affected by such fever or disorder, in such a manner as may from time to time be ordered by the officer appointed by the said Commissioners of Police for inspecting common lodging-houses.

17. Every such lodging-house shall be furnished with a dust-bin of sufficient size to contain the dust, ashes, &c., that accumulate in the intervals of its being cleared away, which shall not exceed two weeks.

18. A watercloset or privy shall be provided for every such lodging-house having a yard or other facilities for erection thereof; and where such facilities do not exist, or where the closet or privy is used in common by the lodgers of two or more houses, the privy or closet must be provided in some place conveniently contiguous, to the satisfaction of the person appointed by the Commissioners of Police of the Metropolis for inspecting common lodging-houses; and for every 20 lodgers to be accommodated a separate closet or privy shall be provided.

19. The drains, the closets, and sinks shall be trapped, so as to prevent the effluvia coming up from the sewers or cesspools. The sink in the yard shall be so placed as to take all the waste water through the drain from the

closets. And where no sewer is available, the cesspool is
to be emptied as often as required.

20. The watercloset or privy-seat, floor, and walls,
shall be kept free from filth, and clean in all other respects.

21. The yards and areas of every such lodging-house
shall be properly paved, so as to run dry, and effectually
take off all waste water.

22. Every such lodging-house shall have a proper
drain communicating with a common sewer, where such
sewer is within 100 yards of the premises.

RICHARD MAYNE,
W. HAY,

Commissioners of the Police of the Metropolis.

Metropolitan Police Office,
Whitehall-place, 31 *October,* 1851.

I confirm the foregoing Regulations.

G. GREY.

Whitehall,
10 *November,* 1851.

1. Name of Patient. _____ Ward.
2. Circumstances. 3. ___ yrs. 4. of ___ temp. Res. in Lon. habs.
5. Aspect and state of Nutrition
6. History of Health
7. Brain and Nervous System
8. Heart and Circulation
9. Lungs and Respiration
10. Organs of Digestion
11. Secretions, &c.
12. Diet No. _____ Discharged. Extras

186

INFIRMARY
OF
HAMPSTEAD WORKHOUSE.

Admitted _____ 186 _____ Aged _____
Under the care of Dr. W. H. Cook for _____

186 .   186 .

LONDON:
STRANGEWAYS AND WALDEN, PRINTERS,
28 Castle St. Leicester Sq.

Works recently Published.

BY THE AUTHOR OF "LENDING A HAND."

Fifth Thousand, crown 8vo. Frontispiece, 5s. cloth,

THE POST OF HONOUR.

The Nineteenth Edition, with Portrait, small 8vo. cloth, 3s. 6d.

DOING AND SUFFERING: Memorials of Elizabeth and Frances, Daughters of the late Rev. E. Bickersteth. By their SISTER. With a Preface by the Right Rev. the Lord Bishop of RIPON.

The Second Edition, with Portrait, in small 8vo. cloth, 2s. 6d.

DAWN AND SUNRISE: Brief Notices of the Life and Early Death of Barbara Sophia Gordon, Daughter of James E. Gordon, Esq. By C. B. With a Preface by J. C. COLQUHOUN, Esq.

Third Edition, with Frontispiece, cloth, price 5s.

SCHOOL AND HOME; or, Leaves from a Boy's Journal. A Tale for Schoolboys. By the Author of " England's Daybreak," " Plain Reading for Ploughboys," &c.

Fourth Edition, with Frontispiece, cloth, price 3s. 6d.

WOMAN'S SERVICE ON THE LORD'S DAY. With a Preface by the Right Rev. the Lord Bishop of Ro-CHESTER.

" It is replete with wisdom and good sense, full of interesting anecdote and detail, and breathes the practical Christianity of one who has not been so cumbered with much serving as to have overlooked the privilege and enjoyment of sitting at the Master's feet."—*Record.*

Second Edition, with Engravings, cloth, price 5s.

ENGLAND'S DAYBREAK: Narrative of the Reformation in the Fourteenth and following Centuries. By the Author of " Come to the Supper," " A Working Man's Fireside," &c.

Second Edition, with Engraved Title, small 8vo. cloth, 3s. 6d.

MOTHERS IN COUNCIL; or, Scripture Light on Home Questions. By the Author of " Plain Words about Sickness," &c.

" A practical book of a most useful character, and equally to be commended for its style and contents."—*The Quiver.*

CPSIA information can be obtained
at www.ICGtesting.com
Printed in the USA
BVOW06s1456271217
503804BV00009B/81/P